P9-CQQ-956

Alibaba

Alibaba

THE HOUSE THAT JACK MA BUILT

DUNCAN CLARK

An Imprint of HarperCollins*Publishers*

 For information address HarperCollins Publishers, 195 Broadway, New York, NY, 10007.

HarperCollins books may be purchased for educational, business, or sales promotional use. For information please e-mail the Special Markets Department at SPsales@harpercollins.com.

FIRST EDITION

Designed by Suet Yee Chong

Library of Congress Cataloging-in-Publication Data has been applied for.

ISBN 978-0-06-241340-6

16 17 18 19 20 OV/RRD 10 9 8 7 6 5 4 3 2 1

Contents

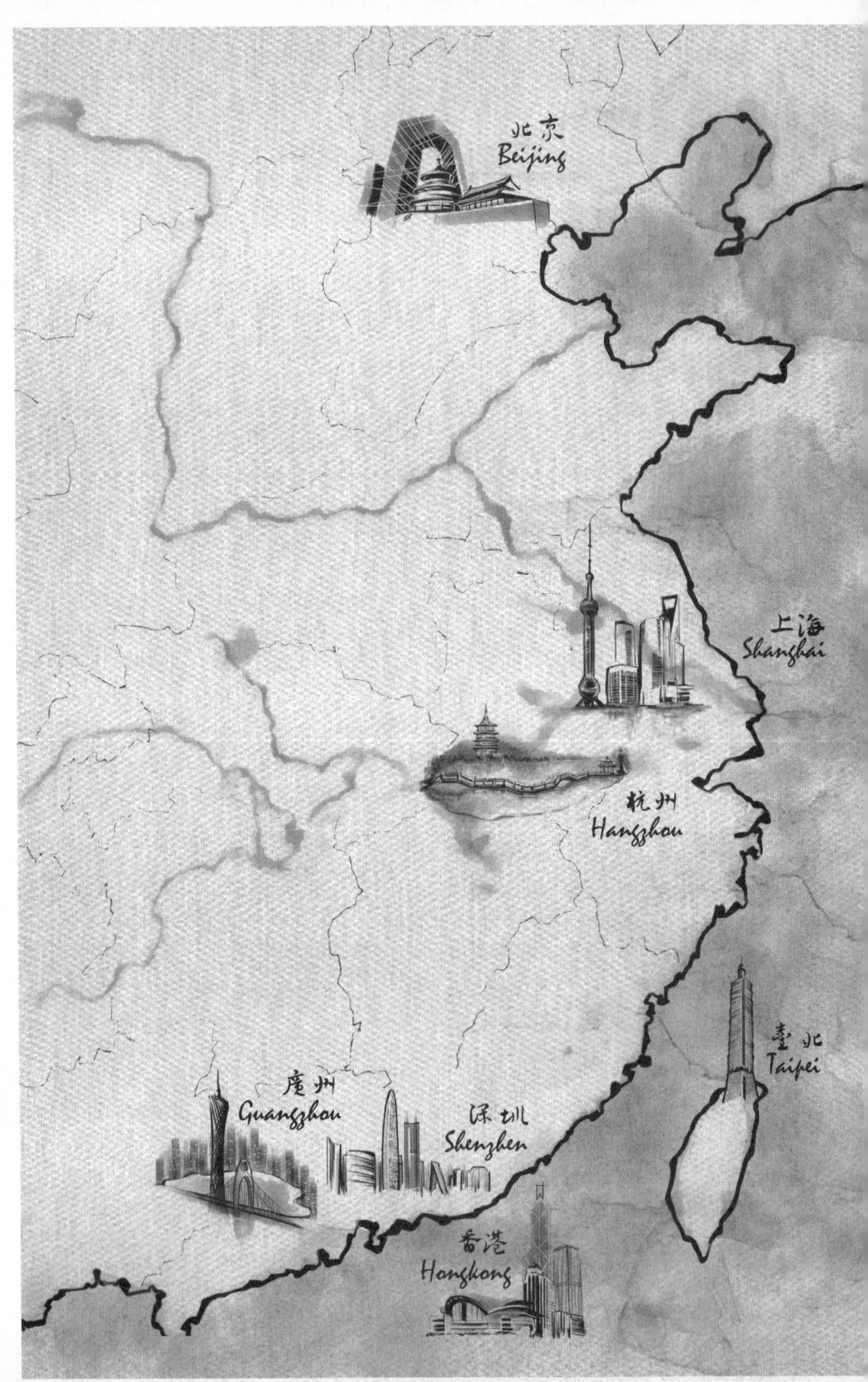
北京
Beijing
上海
Shanghai
杭州
Hangzhou
臺北
Taipei
廣州
Guangzhou
深圳
Shenzhen
香港
Hongkong

朝鲜
orth Korea
韩国
South Korea
东京
Tokyo

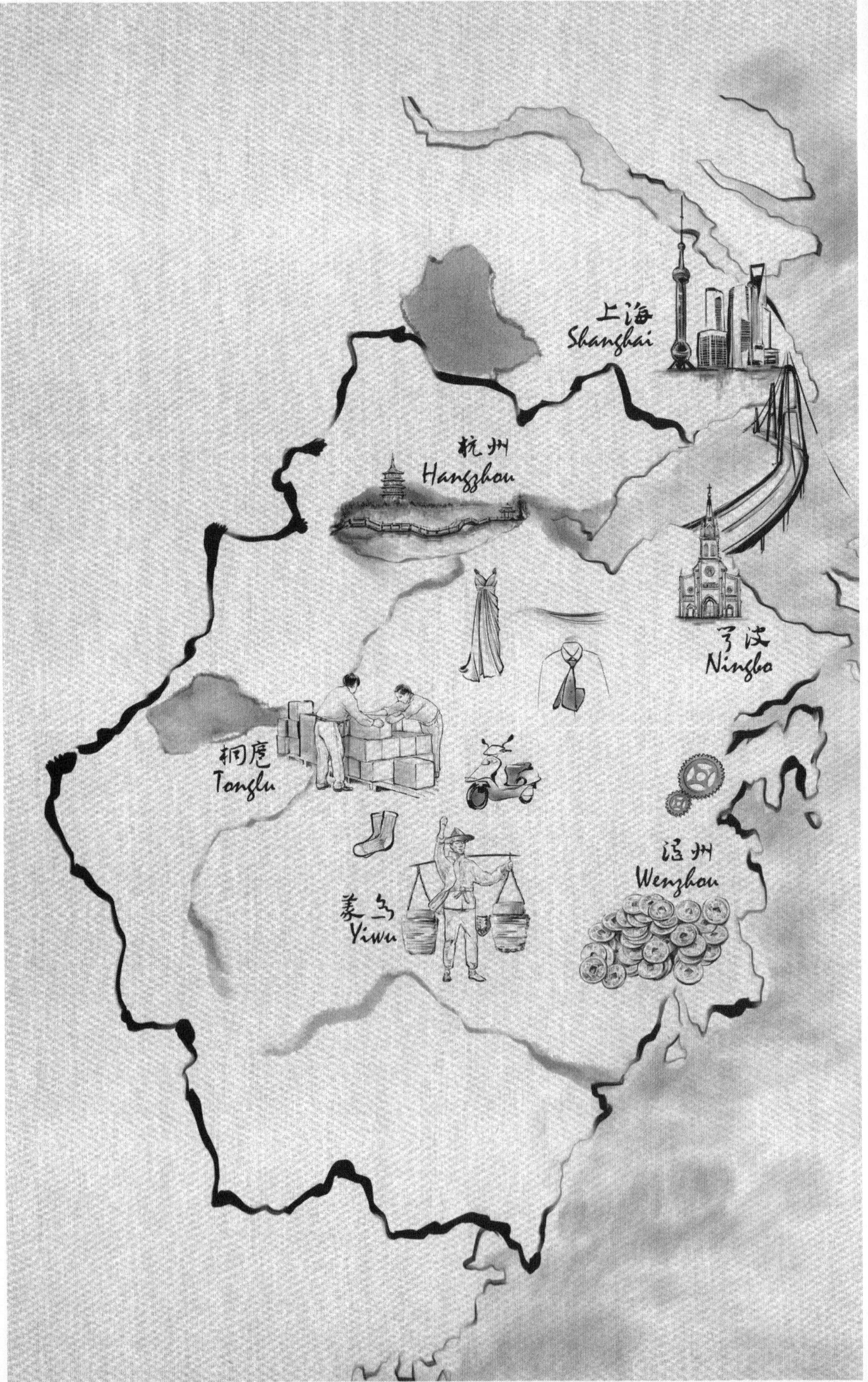

上海
Shanghai
杭州
Hangzhou
Ningbo
Tonglu
Wenzhou
Yiwu

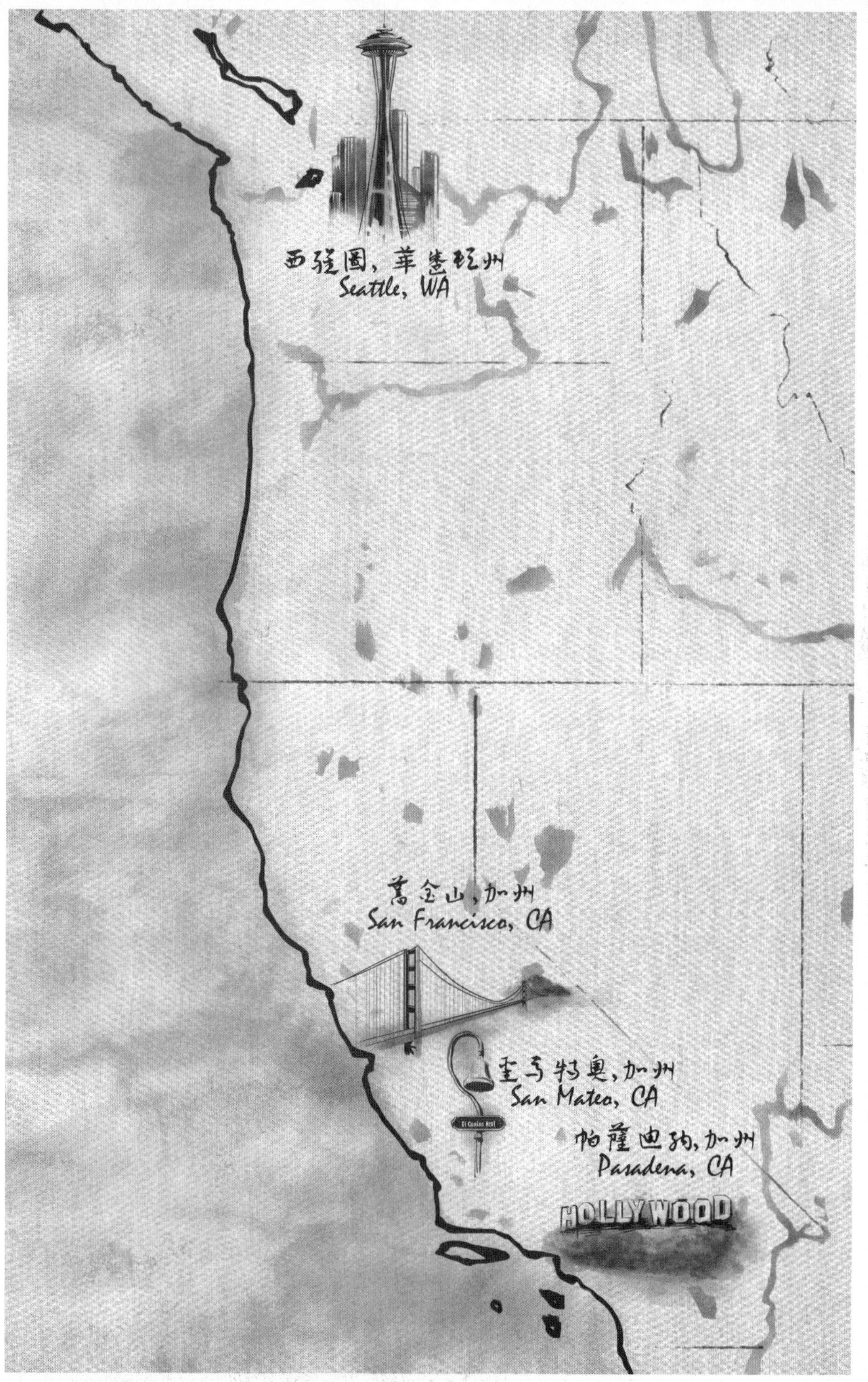

西雅圖, 華盛頓州
Seattle, WA
舊金山, 加州
San Francisco, CA
聖馬特奧, 加州
San Mateo, CA
El Camino Real
帕薩迪納, 加州
Pasadena, CA
HOLLYWOOD

Introduction

Alibaba is an unusual name for a Chinese company. Its founder, Jack Ma, a former English teacher, is an unlikely corporate titan.

Yet the house that Jack built is home to the largest virtual shopping mall in the world, soon to overtake Walmart in the amount of goods sold. The company's IPO on the New York Stock Exchange in September 2014 raised $25 billion, the largest stock market flotation in history. In the months that followed, Alibaba's shares soared, making it one of the top ten most valuable companies in the world, worth almost $300 billion. Alibaba became the most valuable Internet company in the world after Google, its shares worth more than Amazon and eBay combined. Nine days before the IPO, Jack celebrated his fiftieth birthday, the soaring value of his stake making him the richest man in Asia.

But since that peak Alibaba's life as a publicly listed company has not gone according to plan. Its shares fell by half from their post-IPO peak, even briefly falling below the initial offer price. Investor concerns were sparked in early 2015 by a surprising entanglement with a government agency over intellectual property, then fueled by the slowing Chinese economy and volatile stock markets, which dragged down Alibaba's shares in their wake.

Despite the ups and downs of the stock market, with a dominant share of the e-commerce market, Alibaba is uniquely well positioned to benefit from the rise of China's consuming classes. Over 400 million people, more than the population of the United States, make purchases on Alibaba's websites each year. The tens of millions of packages generated each day account for almost two-thirds of all parcel deliveries in China.

Alibaba has transformed the way Chinese shop, giving them access to a range and quality of items that previous generations could only dream of. Like Amazon in the West, Alibaba brings the convenience of home delivery to millions of consumers. Yet this comparison understates Alibaba's impact. Taobao, its online shopping website, has given many Chinese people their first sense of being truly valued as a customer. Alibaba is playing a pivotal role in China's economic restructuring, helping move the country away from a "Made in China" past to a "Bought in China" present.

The Old China growth model lasted three decades. Based on manufacturing, construction, and exports, it delivered hundreds of millions out of poverty but left China with a bitter legacy of overcapacity, overbuilding, and pollution. Now a new model is emerging, one centered on catering to the needs of a middle class expected to grow from 300 million to half a billion people within ten years.

Jack, more than any other, is the face of the new China. Already something of a folk hero at home, he stands at the intersection of China's newfound cults of consumerism and entrepreneurship.

His fame extends well beyond China's borders. A meeting (and a selfie) with Jack is coveted by presidents, prime ministers and princes, CEOs, entrepreneurs, investors, and movie stars. Jack regularly shares the stage with the world's political and corporate elite. A masterful public speaker, more often than not he outshines them. To go onstage after Jack is a losing proposition. In a remarkable reversal of protocol, President Obama even volunteered to act as moderator for Jack at a Q&A session during the November 2015 APEC meeting in Manila. At

Tom Cruise and Jack Ma in Shanghai, September 6, 2015, at the Chinese premiere of *Mission: Impossible—Rogue Nation,* which was financed in part by Alibaba Pictures. *Alibaba*

the World Economic Forum in Davos in January 2016, Jack dined with Leonardo DiCaprio, Kevin Spacey, and Bono, along with the CEOs of the Coca-Cola Company, DHL, and JPMorgan Chase. The founder of another China Internet company remarked to me: "It was almost as though Alibaba's PR department was writing Obama's script!"

Facebook founder Mark Zuckerberg has been demonstrating his commitment to learning Mandarin Chinese in speeches he has made since 2014, starting at Tsinghua University in Beijing. But Jack, English teacher turned tycoon, has been wowing crowds in both English and Chinese at conferences around the world for over seventeen years.

I first met Jack in the summer of 1999, a few months after he founded Alibaba in a small apartment in Hangzhou, some hundred miles southwest of Shanghai. On my first visit, I could count the number of cofounders by the toothbrushes jammed into mugs on a shelf in the bathroom. In addition to Jack, there included his wife, Cathy, and sixteen others. Jack and Cathy had wagered everything they owned on the company, including their home. Jack's ambition then, as it remains today, was breathtaking. He talked of building an Internet company that would last eighty years—the typical span of a human life. A few years later, he extended Alibaba's life expectancy to "a hundred and two" years, so that the company would span three centuries from 1999. From the very beginning, he vowed to take on and topple the giants of Silicon Valley. Within the confines of that modest apartment this should have seemed delusional. Yet there was something about his passion for the venture that made it sound entirely credible.

I became an adviser to Alibaba in its early years, helping Jack and his right-hand man, Joe Tsai, with the company's international expansion strategy and recommending to them some of its first foreign employees. Alibaba has assisted me in my research for this book by arranging interviews with senior management and providing access to the company in various locations. But this is an entirely independent account. I have never been an employee of the company and have no professional relationship with them today. My insights come in part from my brief role during the dot-com boom as an adviser to Alibaba and from the proximity that this early contact has afforded since. Yet in writing this book, I have been guided also by my personal experience living in China since 1994, when the Internet first came to the country's shores, and by my professional career. With support from my previous employer Morgan Stanley,[1] in the summer of 1994, I founded BDA China, a Beijing-based investment advisory firm, which today numbers more than one hundred professionals, consulting to investors and participants in China's technology and retail sectors.

As part of the remuneration for my advisory service, in early 2000, Jack and Joe granted me the right to buy a few hundred thousand shares in Alibaba at just thirty cents each. When the deadline was up to buy the shares, in early 2003, things weren't looking so good for the company. The dot-com bubble had burst and Alibaba's (original) business was struggling. In an error of colossal proportions, I decided not to buy the shares. In the weeks after the company's September 2014 IPO, this mushroomed into a $30 million mistake.[2] I would like to thank you very much for purchasing this book. Writing it has proved (somewhat) cathartic as I explore the stories of others, like Goldman Sachs, who underestimated Jack's tenacity and sold their early stake too soon, and eBay, who dismissed his firm as a rival, only to be forced out of the China market within a few years.

Jack is different from most of his Internet billionaire peers. He struggled in math as a student and wears his ignorance of technology as a badge of honor. His outsize ambitions and unconventional strategies won him the nickname "Crazy Jack." In this book, we will explore his past and quirky personality to learn the method to his madness.

China's e-commerce market differs in important ways from the United States and other Western economies, the legacy of decades of state planning and the important role still played by state-owned enterprises. Alibaba has sought out and exploited the inefficiencies these have created, first in e-commerce, now in media and finance. His vision for the company—or his own philanthropic endeavors—now extends to grappling with China's greatest challenges, in reforming health care, education, and its approach to the environment.

Yet Alibaba's main business today remains e-commerce, a market it helped create and which it currently dominates. Is there more room for it to grow? Competitors are waiting in the wings. Also watching closely is the Chinese government. As Alibaba consolidates more market power than any other private company ever has, can Jack keep the government on his side?

Although most of its operations are in China, Alibaba is pursuing an ambitious international expansion. Newly appointed president Michael Evans: "We like to say that Alibaba was born in China, but we were created for the world."

Before we look at the remarkable story of how Alibaba came to be, and its goals for the future, let's start by taking a tour of what Jack calls the "iron triangle," the key underpinning of the company's dominance today: its strengths in e-commerce, logistics, and finance.

Chapter One

The Iron Triangle

China changed because of us in the past fifteen years.
We hope in the next fifteen years, the world changes because of us.
—Jack Ma

On November 11, 2015, in Beijing, in the iconic bubble-like structure bathed in blue light known popularly as the "Water Cube," the venue for the aquatics events in the Beijing Olympics held seven years earlier, it wasn't water that flowed but streams of data. For twenty-four hours, without interruption, a huge digital screen flickered with maps, charts, and news crawls, reporting in real time the purchases of millions of consumers across China on Alibaba's websites. In front of hundreds of journalists broadcasting the event across China and around the world, the Water Cube had been repurposed as mission control for the Chinese middle class and the merchants marketing to them. A four-hour live TV special, the 11/11 Global Festival Shopping Gala, was broadcast to help keep shoppers up until midnight, featuring actors such as Kevin Spacey, who appeared in a filmed montage as his character from *House of Cards,* President Frank Underwood, endorsing Alibaba as the place to buy disposable "burner" cell phones. The gala show culminated in a skit featuring Jack's face as the new Bond girl before he appeared in a tuxedo walking alongside Bond actor Daniel Craig for some onstage antics in the final countdown to midnight.

In the first eight minutes of 11/11/15, shoppers made more than $1 billion in purchases on Alibaba's sites. And they kept on shopping. As the world's largest cash register tallied the takings, Jack—seated next to his friend, the actor and martial artist Jet Li—couldn't resist taking a photo of the huge screen with his cell phone. Twenty-four hours later, 30 million buyers had racked up over $14 billion[1] in purchases, four times greater than 11/11's U.S. equivalent, Cyber Monday, which occurred a few weeks later, after Thanksgiving's Black Friday discount day.

Shortly after midnight, Chinese media reporting the sales figures recorded by Alibaba's Singles' Day promotion on November 11, 2015. *Duncan Clark*

In China, November 11 is Singles' Day,[2] a special annual promotion.[3] In the West, the date commemorates veterans of past wars. But in China, November 11 is the most important day of the year for the merchants fighting for the wallets of the country's newly minted consumer class.

On this day, also known as Double Eleven (*shuang shiyi*),[4] people in China indulge in a frenzy of pure, unadulterated hedonism. Jack summed up the event: "This is a unique day. We want all the manufacturers, shop owners to be thankful for the consumers. We want the consumers to have a wonderful day."[5]

From just twenty-seven merchants in 2009, over forty thousand merchants and thirty thousand brands now participate in Singles' Day. Total sales in 2015 were up 60 percent from the $9 billion of the previous year. On that occasion, celebrated at Alibaba's Wetlands campus in Hangzhou, the company's chief strategy officer Dr. Zeng Ming described the scene in terms reminiscent of Dr. Frankenstein watching his creation stirring from the dead: "The ecosystem has its own will to grow." Alibaba's executive vice chairman Joe Tsai echoed the sentiment: "You're seeing the unleashing of the consumption power of the Chinese consumer."

This power has long been suppressed. Household spending in the United States drives two-thirds of the economy, but in China it barely accounts for one-third. Compared to developed countries, Chinese people don't consume enough. The reason? They save too much and spend too little. To fund their future education, medical expenses, or retirement, many families accumulate substantial amounts of mattress money or "precautionary savings." Also, lacking the range or quality of products on offer in the West, consumers in China until relatively recently had little enticement to spend more on themselves.

Addressing an audience at Stanford University in September 2015, Jack observed that "in the U.S. when the economy is slowing down it means people don't have money to spend." But, he joked, "You guys know how to spend tomorrow's money or future money or other people's money. China's been poor for so many years, we put our money in the bank."

Old habits die hard, but a new habit—buying online—is changing the way consumers in China behave. Alibaba is at the forefront of this shift. Its most popular website is Taobao.com, China's third most visited website and the world's twelfth. A common saying today in China is *wanneng de taobao,*[6] meaning "you can find everything on Taobao." Amazon has been called "the Everything Store." Taobao too sells (almost) everything, everywhere. Just as Google is synonymous with searching online, in China to "*tao*"[7] something is shorthand for searching for a product online.

Alibaba has a much greater impact on China's retail sector than Amazon does in the United States. Thanks to Taobao and its sister site, Tmall, Alibaba is effectively China's largest retailer. Amazon, by contrast, only became one of the top ten retailers in America in 2013.

Although Alibaba launched Taobao in 2003, it was only five years later that it really came into its own. Until then China's countless factories churned out products mostly for buyers overseas, shipped to stock the shelves of retailers like Walmart and Target. But the global financial crisis in 2008 changed everything. China's traditional export markets were thrown into a tailspin. Taobao pried open the factory gates to consumers in China instead. The Chinese government's response to the 2008 crisis was to double down on the Old China model—pumping money into the economy that fueled a massive real estate bubble, excess capacity, and yet more pollution. As the bills came in, it became clear that the much-needed rebalancing of the Chinese economy toward consumption could no longer be postponed. And Alibaba is one of the biggest beneficiaries.

Jack likes to say that his company's success was an accident: "Alibaba might as well be known as 'one thousand and one mistakes.'" In its early years, he gave three explanations as to why the company survived: "We didn't have any money, we didn't have any technology, and we didn't have a plan."

But let's look at the three real factors that underpin Alibaba's success today: the company's competitive edge in e-commerce, logistics, and finance, what Jack describes as Alibaba's "iron triangle."

Alibaba's e-commerce sites offer an unparalleled variety of goods to consumers. Its logistics offering ensures those goods are delivered quickly and reliably. And the company's finance subsidiary ensures that buying on Alibaba is easy and worry free.

The E-commerce Edge

Unlike Amazon, Alibaba's consumer websites Taobao and Tmall carry no inventory.[8] They serve as platforms for other merchants to sell their wares. Taobao consists of nine million storefronts run by small traders or individuals. Attracted by the site's huge user base, these "micro merchants" choose to set up their stalls on Taobao in part because it costs them nothing to do so. Alibaba charges them no fees. But Taobao makes money—a lot of it—from selling advertising space, helping promote those merchants who want to stand out from the crowd.

Merchants can advertise through paid listings or display ads. Under the paid listing model, similar to Google's AdWords, advertisers bid for keywords to give their products a more prominent placement on Taobao. They pay Alibaba based on the number of times consumers click on their ads. Merchants can also use a more traditional advertising model, paying based on the number of times their ads are displayed on Taobao.

The old joke about advertising is "I know at least half of my advertising budget works . . . I just don't know which half." But with "pay-for-performance" advertising—and a ready market of hundreds of millions of consumers—Taobao commands an enormous appeal to small merchants.

Keeping order amid Taobao's virtual alleyways are Alibaba's client service managers, the *xiaoer*.[9] Thousands of *xiaoer* mediate any disputes that arise between customers and merchants. These referees, young employees averaging twenty-seven years old, work long hours, often sending messages to vendors late at night.

The *xiaoer* have great powers of enforcement, including the ability to shut down a merchant entirely. They can also offer merchants a carrot: the ability to participate in marketing campaigns. Inevitably, some merchants have sought to corrupt the *xiaoer* by offering bribes. Alibaba periodically shuts down merchants caught in the act, and an internal disciplinary unit is constantly on the lookout to root out graft among its employees.

But Taobao's success is not explained by the *xiaoer* alone. The site works because it succeeds in putting the customer first, bringing the vibrancy of China's street markets to the experience of shopping online. Buying online is as interactive as in real life. Customers can use Alibaba's chat application[10] to haggle over prices; a vendor might hold up a product to his webcam. Shoppers can also expect to score discounts and free shipping. Most packages arrive with some extra samples or cuddly toys thrown in, something I have personally grown so used to that when receiving Amazon packages in the United States I shake empty boxes in vain. The merchants on Taobao guard their reputation with customers fiercely; such is the Darwinian nature of the competition on the platform. When customers post a negative comment about a merchant or a product, they can expect to receive a message and offers of refunds or free replacements within minutes.

Alibaba's e-commerce edge is also honed by another of its websites, Tmall.[11] If Taobao can be compared to a collection of scrappy market stalls, Tmall is a glitzy shopping mall. Large retailers and even luxury brands sell their goods on Tmall and, for those customers not yet able to afford them, build brand awareness. Unlike Taobao, which is free for buyers and sellers, merchants pay commissions to Alibaba on the products they sell on Tmall, ranging from 3 to 6 percent depending on the category.[12] Today Tmall.com is the seventh-most-visited website in China.

In Chinese, the site is called *tian mao,* or "sky cat." Its mascot is a black cat, to distinguish it from Taobao's alien doll. Tmall is increasingly important for Alibaba, generating $136 billion in gross merchandise volume for the company,[13] closing in on the $258 billion sold on Taobao. Alibaba earns almost $10 billion a year in revenue from these sites, nearly 80 percent of its total sales.

Tmall hosts three types of stores on its platform: flagship stores, run by a brand itself; authorized stores, set up by a merchant licensed to do so by the brand; and specialty stores, which carry the goods of more than one brand. The specialty stores account for 90 percent of Tmall vendors. More than seventy thousand brands, from China and overseas, can be found today on Tmall.

In the Singles' Day promotion on Tmall, the most popular brands included foreign names such as Nike, Gap, Uniqlo, and L'Oréal as well as domestic players such as smartphone vendors Xiaomi and Huawei, and consumer electronics and home appliances company Haier.

Tmall is a veritable A to Z of brands, from Apple to Zara. Luxury brands also sell on the website, although they are careful[14] not to cannibalize sales in their physical stores. The presence of Burberry on the site is a sign that Alibaba is no longer just about cheap goods.

U.S. retailers like Costco and Macy's are also on Tmall, part of a drive by Alibaba to connect them along with other overseas stores to customers in China. Costco's Tmall store drew over 90 million visitors to its site in the first two months.

Even Amazon is on Tmall, selling imported food, shoes, toys, and kitchenware since 2015. Amazon has long had designs on the China market but has had to settle for just 2 percent of it.

In addition to Taobao and Tmall, Alibaba operates a Groupon-style[15] site called Juhuasuan.com.[16] Juhuasuan is the largest product-focused group-buying site in China. Buoyed by the huge volume of goods on Alibaba's other sites, it has signed up more than 200 million users, making it the largest online group-buying site in the world. Together, Taobao, Tmall, and Juhuasuan have signed up over 10 million merchants, offering more than one billion individual items for sale.

Alibaba's websites are popular in part because, as in the United States, shopping online from home can save time and money. More than 10 percent of retail purchases in China are made online, higher than the 7 percent in the States. Jack has likened e-commerce to a "dessert" in the United States, whereas in China it is the "main course." Why? Shopping in China was never a pleasurable experience. Until the arrival of multinational companies like Carrefour and Walmart, there were very few retailing chains or shopping malls. Most domestic retailers started as state-owned enterprises (SOEs). With access to a ready supply of financing, provided by local governments or state-owned banks, they tended to view shoppers as a mere inconvenience. Other retailers were set up by real estate companies more concerned with the value of the land underneath their store than with the customers within.

A key factor in the success of e-commerce in China is the burden of real estate on traditional retailers. Land is expensive in China because it is a crucial source of income for the government. Land sales account for one-quarter of the government's fiscal revenues. At the local government level they account for more than one-third. One prominent e-commerce executive summed it up for me: "Because of the way our economy is structured, the government has a lot of resources. The government decides the price of land. The government decides how resources are channeled, where money is spent. The government relies too heavily on taxes and fees associated with selling land. That almost destroyed the retail business in China, and pushed a lot of demand online. They deprived offline retailers of the opportunity to benefit from rising consumer demand—which they effectively channeled to e-commerce players." Successful brick-and-mortar retailers—from department stores to restaurants—suffer from success: If they bring in lots of customers to their store, they can expect a hefty rent hike when their lease is up for renegotiation.

As a consequence, there has been far less investment in marketing, customer service, human resources, or logistics in China's traditional retail sector than in the West. The result? China's retail market is highly fragmented and inefficient. In the United States, the top three grocery chains account for 37 percent of all sales. In China, they account for just 7 percent. The largest department stores in the United States represent 44 percent of total sales in that segment. In China? Just 6 percent.

Despite massive construction of shopping malls, supermarkets, and corner stores, China's offline retail penetration is still extremely low. For every person in China there are only six square feet of retail space, less than one-quarter the space in the United States.[17]

China will likely never close the gap. Why should it? Traditional retail is hardly a paragon of efficiency. With the burdens of inventory and rental costs, offline stores are rapidly losing sales to online players in many product categories.

In China today, some shop owners are too busy taking care of customers online to bother with those who actually wander into their store. Many vendors in China have simply dispensed with the shop entirely: Why rent an expensive space that is only open at most half of every day when your Taobao storefront is open 24/7?

Nature abhors a vacuum and in China the Internet is filling the voids created by a legacy of state ownership and state planning. That's why shopping online in China is even more popular than in the West. Jack summed it up: "In other countries, e-commerce is a way to shop; in China it is a lifestyle."

Taobao opened the door to online shopping in China, and Tmall has widened it even further. Taobao's early adopters were young, digital natives, but increasingly their parents and grandparents are buying online, too. As the mix of people buying online has broadened, so has the mix of products. The most popular items on Alibaba's sites are shoes and clothing, ranging all the way up from socks and T-shirts to dresses costing tens of thousands of dollars. The day after the country's biggest television broadcast, the Spring Festival Gala on China Central Television, the dresses worn by the celebrities—or approximations of them—are already on sale on Alibaba's sites. Many storefronts feature photos of people—including the merchants themselves—modeling a wide range of body sizes to make it easy to buy online. Customers know that if the clothes don't fit, or are defective, they can return them without charge.

Groceries are another popular category because, as Jack explained, "supermarkets in China were terrible; that's why we have come out on top." Already more than 40 percent of Chinese consumers buy their groceries online as compared to just 10 percent in the United States. In 2014, online grocery sales in China grew by half. Offline, they grew only 7 percent. Tmall offers grocery items in more than 250 cities in all but six of China's thirty-two mainland provinces, typically at cheaper prices than in a supermarket. Alibaba already offers next-day delivery of refrigerated items in more than sixty cities and also features a wide range of imported foods. Working with the Washington State Apple Commission, Alibaba secured more than eighty-four thousand individual orders for apples that were picked, packed, and freighted to customers in China within seventy-two hours, amounting to 167 metric tons and equivalent in volume to the capacity of three Boeing 747s.

Young mothers are a key customer base for Alibaba. James Chiu, a representative from the Dutch infant formula company Friso, which was showcased by Alibaba on Singles' Day 2015, said that for young mothers in China, "e-commerce is not a channel, it's a lifestyle, an ecosystem." The group sold almost $10 million worth of products on Singles' Day by 6 A.M. alone, more than their 2014 total.

Computers, communication products, and consumer electronics are popular items on Taobao, as are household goods, from hair dryers and microwave ovens to TVs and washing machines. Here the impact on offline retailers has been especially dramatic. On Singles' Day, Alibaba's sales of home appliances regularly exceed half of the annual sales of the country's largest consumer goods retailers. In August 2015, Alibaba acquired 20 percent of retailer Suning for $4.6 billion. Selling electronics and white goods as well as books and baby products, Suning operates more than sixteen hundred stores in almost three hundred cities. The deal with Alibaba, part of the growing "omni-channel" or "online to offline" ("O2O") trend, means that even if customers go to Suning merely to test out a product, the company can capture some of the revenue when they buy the item online.

Alibaba sells automobiles online, too. General Motors brands Chevrolet and Buick both operate stores on Tmall, where they also market interest-free auto loans, a critical competitive tool in a market that is already GM's largest. Automobiles are a popular category on Singles' Day, as buyers can expect to score discounts as well as beneficial payment terms. Real estate is another category. The super-rich can browse lists of entire islands for sale in Canada, Fiji, or Greece.

Taobao is famous for offering all sorts of outlandish items, too. One university student gained notoriety for offering earrings that feature dead mosquitoes—like the insects, each pair is unique. Another vendor even sold bottled farts online.

Taobao isn't just about products. Customers can also buy services, too. Artists and musicians find commissions on the site. The sheer variety of services on offer provides a revealing insight into China's fast-changing social mores. Young men can hire a fake girlfriend to attend social events, or outsource a breakup with their real girlfriend to a specialist on Taobao. Wives worried about a straying husband can subscribe to a counseling service offering techniques to fend off a mistress. Busy young urbanites can hire surrogates on Taobao to visit their parents. To overcome a chronic lack of donors, Alibaba's group buying site, Juhuasuan, even teamed up with sperm banks in seven provinces to entice qualified donors with an offer of more than eight hundred dollars. This is the going rate offline, but with the power of online marketing more than twenty-two thousand men had applied within forty-eight hours.

Feel-good items such as cosmetics and jewelry are popular items on Taobao, too. Merchants are drawn to the category for commanding some of the highest margins for any product sold online. Today an estimated 42 percent of skin-care products in China are sold online, a number boosted by the wide availability of goods sold by merchants who have found a way to circumvent high import duties.

Counterfeit goods are thought to be the world's largest illicit industry, more profitable by some estimates than the drug trade. Sales by merchants of pirated goods on Taobao helped boost the early popularity of the website and continue to be a bone of contention for brand owners. China's fake goods can be so high quality that they defy detection even by legitimate manufacturers, made by "extra shift" production runs in the same plant as the real items, typically using leftover materials. As workshop to the world, China is a big part of the piracy problem. But as it becomes the world's largest consumer base, it has to be part of the solution, too.

Speaking at a fair for online merchants in Guangzhou, Jack once[18] addressed these concerns: "Are there any counterfeit products [on Taobao]? Of course there are. This is a complicated society. Taobao itself does not make fake products, but Taobao is providing some degree of convenience for those who make fake products. Taobao is a digital platform." Jack then urged the merchants who sell genuine products on Taobao to unite, enforce regulations, and kick out the merchants who sell fakes, telling them: "We keep track of all of you who make and sell fake products. You will be punished."

But Alibaba's efforts have not always convinced brand owners. In November 2011, the same month that Baidu was removed from its list, Taobao was added to the "Notorious Markets List"[19] published by the Office of the United States Trade Representative (USTR), America's chief trade negotiator. Inclusion on the notorious markets list not only threatened to damage Alibaba's reputation with merchants, but also complicated its plans for an IPO. In response, the company ramped up its efforts to weed out the largest traders of counterfeit items from Taobao, prompting a number of them to form an "Anti-Taobao Alliance" and march on Alibaba's offices in Hong Kong in protest. Alibaba also raised the bar for vendors selling on Tmall, increasing service charges and deposits, a move that triggered an angry response from thousands of merchants who accused Taobao of monopoly practices and marched on Alibaba's headquarters in Hangzhou.

To appease the USTR Alibaba also ramped up its lobbying efforts[20] and in December 2012 Taobao was removed from its list—although a number of U.S. software, clothing, and shoe manufacturers have continued since then to push for sanctions against Taobao to be reimposed.

As the perennial tensions over piracy highlight, the sheer volume of goods on sale on its platforms means Alibaba has to strike a delicate balance between serving the interests of consumers and merchants as well as protecting its own reputation. Binding Alibaba even closer to buyers and sellers is the second edge of the iron triangle: logistics.

The Logistics Edge

On Singles' Day 2015, orders placed on Alibaba's websites generated 467 million packages, requiring more than 1.7 million couriers and four hundred thousand vehicles to deliver the goods. China today has a veritable army of couriers. On foot, bicycles, electronic bikes, trucks, and trains they are the unsung heroes of the country's e-commerce revolution.

Chinese consumers spent more than $32 billion on package deliveries in 2014. The number increased by more than 40 percent in a year. But the volume is set to grow dramatically in the years ahead: On average less than one package per month is delivered for every person in China.

Without the low-cost delivery that the courier services provide, Alibaba would not be the giant it is today. To survive in a cutthroat industry, some of the courier firms have adopted clever methods to keep costs at rock bottom. In Shanghai, for instance, couriers shuttle back and forth on the subway, passing packages over the barriers to one another to avoid buying multiple tickets.

But none of these couriers are employed by Alibaba itself. Most of the packages in China are delivered by private couriers. Where for-profit delivery services have yet to be rolled out, mostly in the countryside, China Post handles the rest.

In 2005, Alibaba approached China Post, proposing to work together on e-commerce. But, chief strategy officer Zeng Ming recalled, Jack "was laughed at. They actually told him to stick to his own business. They didn't believe in express delivery." China's courier companies saw the same opportunities that prompted companies like

Wells Fargo to launch their own private parcel delivery and banking services during the California Gold Rush in the mid-nineteenth century, in response to the inefficiency of what was then the United States Post Office. In China, the e-commerce gold rush has stimulated the rise of more than eight thousand private courier firms, of which twenty major companies stand out.

Alibaba's home province of Zhejiang is home also to most of China's largest courier companies. They play a critical role in delivering goods all over the country. Over half of the package delivery market in China is carried out by just four companies, known as the "Three Tongs, One Da": Shentong (STO Express), Yuantong (YTO Express), Zhongtong (ZTO Express), and Yunda. Remarkably all come from the same town, Tonglu, not far from Hangzhou. More than two-thirds of their business comes from Taobao and Tmall. Together with two other smaller delivery companies they are often referred to as the "Tonglu Gang."

The Tonglu Gang along with a company called SF Express[21] have played a major role in Taobao's success. ZTO cofounder Lai Jianfa described the relationship: "Delivery companies are a propeller. We are the strongest force driving Alibaba's fast development."

Alibaba has invested together with these companies and others in a firm called China Smart Logistics, or "Cainiao."[22] The combined hauling power of the fifteen logistics partners in Cainiao is staggering. Together they handle more than 30 million packages a day and employ more than 1.5 million people across six hundred cities.[23] Cainiao is building a propriety information platform that knits together logistics providers, warehouses, and distribution centers across the country. Alibaba owns 48 percent of Cainiao, which, with the involvement of the Tonglu Gang and other self-made billionaires from the province, gives the company a distinctively Zhejiang flavor.[24] The Zhejiang-born billionaire Shen Guojun[25] is a major investor in Cainiao, and served as its inaugural CEO. Fosun, best known overseas for its purchase of Club Med, is a 10 percent shareholder. Fosun's chairman, Guo Guangchang, is also a native of Zhejiang. In December 2015, Guo was apparently detained for questioning by the Chinese authorities before being released several days later with no explanation, causing a sharp decline in Fosun's share price.

When it was launched in 2013, Cainiao announced plans to invest more than $16 billion by 2020 to develop the "China Smart Logistics Network," comprising three networks—Peoplenet,[26] Groundnet,[27] and Skynet. Cainiao has not merged the courier companies, instead its strategy is to integrate the data that each generates—focusing on data packets, not physical packages. The idea is that by sharing orders, delivery status, and customer feedback each member company can improve efficiency and service quality, while remaining separately owned.

By investing in Cainiao, Alibaba aims to lock in vital relationships with its logistics partners while finding outside investors to fund the expansion of the networks themselves. Cainiao neither owns the physical infrastructure of the networks nor employs the personnel who make the deliveries. Those assets are contributed by the consortium's members and partners, allowing Alibaba to pursue an "asset-light" strategy.

A lot is riding on this approach. Alibaba's principal e-commerce competitor, JD.com,[28] is pursuing an "asset-heavy" strategy, investing directly in its own logistics infrastructure. JD's mascot is Joy, a gray metallic dog, chosen no doubt to give symbolic chase to Tmall's black cat. Today JD has built up the largest warehousing capacity[29] of any e-commerce company in China, offering speedy delivery services including same-day[30] delivery in forty-three cities. JD.com runs a truly end-to-end system, controlling its own procurement, inventory, distribution, and warehouse systems, with goods delivered to customers by uniformed couriers riding JD-branded vehicles.

With annual revenues topping $11 billion, JD has a growing share of the consumer e-commerce market. The company is especially strong in tier-one cities like Beijing and in product categories such as home appliances and electronics.

Alibaba's investment in the electronics retailer Suning, which it watches warily, illustrates its concern. Both Alibaba and JD are vying to ensure deliveries in as little as two to three hours in a number of cities.

Alibaba is attempting to build a whole a new competitive playing field by harnessing data technology, including Big Data—the ability to analyze and drive business decisions from the huge volumes of information generated every day on its websites. On Singles' Day, the delivery paths of most of the courier companies within the Cainiao network were analyzed and rerouted in the event of traffic jams. Alibaba justifies its investment in Cainiao by arguing that demand would otherwise have run ahead of the courier companies' ability to deliver the packages. This is borne out by feedback from merchants selling major appliances, such as refrigerators, during Singles' Day in 2015 who reported that less than 2 percent of the shipments handled by Cainiao arrived late or were damaged, compared to 15 percent of the shipments handled by other courier companies. From some 30 million packages on a typical day at present, Alibaba expects it will generate more than 100 million packages of orders a day by 2020.

An estimated 30 percent of current delivery routes are inefficient or uneconomic. Like Amazon in the United States, Cainiao member companies are experimenting with deliveries by drone aircraft—although higher population density in China, especially in coastal areas, means this is not as big a priority as in the United States. In 2015, YTO, one of the Tonglu Gang companies, ran a three-day trial involving deliveries of ginger tea by drone to a few hundred customers within one hour's flight of Alibaba's distribution centers in Beijing, Shanghai, and Guangzhou. For now drones in China remain just a gimmick. Innovations in logistics—such as shaving off delivery times or cutting costs—are likely to be more incremental than revolutionary.

Yet with Cainiao Alibaba has shored up the most important asset of all: trust. Customers and merchants know they can count on the products getting where they need to be, on time.

The Finance Edge

The final edge in the iron triangle is finance. In financial services, Alibaba's most important asset is Alipay, its answer to PayPal. By far the most popular online payment tool in China, Alipay handles more than three-quarters of a trillion dollars a year in online transactions,[31] three times the volume of PayPal and one-third of the $2.5 trillion global online payments market. In the peak early minutes of Singles' Day 2015, Alipay handled over eighty-five thousand payments per second.

As a form of escrow, Alipay diffuses trust throughout Alibaba's e-commerce empire. Consumers know that when they pay with Alipay their accounts will be debited only when they have received and are satisfied with the products they have ordered. Only then, after freezing the amount on the account, will Alipay release the funds to the merchant. Customers buying on Alibaba's consumer sites can return goods up to seven days after purchase, provided they are not damaged.

No longer owned by Alibaba,[32] Alipay is the largest asset of a company, controlled personally by Jack, which has been valued by one analyst at $45 billion. Alibaba websites account for more than one-third of its revenues, but other sites also rely heavily on Alipay to process their online payments. People use Alipay to make money transfers, top up their cell phone accounts, and make cashless purchases using bar codes at retailers and restaurants, like KFC. Twenty percent of all

Alipay transactions involve paying for utilities, such as water, electricity, and gas bills. Customers can also buy train tickets, pay traffic fines, or purchase insurance using Alipay, making it the de facto currency of an increasingly digital China. Thanks to commissions on payments it handles, Alipay, which is already highly profitable, is expected to generate almost $5 billion a year in revenues[33] by 2018.

With the growth of smartphones in China, used by more than 830 million people, the value of Alipay goes far beyond that of a simple payment tool. Because consumers keep cash balances on their accounts, Alipay has become a virtual wallet for over 300 million people, the thin end of a wedge that Alibaba is driving into China's financial services market.

In the same way Alibaba has exploited the inefficiency of offline retail, offline banking has proved a ripe fruit for it to pick. Just as state-owned shops paid little interest in their customers, China's state-owned banks paid little heed to the needs of individuals and small businesses. Until recently, they had no choice but to place their cash deposits with the banks that were focused on state-owned enterprises. The political masters of the SOEs are also their own.

The "big four" state-owned banks—the Industrial and Commercial Bank of China (ICBC), Construction Bank, Bank of China, and Agricultural Bank of China—control about 70 percent of the market. The disdain of these banks for their customers has fueled popular jokes such as the one about ICBC's initials standing for, in Chinese, "*ai cun bu cun,*" translating loosely as "who cares if you save with us or not, whatever." Traditionally, these and other state-owned banks paid out very low rates of interest, at times below the rate of inflation. This "financial repression" has skewed China's economy, transferring wealth from consumers to the SOEs, which have squandered much of it in the loss-making investments of the Old China model.

The Chinese government recognizes the need for reform, and the need for more rational capital allocation. But to do so it has to take on a powerful vested interest: itself. Alibaba has already been caught in the middle. Offering much higher returns on deposits than the meager returns paid by the banks, Alibaba's Yu'e Bao online mutual fund proved so popular when it launched in 2013 that it stirred China's stagnant financial service industry into a frenzy of activity. Yu'e Bao, whose name translates in English as "savings balance treasure," sounds innocuous enough: a place to deposit your loose change. But when it launched the product Alibaba set no limits on the amount customers could deposit. Not only were the rates it offered much higher than the banks—as much as two percentage points higher—but Yu'e Bao allowed customers to make withdrawals at any time without penalty. As a result, individual customers transferred tens or hundreds of thousands of dollars into the fund. The banks became alarmed at the outflows. By February 2014, Yu'e Bao[34] had attracted over $93 billion from 80 million investors, more than the combined total accounts of all other money managers in China. The inflow was so huge that in only ten months Yu'e Bao was ranked the fourth largest money manager in the world, closing in on global industry stalwarts such as Vanguard, Fidelity, and J.P. Morgan.

Prior to the fund's launch Jack took the unusual step, for a private sector entrepreneur, of penning an opinion piece in the Communist Party journal *People's Daily* arguing, "The finance industry needs disrupters, it needs outsiders to come in and carry out a transformation." Soon after, the SOE empire struck back, denouncing the fund managers behind Yu'e Bao as "vampires sucking blood out of the banks." Starting in March 2014, the state-owned banks, holding collectively more than $100 trillion in deposits, imposed limits on the amounts their customers could transfer into third-party online payment accounts. Other government-imposed restrictions followed soon after. Pulling no punches, Jack posted a message on social media criticizing the banks by name and blaming them for failing to participate in China's market-oriented financial liberalization: "The decision of who wins and who loses in the market shouldn't be up to monopoly and authority, but up to customers." Jack deleted it soon after, but the message was reposted widely. Alibaba has continued to push the boundaries of private sector involvement in financial services, including providing microloans to the merchants and consumers trading on its platforms. Still relatively new, the lending business is expected to grow into a billion-dollar business within a few years. Offering credit also increases the "stickiness," or loyalty from customers, of Alibaba's e-commerce platforms.

Because it has access to the entire trading history of its customers, Alibaba is in a much better position to assess credit risk than the banks. A new business, Sesame Credit Management, provides credit ratings on consumers and merchants to third parties.

Other financial services offerings[35] include wealth management, peer-to-peer lending businesses, and insurance.[36] In 2015 Jack launched an Internet-only bank called MYbank, which gets rid of the need for branches entirely. MYbank plans to use smartphones to authenticate customers' identities.[37]

The iron triangle is a key factor in making Alibaba such a dominant player in China's e-commerce market. But it is the charisma of the company's founder—his "Jack Magic"—that bound together the people and capital who would build on these foundations.

Chapter Two

Jack Magic

Come up with an idea, make it fun, and breathe something into it which otherwise is still just an idea. That's Jack Magic.

—Jan Van der Ven

Most companies bear the imprint of their founders, but few more than Alibaba. Jack Ma's outsize influence stems from his passion for teaching. Although he left the profession two decades ago, Jack has never really stopped being an educator. He used to joke that in his case CEO stood for "Chief Education Officer." Fourteen years after founding the company Jack relinquished the title to become chairman. But the switch served only to heighten his authority. His chosen successor as CEO lasted barely two years in the job.

E.T.

Jack is, without doubt, the face of Alibaba. Short and thin, Jack has been described in the media over the years as an "imp of a man," "a tiny figure with sunken cheekbones, tussled hair and a mischievous grin," his looks "owlish," "puckish," or "elfish." Jack has turned his distinctive looks to his advantage. At the launch of MYbank, which aims to sign up customers exclusively through facial recognition technology, Alibaba showcased the fact that Jack "who had been unable to live off his face was now going to live off his face."

Some in China like to refer to Jack as "E.T.," after a supposed resemblance to the lead creature in the Steven Spielberg movie. Even his Zhejiang-born billionaire friend Guo Guangchang[1] has called Jack an "alien," but only before dismissing himself as "just a normal guy . . . no one is as smart as Jack Ma."

So, Jack doesn't look the part of a corporate chieftain. He possesses all the trappings, including luxury homes around the world and a Gulfstream jet, but otherwise Jack doesn't really act the part, either. One of the most circulated images of Jack on the Internet is a photo of him sporting a Mohawk, nose ring, and makeup, including jet-black lipstick. On that occasion, a celebration of Alibaba's tenth anniversary, Jack sang Elton John's "Can You Feel the Love Tonight" to a stadium full of seventeen thousand cheering employees and ten thousand other spectators.

Jack combines a love of showmanship with a relish for defying stereotypes. Where other business moguls like to talk up their connections or academic credentials, Jack enjoys talking down his own: "I don't have a rich or powerful father, not even a powerful uncle." Having never studied abroad, he likes to describe himself as "one hundred percent Made in China." He stands out as a tech company founder with no background in technology. At Stanford University in 2013 he confessed, "Even today, I still don't understand what coding is all about, I still don't understand the technology behind the Internet."

Jack has made a career out of being underestimated: "I am a very simple guy, I am not smart. Everyone thinks that Jack Ma is a very smart guy. I might have a smart face but I've got very stupid brains."

Blarney Meets Chutzpah in China

His achievements have proved otherwise—this dumbing down is of course just a feint. Jack once explained[2] that he loves the lead character of the movie *Forrest Gump* because "people think he is dumb, but he knows what he is doing." In his early speeches promoting Alibaba, Jack referred so often to Forrest Gump that I came to think of his stump speech as his "Gump speech." Much has changed for Alibaba, but Gump's appeal endures. On the first day of trading of Alibaba's shares, Jack was interviewed by CNBC live on the floor of the New York Stock Exchange. When he was asked which person had most inspired him, Jack replied without hesitation, "Forrest Gump." His interviewer paused, then said, "You know he's a fictional character?"

Jack's ability to charm and cajole has played an important role in attracting talent and capital to the company, as well as building his own fame. Jack has a unique Chinese combination of blarney and chutzpah. One of his earliest foreign employees[3] summed up for me his qualities in two words: "Jack Magic." In this respect, Jack shares a characteristic with Steve Jobs, whose charisma and means of getting his way were famously described by a member of the original Apple Macintosh design team as a "Reality Distortion Field."

Central to Jack's own distortion field are his skills as a communicator. Jack's speaking style is so effective because his message is so easy to agree with, remember, and digest. Collections of his quotes circulate widely online, in English as well as in Chinese. Most are bite-size messages of inspiration, words that wouldn't be out of place on a motivational poster, such as "Believe in your dream and believe in yourself," or "Learn from others the tactics and the skills, but don't change your dream." Other popular quotes read more like an Aesop fable: "If there are nine rabbits on the ground, if you want to catch one, just focus on one. Change your tactics if you need to, but don't change the rabbit.

. . . Get one first, put it in your pocket, and then catch the others." People have even taken to inventing carpe diem–style quotes from Jack to justify, for example, the purchase of a pair of expensive shoes.

Jack always speaks without notes. His oratorical skills are so effective because his repertoire is so narrow. Jack can dispense with notes because he already knows much of his material: a well-honed stable of stock stories, mostly tales from his childhood or Alibaba's own infancy. A close inspection of all of his speeches reveals he has essentially been giving the same speech for the last seventeen years. Yet by subtly tweaking his message to match the mood and expectations of the crowd, he somehow manages to make each speech sound fresh.

Jack is a master at appealing to people's emotions, which is not something you'd expect from the founder of a company that started out focusing on international trade. Sometimes, as he's launched into a familiar story, I have turned around to look at the faces of the audience, trying to understand what explains his enduring appeal.

Humor is a big part of it. As a quick look at any of the hundreds of videos available on YouTube of his most popular speeches will reveal, Jack is very funny. Back in the early days, after he came offstage at an event we'd both spoken at, I joked to him that if his day job at Alibaba didn't work out he had a promising career as a stand-up comedian.[4] Jack's set pieces, his one-liners and anecdotes, and the way he combines them are essentially the same as the "bits" that comedians use to make up their routines.

With his tales of overcoming challenges and defying the odds, Jack regularly drives some in his audience to tears, even hardened business executives. After giving a talk to a group of students in South Korea, Jack himself appeared to be consumed by emotion when asked about his biggest regrets in life, replying that he regretted not spending more time with his family. After composing himself, he added, "Normally *I* make other people cry."

Jack's speeches, like that one in Seoul, reach a much wider audience than speeches by many public figures in China in part because he is able to deliver them in fluent English. Other tech executives in China speak English, too, many having been educated overseas, but Jack's message has much greater resonance in both languages. Jack's long-term business partner, Joe Tsai, told me: "Jack today is still one of the only international businesspeople who is as attention-grabbing in both English and Chinese."

To build a connection to foreign audiences, Jack often peppers his speeches with pop-culture references—including citing more recent movies than *Forrest Gump,* some of which Alibaba is now financing. As his company expands its presence in Hollywood, Jack now regularly enlists the support at his public appearances of famous actors like Daniel Craig, Kevin Spacey, and Tom Cruise, the star of Paramount Pictures' *Mission: Impossible* franchise—in 2015 Alibaba invested in *Rogue Nation,* the franchise's latest title. To audiences in China, Jack often draws on stories from his favorite martial arts novels, or Chinese revolutionary history. An American colleague once asked Jack about his references to Mao in his speeches in China. Jack explained, "For me to motivate you I would talk about George Washington and the cherry tree."

Jack's Mantra

Perhaps the most famous lesson of Jack the teacher is known by heart by every Alibaba employee: "Customers first, employees second, and shareholders third." Jack describes this as Alibaba's philosophy.

Customers, especially the "shrimp," come first in his mantra. When asked by the journalist Charlie Rose if he saw himself as an "apostle for small business," Jack agreed, "I'm a strong believer. It's my religion." Many small businesses in China don't just use Alibaba's websites as a marketing channel, they depend entirely on them to make a living. Jack has always insisted on offering most of Alibaba's services for free.

Employees may come second to customers for Jack, but an ability to motivate his team to overcome obstacles has been critical to Alibaba's success. Joe Tsai didn't hesitate in describing them to me as "disciples," when recalling his first impression in 1999 of Alibaba's earliest employees, some of whom had already followed Jack for years. Jack doesn't sugar coat the challenges to his employees. One of his favorite messages to them, and a "bit" in his comedy routine, is "Today is brutal, tomorrow is more brutal, but the day after tomorrow is beautiful. However, the majority of people will die tomorrow night." The goal for Alibaba to survive for 102 years might seem weird to outsiders but not to his employees, especially the Aliren (the "Ali People")—those with more than three years of service—for whom it is an accepted part of the Alibaba culture.

Shareholders come third in Jack's ranking because he refuses to be diverted from his lofty ambitions by short-term pressures to generate profit. In public, Jack likes to make fun of his shareholders and investors, a means to burnish his credentials as a maverick with his employees and the general public. When the share price of Alibaba's first business, alibaba.com, languished on the stock market in 2009, Jack cried out at the rock concert–style gathering for the company's employees, "Let the Wall Street investors curse us if they wish!" Not exactly standard behavior for the senior executive of a publicly listed company.

Yet despite the populist rhetoric, Jack has assiduously created opportunities at regular intervals—on average every four years or so—for employees and long-term shareholders to turn a profit from the sale of their shares. Investors who supported Alibaba early on and stuck with the company for years have been richly rewarded, much less so those public investors who purchased the company's shares in their post-IPO peak.

Company Campus and Culture

Jack's imprint can also be seen in the design of Alibaba's 2.6-million-square-foot Wetlands headquarters campus. From the main south gate visitors enter a massive complex of futuristic glass towers. At the base of the office towers lie a large gym, Starbucks, and a country-style store stocked with organic fruit and vegetables that could be straight out of Silicon Valley. Farther to the north lies a huge, man-made lake. Dotted with lotuses and lily pads and bordered with reeds, the lake is overlooked on one side by a cluster of elegant, white-walled villas topped with curved, black-tiled roofs, a scene reminiscent of Jack's much-loved classical novels, like the sixteenth-century work *The Water Margin*.

The lake reflects Jack's newfound passion for environmental protection. When asked by President Obama in Manila what spurred his interest in the environment, Jack told the story of a lake in which he had last swam when he was twelve years old. "I went to swim in a lake and almost died in the lake because the water was so deep, much deeper than I thought. Five years ago I went to the lake, the total lake was dry."

On a visit in the spring of 2015 to the campus, I had to step gingerly to avoid squashing the tiny baby frogs that had hopped out of the man-made lake onto the walkway leading to the office towers. On my way I also stopped by Alibaba's large library and bookstore. Jack is a keen reader, particularly of titles by the Hong Kong–born martial arts writer (Louis) Cha Leung-yung, known in China by his pen name Jin Yong. His works are featured in the library along with classical works and the latest books on management theory or Silicon Valley icons like Steve Jobs and Elon Musk.

But beyond the design of the campus, it is in the culture of Alibaba that we can most clearly see the influence of its principal founder. To zip around the Wetlands headquarters complex, Alibaba's employees make frequent use of the free bicycles the company provides, a perk no doubt inspired by Google's fleet, which is decked out in the U.S. giant's signature blue, yellow, green, and red colors. The bicycles at Alibaba are orange and include tandems: the two seats illustrating the company's emphasis on teamwork above individual achievement.

A sense of subjugating one's own needs for the interest of the customer is a cornerstone of Alibaba's corporate culture. Just as Disney refers to all of its executives and employees as "cast members," Alibaba places a big emphasis on camaraderie and a commitment to the greater good.

Every May 10, around the time of the annual "Aliday," a company anniversary that celebrates the spirit of teamwork shown by the company's employees as they emerged from the spectre of the SARS virus, Jack presides as chief witness over a ceremony to celebrate recent weddings of company employees. Alibaba covers the lodging and meal expenses of the immediate family members who are invited to join. The photos of a hundred plus couples celebrating their matrimonials together at one company has inevitably invited comparisons to cults such as Rev. Sun Myung Moon's Unification Church. But Alibaba takes pains to point out that the event is just a celebration, not a replacement, of the couples' official marriage registrations.

A more tangible benefit for the couples and other Alibaba employees is the interest-free loan of up to $50,000 offered to finance the down payment on a new apartment, an increasingly valued perk for staff members working in high-cost cities like Hangzhou and Beijing. Thousands of employees have taken advantage of the loans, amounting to several hundred millions dollars today.

Alibaba encourages a sense of informality at work. Every employee is asked to adopt a nickname. The practice is so widespread that it can invite confusion when they have to search to find out the actual names of their colleagues to communicate to people outside the company. Initially, the nicknames were drawn from characters in the novels of Jin Yong or other stories of martial arts and bygone eras. As Alibaba grew this pool of names was soon exhausted. Using their nicknames, employees post comments about the company's products or culture on Aliway, the company's internal bulletin board. They can even initiate polls or invite the support of their colleagues to dispute assessments or management decisions, and address suggestions or complaints directly to Feng Qingyang. That is the name of Jack's online persona, a swordsman from one of his favorite martial arts novels.

Employees are discouraged from ever complaining—a pet peeve of Jack's—and encouraged instead to shoulder personal responsibility, carrying out or delegating tasks rather than waiting for orders from on high.

Military terms crop up a lot at Alibaba. Top-performing individuals at Alibaba are known as King of Soldiers (*bing wang*). Fictional character Xu Sanduo is sometimes used to illustrate management's message. In the 2007 TV drama *Soldier's Sortie,* Xu, a shy village boy, rises despite the odds to become an elite soldier in the People's Liberation Army.

Six Vein Spirit Sword

Alibaba has codified its own company values in something it calls the Six Vein Spirit Sword. The term originates in the work of Jack's favorite novelist, Jin Yong. The sword he writes about is not an actual weapon, but the art of building up one's own internal strengths in order to defeat any opponent. In Alibaba's case, the strengths that form the Six Vein Spirit Sword are akin to those outlined in the "Mission, Vision, and Values" of Jack's favorite corporate guru, Jack Welch, the former CEO of General Electric (GE).

Welch's 2005 book, *Winning,* recommends an almost messianic culture in the workplace: "Leaders make sure people not only see the vision, they live and breathe it." Jack (Ma) has always held GE in high regard.

The "Six Veins" of Alibaba's "Spirit Sword" are "customer first, teamwork, embrace change, integrity, passion, and commitment." Generic-sounding as they are, the company treats them very seriously. Commitment to the Six Vein Spirit Sword accounts for half of employee appraisals.

"Customer first" is reflected in the power given to Taobao's *xiaoer* referees and in the composition of Alibaba's workforce. Most of Alibaba employees work in sales, a much higher proportion than the more technical bent of competitors like Tencent and Baidu. Face-to-face visits are a key part of Alibaba's sales methods.[5]

"Teamwork" at Alibaba means regular group games, songs, and outings. These can come as quite a culture shock to employees joining Alibaba from firms based in Silicon Valley. But for those fresh out of college, the system of apprentices and mentors is well received, including the routine of holding regular meetings to "kick off in the morning and share in the evening." One former employee summed it up: "Lots of companies focus only on results: You have to complete a certain number of orders. Alibaba takes the opposite approach: If you want to complete a certain number of orders this month, what do you need to do every day? By breaking it down into phases, each day could be dedicated to one key step in the process—and eventually you wouldn't be far off from your goal." Recognition of high performers in company-wide announcements helps, too, as do the prizes awarded to the "A-teams" (*lao A,* a military reference), ranging from Louis Vuitton wallets, belts, and limited-edition sneakers to monthly bonuses of tens of thousands of yuan or even a car.

The call to "embrace change" is reflected in Alibaba's frequent rotation of its employees, switching them regularly between various new products or between regions of the country, regardless of performance. This creates lots of challenges, but Alibaba asks its employees to "embrace setbacks," a radical departure from traditional Chinese culture, where failure is seen as something shameful. Alibaba's approach is in line with the Silicon Valley practice of entrepreneurs celebrating previous failed ventures on their T-shirts, a recognition that on the fast-moving battle lines of the China Internet, some failure is unavoidable, or even desirable.

The "integrity" vein of the sword highlights the fact that corruption is a constant risk for Alibaba: Millions of merchants are constantly looking for ways to promote their wares on Taobao, overseen by only a few thousand *xiaoer* referees. The Communist Party of China regularly uses rotation of personnel to avoid alternative centers of power from developing, in an effort to keep corruption under control. David Wei, who served as the CEO of Alibaba.com, experienced Jack's penchant for rotation even before he had joined the company. In the nine months between leaving his previous employer and joining Alibaba, David recalled, "[m]y job description and titles changed four times before I joined. First I was going to be head of Taobao, then head of Alipay. I didn't know what I was doing until one month before I was on board." Once he finally joined as CEO of Alibaba's B2B business, David joked to Jack, "You changed my job so many times before I joined you couldn't change it anymore."

Whatever the inspiration for regular rotation, Alibaba devolves a lot of autonomy to its business units, an effort to maintain a relatively flat management hierarchy and minimize the temptation to shame and blame.

The need to demonstrate "passion" when working for Alibaba was summed up by one employee as "being a swordsman is all about being hot-blooded." Compared to other firms, "people at Alibaba are more passionate about their work, more honest, and more hardworking." Jack's emphasis on "commitment" is reflected in his frequent invocation of the phrase to "work happily but live seriously." The whimsical approach he encourages at Alibaba is, he says, in stark contrast to most companies who emphasize "working seriously but living happily."

Measuring how employees live up to the Six Vein Spirit Sword is the job of Alibaba's human resources department, which plays a critical role, overseeing the hiring of twelve thousand people in one year alone. Relegated in some companies to a purely administrative function, HR at Alibaba has tremendous power over promotions and hiring. With its constant emphasis on culture and ideology, people at Alibaba refer to HR informally as the "Political Commissar" (*zheng wei)*. The HR department also oversees extensive training, with manuals of more than one thousand pages for new employees and a sophisticated database, matching performance closely with promotions and pay raises.

The culture of Alibaba endures even in the employees who have left the company. Given the long history and rapid growth of the company, they number over twenty-five thousand. Many have banded together in a nonprofit organization called the Former Orange Club (*qian cheng hui)* to help its members share investment opportunities and career advice. One member, Hu Zhe, who left Alibaba in 2010 after working there for five years, described[6] his reason for joining: "Former Alibaba employees are closely connected, as if there is a bond linking us together. The club serves as a very important platform for us to communicate and exchange ideas."

A number of members[7] have founded their own Internet companies or investment vehicles, some of which have established links with one another, active in a range of sectors including e-commerce, online travel booking, Internet financial services, online music, online recruiting, O2O, venture capital, and health care. A search in a database[8] of Chinese Internet-related start-ups reveals that former Alibaba employees have been associated with 317 start-ups, compared to 294 from Tencent and 223 from Baidu. While not all of these start-ups will be successful, indeed some of them have already failed, the web of entrepreneurial activity is important both as a source of future innovation and acquisition targets for Alibaba.

A common thread in many of the ventures founded by Alibaba veterans is what some have described as a "Long March" culture, an ambitious management ethos that involves personal sacrifice, and huge investments of personnel and time. In contrast, in their new businesses, the veterans of Alibaba's rivals such as Tencent are known to focus more on reducing "time to market," launching products that they can perfect later, an approach some refer to as "running with short steps."

Alibaba has been a team effort from the start. Jack doled out much more equity, and at an earlier stage, than many of his Internet founder peers. But he has kept a firm control on the company through his gift for communicating and his lofty ambitions. A modern-day Don Quixote, Jack relishes tilting at windmills, from retail to finance, to entertainment, health care, and beyond. To gain a sense of how likely Alibaba is to conquer these new horizons, let's look at the events that made Jack and the company what they are today.

Chapter Three

From Student to Teacher

If you are one in a million in China, you're one of 1,300 people.

—Bill Gates

Barrow Boy

Jack Ma was born on September 10, 1964, the Year of the Dragon, in Hangzhou, a city one hundred miles to the southwest of Shanghai. His parents named him "Yun," meaning "cloud." His surname, "Ma," is the same as the Chinese word for horse.

Jack's mother, Cui Wencai, worked on a factory production line. His father, Ma Laifa, worked as a photographer at the Hangzhou Photography Agency. But both share a passion for *pingtan,* a form of Chinese folk art performance that involves the singing of ballads and comedic routines punctuated by the sound of wooden clappers. Exposure to the art form may help explain Jack's abilities as a communicator. *Pingtan* no doubt provided Jack's parents a welcome escape from the hardscrabble life of postrevolutionary China, a window to a richer and more colorful past.

A future icon of Chinese entrepreneurship, Jack came into the world at a time when private enterprise had almost been completely extinguished. Ninety percent of industrial production had been taken into the hands of the state. China was alone in the world, struggling to recover from the Great Leap Forward. Faced with the starvation of millions across the country, Mao Zedong had been forced to make a "self-criticism" and was relegated to the margins of power. Deng Xiaoping was among those tasked with reversing the most damaging aspects of collectivization, a foreshadowing of the pivotal role he would play in unleashing the country's economic miracle, which, two decades later, would provide the opening for Jack's entrepreneurial career.

But when Jack was two, Mao was back in power and China was subjected to the ravages of the Cultural Revolution. Mao launched an attack on the "Four Olds"—old customs, culture, habits, and ideas—and Red Guards marched to destroy cultural sites and antiquities, including in Hangzhou, where they attacked and badly damaged the tomb of Yue Fei, a famous Song dynasty general. But even the Red Guards were not immune to the charms of the city, taking breaks from their violence with boat trips on West Lake. Mao himself developed a strong attachment to Hangzhou, visiting it on more than forty occasions and staying up to seven months at a time. He enjoyed performances of *pingtan*. Despite Mao's fondness for the art form in private, old customs like *pingtan* became a target of the Red Guards and its practitioners were denounced. Jack's family was at risk of persecution, particularly as his grandfather had been a local official[1] under the Nationalist (KMT) government. During the Cultural Revolution Jack was taunted by his classmates, although fortunately the family was not broken up like many were at the time.

In February 1972, President Nixon traveled to Hangzhou as part of his historic visit to China to meet Mao. Nixon was accompanied on the trip by almost one hundred reporters, including Walter Cronkite, Dan Rather, Ted Koppel, and Barbara Walters, their live broadcasts generating support for the normalization of relations with China, leading eventually to cities like Hangzhou reemerging as a destination for foreign tourists.

As a boy, Jack fell in love with the English language and literature, particularly readings of Mark Twain's *The Adventures of Tom Sawyer* that he listened to on a shortwave radio. Later it was the arrival of foreign tourists in China that provided Jack with his opening to the outside world. In late 1978, when Jack was fourteen, China launched the new "open door" policy, initiated by Deng Xiaoping, in pursuit of foreign trade and investment. After a decade of turmoil the country was on the verge of bankruptcy, and desperately needed hard currency.

In 1978, only 728 foreign tourists visited Hangzhou. But the following year more than forty thousand came to the city. Jack relished any opportunity to practice his English. He started waking up before dawn and riding his bicycle for forty minutes to the Hangzhou Hotel to greet foreign tourists. As he recalled, "Every morning from five o'clock I would read English in front of the hotel. A lot of foreign visitors came from the USA, from Europe. I'd give them a free tour of West Lake, and they taught me English. For nine years! And I practiced my English every morning, no matter if it snowed or rained."

An American tourist whose father and husband were named Jack suggested the name and Ma Yun became known in English henceforth as Jack. He is dismissive of the quality of his English: "I just make myself understood. The grammar is terrible." But Jack never dismisses how much learning the language has helped him in life: "English helps me a lot. It makes me understand the world better, helps me to meet the best CEOs and leaders in the world, and makes me understand the distance between China and the world."

Among the many tourists who came to Hangzhou in 1980 was an Australian family, the Morleys. Ken Morley, a recently retired electrical engineer, had signed up for a tour of China offered by the local branch of the Australia China Friendship Society. He took along his wife, Judy, and their three children, David, Stephen, and Susan, for whom it would be their first overseas trip. For Jack, their visit would change his life.

Today, David runs a yoga studio in Australia, where I managed to track him down. He kindly shared his memories and the photos of his family's visit to China and their enduring friendship with Jack.

On July 1, 1980, the Morleys' Australian tour group arrived by plane in Hangzhou from Beijing and was transferred by bus to the Shangri-La Hotel on West Lake, the same hotel (then the Hangzhou Hotel) where President Nixon and his entourage had stayed eight years earlier. David recalls being shown the suite where the First Couple had stayed, allocated to their tour leader, complete with "plush, red velvet toilet seats, which we three children were fascinated by."

The next day the Australian group's itinerary included a boat trip on West Lake, followed by a visit to the nearby tea plantations and on to the Liuhe (Six Harmonies) Pagoda before returning to the hotel for dinner at 6:30 P.M. Taking advantage of the "free evening," David and a young woman called Keva whom he had befriended on the trip snuck across the road from the hotel to the park opposite, overlooking West Lake. There they proceeded to play with matches, practicing the art of "match flicking" that she had taught him. This involved standing a match upside-down with its head on the striking surface and flicking it with your fingers and watching it spiral off to, David recalls, "hopefully an uneventful extinguishment." Fortunately that day, the park didn't catch fire. But David and Keva's antics *did* catch the attention of a fifteen-year-old boy—Jack Ma.

David recalls, "It was on that free evening, flicking matches in the park, that I was approached by a young man wanting to try his newly acquired English skills on me. He introduced himself; we swapped pleasantries and agreed to meet in the park again."

On July 4, their last day in Hangzhou, David introduced Jack to his sister, Susan, and invited him and some other local children to play Frisbee with them in the park. David described the scene to me: Marking out a playing area with shoes and other items "we were soon surrounded by hundreds of Chinese spectators." Jack's father, Ma Laifa, took photos of the game.

David's father, Ken Morley, once described his first impressions of Jack as a "barrow boy," or a street hawker. "He really wanted to practice his English, and he was very friendly. Our kids were very impressed."

David described how the family stayed in touch: "What followed that meeting was a pen pal relationship that I kept up for a few years until my father started to take an interest in helping this young man." Jack would correspond regularly with Ken, referring to him as "Dad," who asked him to "double space his letters so that any corrections could be sent back in the spaces." David explained, "The original with corrections was returned for learning purposes with the reply letter. I believe this greatly helped and encouraged Jack to continue with his English studies."

Armed with his improving English, rich knowledge of the history

Jack Ma, age fifteen, with his new Australian friend David Morley by West Lake. David is wearing his Australia China Friendship Society ID card. *The Morley Family*

of the area, and a knack for storytelling, Jack embraced the opportunity to show more foreign tourists around the sights of West Lake. He relished visiting Hangzhou's teahouses, where locals would play Chinese chess and cards and recount "tall tales."

Jack would often accompany his grandmother to Buddhist temples to burn incense and worship the gods. He developed a passion for tai chi and reading *The Water Margin,* a classic Chinese tale that features 108 heroes—the number of employees he later would set as an early head count target for Alibaba.

But by far his favorite works are those of Hong Kong author Louis Cha, who writes under the pen name Jin Yong. Born in Zhejiang Prov-

Dear David: ① 15th March 82

It's a pleasure to read your letter and to know about your trip to China. The weather in January in Hangchow is in winter. So it is very cold and it maybe have snow. I think it is a good time for you to come. I guess there is no snow in your city. The snowing view in Hangchow is very beautiful and very famous in our country. I hope you will come to see us David. I think April and May are the best season to visit China. There is hale near our city, is very beautiful. In the hale it has all kinds of stones. They are very strange and it It is like a fairy land. We often go for an spring outing in April or May. On 5th April our school plan to have an outing. I don't know where we should go. I will write to tell you about it.

Thank you for the Rubik cubes. We like them very much. We called it "Mou Fang" 魔方 in China. People enjoy them very much and they often competition each other to see who do them the fastest.

Thank you for the books and diaries and a calendar cloth

One of Jack's childhood pen pal letters to David Morley. *The Morley family*

ince in 1924, Jin Yong cofounded in 1959 the Hong Kong newspaper *Ming Pao,* which published many of his early works. In total, he authored fifteen novels, all in the *wuxia* genre, which blends historical and fictional tales of martial arts and chivalry. Jin Yong is highly popular in the Chinese-speaking world. Worldwide sales of his books have topped 100 million copies. There have been more than ninety television series and film adaptations of his work.

Set between the sixth century BC and the eighteenth century, Jin Yong's works contain strong elements of Chinese patriotism, pitting heroic peoples against northern invaders such as the Mongols and Manchus.

Yi Zhongtian, a well-known writer and a professor at Xiamen University, summarized the popular appeal of traditional stories and martial arts as follows: "In traditional Chinese society, people have three dreams. The first is a wise emperor. People hope to have a good leader so that they can have peace in the country. The second dream is clean officials. If there are no clean officials, then comes the third dream, chivalrous heroes. People hope that the heroes could stand for them, kill the greedy officials, and bring justice back to the society. However, if there are no heroes, people can only seek comfort from martial arts fiction. That's why many Chinese people like kung fu novels."

Jin Yong's writing is suffused with traditional elements of Chinese culture and arts, as well as Buddhism, Taoism, and Confucianism. Jack found inspiration in Jin Yong's legendary warrior Feng Qingyang. Feng was a teacher. His martial arts moves were never performed to any set plan.

In his own practice of martial arts, Jack was trained in tai chi[2] by a woman in her seventies who, according to Chen Wei—a former student of Jack's who is now his personal assistant—was so skilled that she could defend herself against two or three younger men. Every morning she would close her eyes to meditate before practicing tai chi, "listening to the sound of flowers blooming." Today Jack often travels with a personal tai chi coach.

But these skills were of little use against one of Jack's earliest foes: math. In China, all high school students hoping to go on to higher education have to pass a merit-based national higher education entrance exam, commonly known as the *gaokao,* literally the "high test." The *gaokao* takes place over two or three days. Math, along with Chinese and a foreign language, is mandatory.

The *gaokao* is widely seen as one of the most challenging in the world, requiring a huge amount of preparation and memorization. Today there is growing criticism of the exam's negative social consequences, including depression and suicide.

Jack took the *gaokao* but failed badly, scoring 1/120 in math. His hopes crushed, he took to menial labor delivering heavy bundles of magazines from printers to the Hangzhou train station on a pedicab, a job Jack managed to land thanks only to his father's connections. Jack was rejected from numerous other jobs, including as a waiter in a hotel. He was told he was not tall enough.

Chen Wei relates in his biography of Jack, *This Is Still Ma Yun,* how his boss found inspiration in the book *Life,* written by the Chinese author Lu Yao. Published in 1982, and made into a film in 1984, the book relates the story of Gao Jialin. A talented man living in a village, Gao struggles but ultimately fails to escape the clutches of poverty. Jack resolved to have a different fate, and took the *gaokao* again. This time his math score improved slightly, to 19/120, but his overall score dropped considerably.

Jack once again set about applying for jobs to make ends meet. He sent out eleven job applications but all met with rejection. Jack likes to tell the story of how even KFC turned him away, the only one of twenty-four candidates they didn't like.

Undeterred, Jack became a regular every Sunday at the library of Zhejiang University, where he committed to memory the formulas and equations he would have to master to pass the test.

Jack never gained admission to a prestigious university in Beijing or Shanghai. But in 1984, when he was nineteen, he raised his math score sufficiently to win acceptance to a local university, the Hangzhou Teachers College. On his third attempt at the *gaokao* he scored 89 in math. His score was several points below the normal acceptance rate at other universities for a full four-year undergraduate degree.[3] Normally he would have been relegated to a two- to three-year associate's degree course,[4] but Hangzhou Teachers College had a few spaces left for male students, and Jack squeaked in. The college was not a prestigious one. Jack recalled that "it was considered the third or fourth class of my city." In his public appearances, Jack often speaks of his twice failing the *gaokao* as a badge of honor.

Teacher

In his sophomore year, Jack was elected president of the school's student union, where he launched a Top Ten Campus Singers Competition, and was later president of the Hangzhou Students Federation.

In 1985, Jack also received an invitation from Ken Morley to stay with his family at their home in New Lambton, Australia, a suburb of Newcastle in New South Wales. It was the first time Jack had left China. He stayed for a month and returned a changed man.

"Everything I'd learned in China was that China was the richest country in the world," Jack later said. "When I arrived in Australia, I realized it was totally different. I started to think you have to use your own mind to judge, to think."

Jack has never shown any hint of shyness toward foreigners. During his trip to Australia, Jack gave a demonstration to a local

Stephen Morley, Jack, and Anne Lee, a cousin of the Morleys. *Louis and Anne Lee*

tai chi group gathered in a suburban hall, showing off his skills at monkey- and drunken-style kung fu. "I'd often request he do his drunken boxing routine, it was great to watch," Stephen Morley recalls.

Jack's friendship with the Morleys blossomed. After Jack's trip to Australia, Ken Morley made a return visit to Hangzhou with Stephen. As the Ma family home was too small to host guests, Jack arranged accommodation at a student college for the Morleys. "We would have dinner at the Ma household and cycle to the college after dinner," Stephen recalls. "Jack would always help prepare and cook dinner, always making us feel special."

Louis and Anne Lee

During their holiday, Jack planned a trip out to the countryside for his two Australian friends, and they got their fair share of Chinese adventures. For transportation, Jack secured the use of a pickup truck. He and the driver sat up front in the cab while Ken and Stephen sat on two loose chairs that Jack had placed on the open-top cargo bed. On their way out of Hangzhou one day, the driver had to break suddenly to avoid a cyclist who had fallen off his bike, sending Ken and Stephen hurtling forward into the rear of the cab. Fortunately they escaped injury. Back in town later that evening, Jack arranged a banquet for his Australian friends with some local officials and VIPs, looking out over a street below where a festival was taking place. Stephen recalls, "I'd never seen so many people congested in one place. It became clear then that Jack was a bit of a networker, organizing a vehicle and a dinner with the mayor required connections."

Back in Hangzhou, Jack's university life was not carefree. Money concerns were pressing. Once again Ken Morley stepped in to help. While the tuition at the college was free, the compulsory live-in fees were beyond the means of Jack's family. "When we came back to Australia we thought about it," Morley recalled, "and decided we could help. It was not much—five to ten dollars a week, I think—so I would send him a check every six months."

At Hangzhou Teachers College, Jack met and fell in love with Zhang Ying, a fellow student and Zhejiang-native who had taken Cathy as her first name. The relationship was

Ma Yin (Jack's sister), Stephen Morley, Ken Morley, and Jack in Hangzhou. *The Morley family*

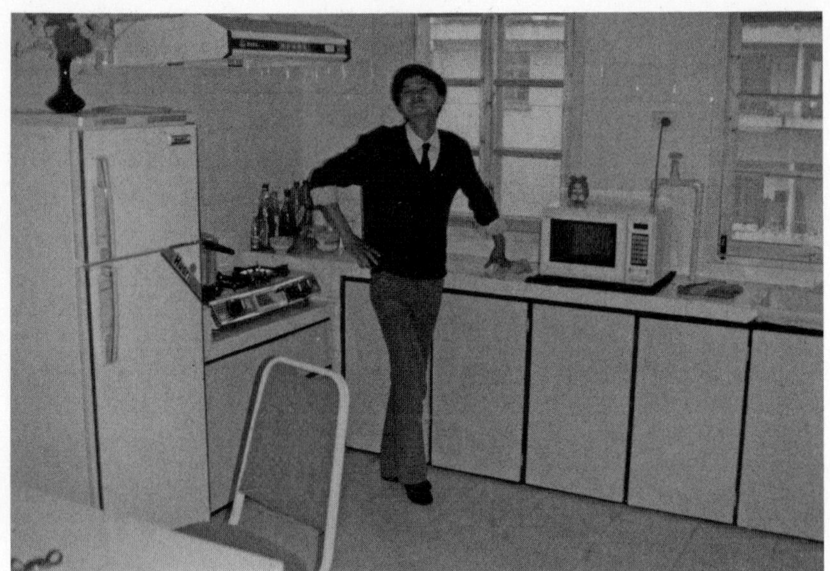

Jack inside the kitchen of the new apartment that Ken Morley helped him purchase in Hangzhou. *The Morley Family*

kept secret from Jack's family. During a dinner one evening in Hangzhou with his father, Jack, and his parents, Stephen Morley recalled, "I blurted out '*nü peng you*' [girlfriend] and gestured towards Jack. Jack looked mortified and probably wanted to kill me at this point. This led to a discussion in Mandarin between Jack and his parents. Jack still reminds me of the time I blabbed on him as a kid."

Despite being outed by their young Australian friend, the relationship between Jack and Cathy endured and they were married soon after. The Morleys once again showed their generosity and gave the couple 22,000 Australian dollars (about $18,000) to help finance the purchase of their first home, two apartments on top of a tower block that they combined together to make a penthouse.

Jack later said that words could not express what Ken and Judy Morley had done for him.

Ken Morley died in September 2004 at the age of seventy-eight.

Jack and a fellow lecturer prepare to host a talk by Jack's mentor, Ken Morley, in April 1991 at the Hangzhou YMCA. *The Morley Family*

His obituary in a local newspaper records that he had taken "his children to China and Cuba and encouraged them to get an education, travel and have a political point of view. This broad-minded, generous approach extended outside the family and Ken is well-known for befriending a poor young Chinese boy. This boy is now a man who heads a successful company in China." At the funeral, a clergyman read out a message from Jack to the Morley family in which he disclosed a plan he had to one day travel the Trans-Siberian Railway with Ken, whom he described as his "Australian 'Dad' and mentor." His son David wrote to me, "It may be a fantasy now, and with his celebrity status something difficult to achieve for Jack incognito, but I would like one day to fulfill the idea of that trip on behalf of my father."

The irony is that Ken Morley, who was instrumental in unlocking opportunities for a man who would become one of China's richest capitalists, was himself a committed socialist. Born the son of a miner and a seamstress, he was a longtime political activist and member of

Jack and Ken Morley sharing some beer. *The Morley Family*

the Communist Party of Australia, presenting himself as a candidate in local elections for the Socialist Alliance. In the years before he died, he would witness some of Jack's early success, expressing his embarrassment at the money and gifts Jack and Cathy liked to shower on him. Instead he treasured most, he said, the honor that Jack and Cathy bestowed on him by naming their eldest child after him (calling him "Kun," an approximation of Ken). China impacted the Morleys, too: Susan Morley went on to study Chinese in Sydney for several years. The Ma and Morley families remain close friends to this day and continue to vacation together.

To Get Rich Is Glorious

In 1992, Deng Xiaoping undertook his famous "southern tour," immortalized[5] in his pronouncement that "to get rich is glorious." For the country's entrepreneurs, relegated to the margins of society, Deng's endorsement was an unambiguous invitation to return to the fold.

But Jack was not yet an entrepreneur. Upon graduating in 1988, with a bachelor's degree in English, he had become a lecturer in English and international trade at the Hangzhou Institute of Electronic Engineering. While his fellow students were all assigned to teach English in middle schools, Jack was the only one among five hundred graduates to be assigned to teach in an institution of higher learning. But he had started to think of a future beyond teaching. Jack recalled the lesson he drew from Deng's southern tour: "You can be rich; you can help other people be rich." Although he was keen to serve out the remaining two years of his contract, Jack began to pursue opportunities outside his school.

After his day job at the institute, he started teaching English classes at the Hangzhou YMCA. According to Chen Wei, who first attended a class in 1992, Jack's English classes were popular because he spent little time teaching grammar, vocabulary, or reading out texts. Instead Jack preferred to pick a topic and engage in conversation. His students came from a wide variety of backgrounds, from high schoolers striving to study overseas, to college students, to factory workers and young professionals. Jack would often spend time with them after class, "drinking tea, playing cards, and chatting."

Hangzhou had a regular "English corner," a gathering of local residents keen to practice their language skills on one another, which met every Sunday morning in the Six Park beside West Lake. Jack would take along his students from night school, but as they were eager to go more often, he decided to launch his own English corner. His sessions were held every Wednesday night, with Jack finding that the anonymity that darkness conferred made his students less self-conscious in practicing their imperfect English.

But Jack's teaching days were coming to an end. Swept up in the enthusiasm that Deng Xiaoping's southern tour had fanned, he resolved to launch his own business before he turned thirty. Working part-time on his new business, after class, he named his first company "Hope."

Chapter Four

Hope and Coming to America

China has a million companies that want to sell abroad,
but they don't know how.
—Jack Ma

In January 1994, at the age of twenty-nine, Jack founded the Hangzhou Haibo Translation Agency. When the company first started there were only five staff members, mostly retired teachers from the institute. He rented two rooms at 27 Qingnian Road, not far from West Lake in a converted church that once housed the YMCA. Today the sign for Hope Translation still hangs outside, where the translation agency maintains a meeting room, adjacent to what has become the YMCA International Youth Hostel.

Jack convinced some students from his English night school to lend a hand with the business, largely to help find his first clients. On opening day, his students went to Wulin Square with banners to help publicize the company.

A few of these students ended up joining the company full-time.

One of the early employees was Zhang Hong. She met Jack in 1993, when he was teaching advanced oral English at the YMCA. She recalled, "Nobody else saw the opportunity in this business. . . . We didn't make much money at first, but [Jack] persevered. . . . I respect him tremendously for he has a great ability to motivate people and he can invest things that seem hopeless with exciting possibility. He can make those around him get excited about life."

Jack's first business was focused on helping local companies find customers overseas. Jack later recalled, "I had to teach during the day, and had no time to help others do translation work. But lots of retired teachers had nothing to do at home, and their pension was low, so I wanted to found a translation company, to be an intermediary." With its narrow focus on translation, Jack would not find commercial success with Hope. But his first venture gave him direct exposure to the entrepreneurial revolution that was transforming Zhejiang and his first tentative steps as an entrepreneur himself.

The Chinese word for Hope was *Haibo,* which literally translates as "vast like the sea." Popular slang for leaving a government job and entering the private sector at the time was to *xia hai,* or to "jump into the sea."

Jack wanted to get his feet wet as an entrepreneur, but he wasn't quite ready to take the plunge and abandon his public sector job as a teacher. Entrepreneurship is such a well-established part of modern Chinese business and culture today that it is easy to forget how much things have changed in the last few decades.

In the earliest days of China's economic reforms, entrepreneurship was viewed as a highly risky, even illegal undertaking. Memories then were fresh of those imprisoned or even executed during the Cultural Revolution for carrying out commercial activities.

From 1978, the establishment of a "household contract responsibility system" allowed farmers to sell surplus crops on the open market.

The first embers of private business started to grow with the township and village enterprises (TVEs). The TVEs were nominally state-controlled but in effect privately run rural enterprises. The spark was lit for a rapid expansion of private sector employment in China.

From the early 1980s, the Chinese government began to recognize entrepreneurs,[1] first individual entrepreneurs then businesses run by entrepreneurs.

The first entrepreneurs, the *getihu,* were not leaving behind a stable government job, but rather were those with nothing to lose. They were mostly agricultural laborers, their low status inviting the pejorative association of "peddlers." As they grew richer they were resented and mocked for their success and lack of class. One early *getihu* even papered the walls of his home with banknotes.

Some of the richest businesspeople in China today started out as lowly *getihu,* many in Zhejiang Province. To understand Alibaba's rise, it is helpful to understand how Jack's home province became the source of so much wealth.

Zhejiang: China's Crucible of Entrepreneurship

Hangzhou, the nearby port of Ningbo, and other industrial clusters dotting northern Zhejiang and southern Jiangsu Provinces form the economic powerhouse of the Yangtze River delta, with Shanghai as its center.

Home to Alibaba's e-commerce empire, Hangzhou has a long tradition as a trading center. The city once served as the southernmost point of the 1,100-mile-long Grand Canal, whose full name in Chinese is Jing Hang Da Yun He, or the Beijing-Hangzhou Grand Canal. For more than a thousand years, the Grand Canal was the main trading artery between south and north China, making Hangzhou one of the most prosperous cities in China.[2]

Hangzhou and the nearby port of Ningbo lie on relatively flat land. But much of Zhejiang Province is mountainous, its elevations and rivers creating a patchwork of isolated communities and dialects. The need to trade and the distance from the country's political rulers have helped make Zhejiang the cradle of private enterprise in China. Today many of the province's entrepreneurs sit atop China's rich list. Most, like Jack, started out living hardscrabble lives.

Zong Qinghou, worth more than $11 billion, is the founder of Wahaha, China's largest beverage manufacturer. From the age of four, Zong grew up in Hangzhou, later working on a salt farm on an island off the coast of Ningbo before graduating from secondary school. In the 1980s he sold ice pops on the street for less than a penny. Li Shufu, worth more than $2 billion, founded Geely, China's first non-state-owned car manufacturer. He started out assembling refrigerators using spare parts, then in 1988 founded Geely. In 2010 Geely purchased Sweden's Volvo Cars. Lu Guanqiu, worth more than $7 billion, is the founder of Wanxiang Group, the Hangzhou-based auto parts manufacturer. He started out as a farmer, then started buying scrap metal from villagers.

Jack's friend Guo Guangchang, a man worth an estimated $7 billion before his unexplained disappearance for several days in December 2015, is the founder of investment firm Fosun. Guo survived the Cultural Revolution only by eating moldy, dried vegetables, later winning entry to Shanghai's prestigious Fudan University, where he sold bread door-to-door in the dorms to make ends meet. Prior to his surprise absence in 2015, Fosun had been described by the *Financial Times* as the "Berkshire Hathaway of China." Guo is an active supporter of Alibaba's forays into logistics and finance.

As we saw in the logistics edge of the iron triangle, one cluster of Zhejiang entrepreneurs has played an important role in Alibaba's success. The Tonglu Gang of logistics companies, located in the town of

Tonglu to the southwest of Hangzhou, account for more than half of all package deliveries in China. Tonglu was the birthplace of the late Nie Tengfei, founder of courier giant Shentong (STO Express). Born into poverty, Nie raised pigs, planted grain, and sold firewood before moving to Hangzhou to work in a printing factory. He moonlighted as a courier delivering bread on his tricycle before spotting an opportunity at the age of twenty to beat China Post,[3] delivering customs forms for trading companies in Hangzhou to the port in Shanghai. Nie died in a car crash in 1998, but Shentong continued to thrive. Two of Nie's relatives and one of his classmates each founded three other large courier companies in the Tonglu Gang.[4]

Hangzhou, the provincial capital, and Ningbo, its largest port, have long been prosperous trading centers. But two other cities in Zhejiang, Wenzhou and Yiwu, though less well known overseas are renowned in China for their newfound wealth. Wenzhou helped legitimize the role of entrepreneurs in society, and Yiwu established the wholesale markets that extended their reach to all parts of the country and indeed the world. Wenzhou and Yiwu have played as important a part in China's entrepreneurial revolution as the cotton mills of Lancashire did in Britain's industrial revolution.

Wenzhou and Yiwu provided the dynamism that inspired Jack to launch his own entrepreneurial career. Innovations in Wenzhou opened the door for Alibaba's future forays into financial services, and the massive wholesale market in Yiwu was a template for Alibaba's first business model, connecting merchants in China with global buyers. Let us take a brief tour.

Wenzhou

Wenzhou lies two hundred miles southeast of Hangzhou. Hemmed in by mountains on one side and the East China Sea on the other,

Wenzhou had always looked to trade, including tea exports, for its livelihood. But after 1949, its proximity to nationalist Taiwan became a liability. With Shanghai a three-hundred-mile ferry ride away, the city suffered from its isolation.

Wenzhou had little arable land and many unemployed or underemployed agricultural workers. But once Deng Xiaoping launched his economic reforms in 1978, the private sector started to boom. Wenzhou's entrepreneurs, often working with family members, started out in light manufacturing. In the 1980s they were some of the first merchants to fan out across China to sell their wares, including knockoffs of Western brands. For many, Chinese goods from Wenzhou were the first items they ever purchased that were not made by the state.

Wenzhou has played a pivotal role in legitimizing entrepreneurship in China. In 1984 the Wenzhou municipal government invited the city's most successful private entrepreneurs to a conference. Although the government wanted to help them showcase their success, many entrepreneurs refused to attend, fearing arrest. Only two years earlier a number of entrepreneurs in the city had been arrested for speculation. They still languished in prison. Of the entrepreneurs who showed up for the meeting with the government a number brought along their toothbrushes, in case they too were detained. But the entrepreneurs were not jailed. After releasing those arrested two years earlier, the Wenzhou government published an unprecedented admission in local newspapers that it had erred. Professor Yasheng Huang at the Massachusetts Institute of Technology writes that "many entrepreneurs cited these two episodes as having convinced them of their personal security."

For decades in China, the country's state-owned banks ignored private enterprises and individuals, making politically directed loans[5] to the state-owned enterprises (SOEs).

Starved for lending, the private sector in Wenzhou began to devise its own private credit market, often adopting illegal structures. The local government actively supported the establishment of private credit associations, cooperatives, and money houses—a form of local financial broker that derives profits from the spread between rates of interest on deposits and loans—forming a system that came to be known as the "Wenzhou model." Wenzhou paved the way for Alibaba's own foray into banking. When Alibaba received its banking license in 2014, two of the other five recipients were from Wenzhou.

Raw entrepreneurial spirit, plus access to capital, fueled an explosion in the city's private sector, which so dominated Wenzhou's economy that the state became completely marginalized. Facing a huge demand for new roads and bridges, the entrepreneurs of Wenzhou didn't wait for funds or instructions from Beijing. They simply built their own, in a surge of construction that bordered on anarchy, lacking any coordinated plan.

In 1990, acting on their own, entrepreneurs even funded the construction of the city's airport. One year later the country's first private carrier, Juneyao Airlines, was launched in the city. In 1998, Wenzhou created China's first privately funded railroad.

Today in China, Wenzhou is synonymous with wealth. The city's residents are resented by some for their mass shopping sprees, always paying cash, which have driven up the prices of apartments in Beijing, Shanghai, Hong Kong, New York City, and beyond.

Yiwu

Yiwu is an unlikely location for one of the world's key trading nodes. It is located inland, far from Hangzhou, Ningbo, or the East China Sea. Like Wenzhou, it was dirt poor, with little cultivable land. Lacking any alternative, local farmers since the sixteenth century turned to trade. Their main product was brown sugar, which they cooked with ginger and cut into chunks. This they bartered for chicken feathers, which they used to make feather dusters or mulched to make fertilizer.

In the winters, when the farmers had little to do and food was scarce, local men would hoist a pole with bamboo baskets on their shoulders and travel the country as peddlers. They carried out sugar chunks, sewing needles, and thread, and brought chicken feathers back to Yiwu. As they walked they would use a rattle drum to attract customers. They became known as "Sugar Shoulder-Pole Men"—a precursor to today's million-strong courier workforce.

Soon there were so many itinerant merchants in Yiwu that they formed a veritable mobile army. To supply them with wares in the 1700s, the first wholesale markets started to appear in the city. Trade flourished for centuries until the dislocation of the Japanese invasion and the communist revolution.

When Deng Xiaoping's reforms started to take effect, the wholesale trade came out of the shadows. In September 1982, traders in Yiwu were allowed access to a patch of land—a ditch that they had first cemented over—to set up their stalls. Seven hundred stalls popped up almost immediately and Yiwu became one of the first wholesale markets of its kind in postrevolutionary China.

Today the city is home to the largest wholesale market in the world and its population has shot up to over two million people. An estimated 40,000 people visit the wholesale market every day. The 700 stalls have become 70,000 outlets, housed today inside the Yiwu International Trade Center. This colossal building spans more than 40 million square feet, generating a turnover of more than $6 billion per year.

On sale inside are an estimated 1.7 million products, from toys to plastic flowers, jewelry to suitcases, clothing to home appliances, anything and everything that is Made in China. Without knowing it, a huge amount of what we consume in the West has passed through Yiwu. Even Christmas is "Made in Yiwu": More than 60 percent of the world's Christmas decorations are manufactured in the city. Although traders travel there overwhelmingly for its cheap prices, part of Yiwu's attraction has been its supply of counterfeit products, for example handbags sold under almost-familiar-sounding names such as "Gussi." The *Financial Times* journalist James Kynge traveled to the city in 2005 to research the problem of fake goods, only to find out that even hotels there were fake: He passed by not the Hyatt but the "Hiyat."

Yiwu attracts traders from all four corners of the world. The town is a favorite of traders from the Middle East, making Yiwu home to the fastest-growing Muslim community in China. With an estimated 35,000 Muslims in the city at any time—Chinese, South Asian, and Arab—Yiwu features dozens of Muslim restaurants and an ornate $4 million mosque featuring marble imported from Iran.

Since 2014, Yiwu is the start of the longest freight railroad line in the world. Taking twenty-one days to traverse end to end, the 8,111-mile line links Yiwu with Madrid.

What makes Yiwu such an essential node is its role marketing the goods of the countless industrial clusters of Zhejiang and other parts of the Yangtze River delta. These single-product towns can represent 80 percent or more of the production of individual commodities—not just in China but worldwide. Shaoxing is "textile city" and Yongkang is "hardware city," churning out 30,000 steel doors and 150,000 motor scooters every day. Taizhou is known as "sewing machine city" and Shenzhou as "necktie city." Haining calls itself "leather city." There is even a "toothbrush city"—in case nervous entrepreneurs get a summons from their local government official—in Hangji.

Yiwu itself claims to be China's "sock city," producing annually more than three billion pairs of socks for companies like Walmart and Disney, although Datang, near Hangzhou, also claims to be "sock city," producing more than eight billion pairs each year.

By the mid-1990s, when Jack was starting his own business career,

Zhejiang was already an entrepreneurial powerhouse. But the province's companies were highly labor-intensive and their average size small. From hardly any entrepreneurs at the beginning of the 1980s, by 1994 Zhejiang arguably had too many. In a population of 44 million people, the province was home to an estimated 10 million economic entities.

Many manufacturers struggled to find enough customers to make a profit. Unlike the factories in southern China set up by wealthy overseas Chinese in Hong Kong and Taiwan, the small factories in Zhejiang had to hustle to find customers and finance.[6] China's state-owned banks denied them any credit. This chronic lack of funding created innovations in private finance, such as the Wenzhou model, and led to the rise of industrial clusters that bound together debtors and creditors, who could dole out capital based on the profit they believed would be generated by a specific contract. By 2004, of the top hundred largest domestic private firms in China, half came from Zhejiang Province.

Jack recognized early on both the region's strengths and its shortcomings, and is a proud advocate for the province. Since October 2015, he serves as the inaugural chairman of the General Association of Zhejiang Entrepreneurs. In his inaugural speech, Jack talked about the six million Zhejiang entrepreneurs in China and the two million Zhejiang entrepreneurs around the world: "The total number of over eight million Zhejiang entrepreneurs might be the largest business association in the world. They have created another economic entity in addition to the local economy in Zhejiang." Their successes weren't won easily though. In an earlier speech to the Zhejiang Chamber of Commerce, Jack summed up the dynamism of his home province: "As entrepreneurs from Zhejiang, our greatest advantages are that we are hardworking, courageous, and good at seizing opportunities. We have these excellent qualities because we were given nothing. We are not like other provinces which have resources of coal and ore. We Zhejiang entrepreneurs have markets. . . . As long as we are in places where there are people, we are always able to find opportunities. It will be the same in the future."

Yet Jack's first effort to tap into Zhejiang's entrepreneurial fizz was not a success. In 1994, his Hope Translation venture had gotten off to a troubled start. While his monthly office rent was almost $300, his first month's income was just over $20. Hope may spring eternal, but cash is king. Jack was facing a crunch. To support his venture, Jack started peddling goods on the streets of Hangzhou, including some he sourced from Yiwu. His translation company also became a trading company. Hope Translation Agency started to sell gifts, flowers, books, and even plastic carpet, a range of items that foreshadows Taobao. Jack recalled, "We did everything. This income supported the translation agency for three years until we started to make ends meet. We believed that as long as we kept doing it, we would definitely have a future."

But it was becoming clear to Jack that translation services alone were not going to sate his entrepreneurial ambitions. Soon an unexpected journey, which looked at first like a disaster, was about to give Jack a lucky break.

With his reputation as an expert English speaker growing from his popular evening classes and his Hope Translation venture, Jack was asked by the government of Tonglu County—some fifty miles to the southwest of Hangzhou and later home to the Tonglu Gang of logistic companies—to assist as an interpreter in helping resolve a dispute with an American company over the construction of a new highway.

In 1994, the company had proposed to invest in a new highway to be built from Hangzhou to Tonglu. After a year of negotiations, no agreement had been reached, and the initial funding promised by the partner in the United States had not materialized. Jack was tapped to find out what was going on, and hopefully end the deadlock.

First Jack traveled to Hong Kong, where he was told that the company's funds were held in the United States, so Jack embarked on his first trip there. He would stay for a month. His mission for the Tonglu government was a failure. But the trip would give him his first exposure to the Internet, and he would return to China a changed man.

Going to America

His first trip to America sounds more like a plot for an *Ocean's Eleven*–style crime caper than an interpreter's business trip, at least according to the version put out five years later during the dot-com boom when media started to take an interest in Jack's background. Upon arriving in Los Angeles, the story goes, Jack met with the unnamed boss of Tonglu's erstwhile U.S. partner. Jack quickly figured out, as *The Economist* related, that the "company he was investigating did not exist, that his host was a crook, and that he himself was in serious danger." Jack has never named the boss, later described in local media only as a "bulky Californian." But after refusing to take a bribe, Jack recalled he was locked in a beach house in Malibu, where his captor flashed a gun. He was then taken to Las Vegas, where he was kept in a form of house arrest in a hotel room on the top floor of a casino. Jack hasn't repeated the details of any of this in recent years. His personal assistant, Chen Wei, has written that it is an episode that Jack prefers to forget. A few years after the incident, when Alibaba was beginning to gain international prominence, Jack told a similar story to Melinda Liu, the Beijing bureau chief for *Newsweek*: "I flew to Hangzhou for an exclusive interview with Jack, and he spent a generous amount of time showing me around the Alibaba headquarters and talking at length about his life. He said that, on his very first trip to the USA, a former business contact (an American) had 'virtually kidnapped' him in a failed attempt to get Jack to work for him. At the time, Jack was pretty matter-of-fact, and the anecdote was just one of many he recounted. I later contacted him requesting more information; he indicated he didn't want to make too much of it and declined to provide additional details." The bizarre story ends with Jack escaping his hotel room and winning $600 on slot machines in the casino. Abandoning his belongings upstairs, he escapes the casino and buys an airline ticket for Seattle. A less colorful version of the story was detailed in an article published in September 1995 in the *Hangzhou Daily,*[7] which says Jack had taken along $4,000 in savings and money borrowed from his wife Cathy's mother and his brother-in-law.

In any event, it was in Seattle that Jack first logged on to the Internet. He had heard about the Internet the previous year from a fellow English teacher in Hangzhou, called Bill Aho. Bill's son-in-law was working on an Internet-related business, which Bill described. Jack recalled that it was Bill who first told him about the Internet, but that he "couldn't explain it clearly either, it sounded very strange. . . . I couldn't really understand it either."

In Seattle, Jack stayed at the house of Bill Aho's relatives, Dave and Dolores Selig.

Jack was shown around the wealthier districts of the city, including the Queen Anne neighborhood. Dolores Selig recalled to the BBC that Jack was impressed by some of the larger houses on the hill: "Jack would point at various houses and say 'I'm going to buy that one, and that one and that one' and we'd just laugh because they were very expensive houses. But he was impressed." Bill Aho remembered, "At that time, he didn't have a nickel."

Jack then met Bill Aho's son-in-law, Stuart Trusty, who had set up an Internet consultancy called Virtual Broadcast Network (VBN), located in the U.S. Bank building on Fifth Avenue near Pike Street in downtown Seattle.

"Jack came and I showed him what the Internet was," Trusty

recalled. "Back then, the Internet was largely a directory for governments and businesses, but he seemed excited."

For Jack the visit to Seattle was a transformative experience: "It was my first trip to the States, the first time in my life I touched a keyboard and computers, the first time in my life I connected to the Internet, and the first time I decided to leave as a teacher and start a company."

Jack recalled his first online session: "My friend Stuart . . . said, 'Jack, this is Internet. You can find whatever you can find through the Internet.' I say really? So I searched the word *beer*. Very simple word. I don't know why I searched for beer. But I found American beer, Germany [*sic*] beer and no Chinese beer. . . . I was curious, so I searched 'China,' and no 'China,' no data."

Intrigued, Jack asked Stuart for help. "I talked to my friend, 'Why don't I make something about China?' So we made a small, very ugly-looking page . . . [for the] translation agency I listed on there."

The site for Hope Translation was just text, without any images, plus a telephone number and the price for translation work.

Jack later recalled to the journalist Charlie Rose: "It was so shocking, we launched it nine forty in the morning, twelve thirty I got a phone call from my friend. 'Jack, you've got five emails.' I said, 'What is email?' " Three emails came from the United States, one from Japan, and one from Germany.

Jack set about formulating the idea for a new business—helping Chinese companies find export channels online—and pitched the idea of a partnership with VBN.

Stuart, who developed a love of tai chi from Jack—he still practices in Atlanta today—recalled Jack as intensely focused on work.

"We'd go down to the office, we'd do our work, then we'd get something to eat, go back home maybe do more tai chi and it was just that way . . . every day. No extra curricular activities."

Jack's dealings with VBN weren't easy. Stuart asked for an up-front deposit of $200,000[8] to grant Jack the exclusive right to make Web pages in China. When Jack explained that he had borrowed money to make the trip to the United States and was now penniless, Stuart signed the agreement without the deposit but on the condition that Jack pay up as soon as possible, even enlisting Bill Aho and his wife as guarantors. To get home to Hangzhou, according to a local media report, Jack had to borrow funds from a Hangzhou student in the States, then flew to Shanghai.

For his client in Tonglu, Jack returned to China empty-handed, with no deal to finance the proposed highway. But inside his suitcase he carried back with him a computer running the Intel 486 processor: "It was the most advanced in China at that time."

Back in Hangzhou he set about building his concept of an online yellow pages. He named the business China Pages. In this, his second venture, he would dive headfirst into the entrepreneurial sea, leaving his teaching days behind.

Chapter Five

China Is Coming On

If traditional industry and e-commerce "successfully merge together, there will be no limit to China's next round of economic development."

—Jack Ma

Soon after returning from Seattle to Hangzhou, Jack resigned his position as a teacher at the Hangzhou Institute of Electronic Engineering. He had realized that his teaching days must end when he ran into the dean, who was riding his bicycle carrying vegetables he had just bought from the market. The dean encouraged him to keep working hard at teaching, but looking at the bicycle and the vegetables Jack realized that even if he were to become dean himself one day, this was a future he couldn't get excited about.

His new dream wasn't teaching or translating. Fresh from his first contact with the Internet, he would build an online index, in English, of businesses in China seeking customers overseas.

As Stuart Trusty had noticed back in Seattle, Jack had a tremendous work ethic. To populate China Pages with entries, he toiled away collecting information on companies, which he would translate into English, then send along with photos to VBN in Seattle for uploading to the website.

In March 1995, Jack convened a gathering of two dozen of his night school students to present his concept and seek their advice, as well as their business. "I asked the most active and capable people from my evening classes to my home. I talked about two hours, they listened to me, obviously confused. . . . Eventually lots of people cast their votes. Twenty-three of them said it would not work out. Only one person—now he is working at Agricultural Bank of China—said to me: If you want to try, then go ahead, but if it doesn't work out, come back as soon as you can."

Undeterred, he pressed ahead. Together with his friend He Yibing, a computer science teacher at the institute Jack had just left, Jack launched China Pages. The two had met the year before when He Yibing was looking for someone to help him practice his English ahead of a training trip to Singapore. There, He Yibing gained exposure to the Internet. When Jack returned from Seattle with a dream of building an Internet company, the two decided to work together.

China Pages

The company they registered, Hangzhou Haibo Network Consulting (HHNC), was one of the first in China devoted to the Internet. To fund his start-up Jack borrowed money from his relatives, including his sister, brother-in-law, and parents. Jack's wife, Cathy, was the first employee.

In April 1995, Jack and He Yibing opened the first office for China Pages in a twelve-square-meter office building at 38 Wen'er Road. To portray their business as a solid concern, Jack and He Yibing printed up several versions of their business cards, each listing different positions[1] that they would use depending on whom they were meeting. During the day, the two partners went out to find clients, returning in the evening to teach an introductory training course about the "information superhighway." This class helped generate some of China Pages' early customers.

On May 10, 1995, they registered the domain name chinapages.com in the United States. In July they officially launched their website, which featured a red-framed map of Asia, with China highlighted under the title "China Business Pages: The Online China Business Directory."

The website's home page indicated chinapages.com was "Broadcast via Seattle, USA from Hangzhou, the Garden City." The site featured tabs including "What's New!," "What's Cool!," "Net Search," and "Net Directory," and a link to Hope, his translation venture.

China Pages started off as a family affair. Jack's wife, Cathy, her sister Zhang Jing, and He Yibing's girlfriend all lent a hand.

Jack's former students also provided a ready pool of talent for China Pages. Jane Jiang (Jiang Fang), whom Jack had taught at the institute a few years earlier, took charge of customer service. One visitor to China Pages in those early days was Cui Luhai, who ran a computer animation business. Now a lecturer at the China Academy of Art, Cui commented, "I can still remember the first scene I saw when I walked into his office. . . . It was a pretty empty space with only one desk set up in the middle of the room. There was only one very old PC desktop surrounded by a lot of people." Cui learned that Jack had spent most of his money on registering the business, leaving little leftover for hardware or other equipment.

China Pages badly needed customers. Cathy signed up one of the first clients, who paid them eight thousand yuan ($960). The company received a boost when Hangzhou was selected in May to hold the Formula One Powerboat World Championship later that year, the first time the event would be held in China. Jack's venture won the contract to make the official website for the race.

To win more clients, as with Hope Translation beforehand, Jack called on his former students to spread the word and bring in business. Two of them duly obliged.

He Xiangyang, a former student of Jack's, was working at the Qianjiang Law Firm. Reluctant to list the firm's name on the Internet, he gave Jack his personal phone number instead. To his surprise, he started to receive phone calls around the clock from prospective clients, many overseas, who told him they'd got his number from China Pages. The once-skeptical lawyer started to think there might be something to Jack's story about the Internet after all.

Another former student was Zhou Lan, who would become Jack's secretary. Zhou was working at the Lakeview Hotel in Hangzhou when Jack made a website for them, featuring the hotel's brand-new fourteen-inch color TVs. Later that year, the United Nations held its Fourth World Conference on Women in Beijing, attended by more than seventeen thousand participants, including First Lady Hillary Clinton. A number of delegates traveled on to Hangzhou after the conference. Booking rooms at the Lakeview, they told the hotel management it was the only hotel in Hangzhou they could find online. By the following spring, the hotel had sold more rooms in the first three months than the previous year, another demonstration of the power of the Internet.

Even with the help of Jack's former students, China Pages needed more clients if it was going to survive. But demonstrating what China Pages was all about was not easy, for one very basic reason: In Hangzhou at the time it was impossible to get online.

Instead Jack came up with an alternative approach. First, he spread the word through friends and contacts about what the Internet could do for their business. He then asked those interested to send him marketing materials to introduce their companies and products. Next Jack and his colleagues translated the materials, and sent the material by mail to VBN in Seattle. VBN then designed the websites and put them online. They then printed out screenshots of the websites and mailed them to Hangzhou. Finally, Jack took the printed materials to his friends and announced that, although they couldn't check this themselves, their websites were now online. But without Internet access in Hangzhou it was a challenge even explaining to his customers what "online" actually meant. As sales pitches go, asking people who had never heard of the Internet to fork over 20,000 renminbi ($2,400) up front to create, design, and host a website they could never see was a challenging one. Jack worried that people thought he was defrauding them. "I was treated like a con man for three years," he said.

First Connection

Finally, in the fall of 1995, Zhejiang Telecom started to provide Internet access services in Hangzhou. By the end of the year there were only 204 Internet users in the whole province. But Jack was among them and was finally able to load a website in front of his first client, the Lakeview Hotel, on the 486 computer he'd brought back from Seattle in his suitcase. "It took three and a half hours to download the front page. . . . I was so excited."

Starting with Deng Xiaoping's reforms, China experienced an entrepreneurial explosion that began to replace Marx with the market, becoming a socialist country "with Chinese characteristics." But this did not mean the Communist Party was going to ease up on a central pillar of its rule, the control of information. China has a long tradition of controlling information, but especially so under the rule of the Communist Party. It is surprising, therefore, that the country ever connected to the Internet at all. The fact that it did illustrates the

Chinese government's often contradictory desires to maintain control while simultaneously unlocking greater economic opportunities.

Without the Internet, Jack's vision of connecting entrepreneurs with global markets would have never been realized.

On September 14, 1987, while Jack was still a university student, the very first email from China was sent by Professor Qian Tianbai at Peking University to Karlsruhe University in what was then West Germany. The email, in English and German, read, "Across the Great Wall we can reach every corner in the world." The email was sent at 300 bits per second (bps), an impossibly slow connection by today's typical consumer broadband speeds measured by the tens or hundreds of millions of bps. It would be another seven years before China was connected to the Internet proper.

While the Chinese government was thinking about what to do about the Internet—wrestling with issues of ideology, control, and infrastructure—the U.S. government was pondering the wisdom of bringing a communist country online. In the end, it was not politicians but scientists,[2] on both sides of the Pacific, who took the lead. After years of efforts, the Stanford Linear Accelerator Center (SLAC) in Menlo Park, California, connected[3] with the Institute of High Energy Physics (IHEP), 5,800 miles away in Beijing.

While this was just a connection between two institutions, other scientists wanted to set up their own links. Connecting SLAC-IHEP to the Internet was a much easier solution than stringing up new links from other locations in the United States to IHEP. As Dr. Les Cottrell at SLAC recalled, "We explored this only to find out that the DOD [Department of Defense], the DOE [Department of Energy], the State Department all were very concerned about this." But eventually the U.S. government agreed, "They said okay, you can do this as long as you tell everybody who is on the Internet that China's coming on."

Les wasn't quite sure how to "tell everybody" on the Internet but eventually it was agreed that he would send an email to a particular distribution list. On May 17, 1994, the first real Internet connection to China was established.

Although IHEP was host to China's first Web pages, the Internet soon became more than a privilege reserved for particle physicists.

At the same time as this first connection was being established, China was on the verge of a massive expansion in its communications infrastructure, a policy it called "informatization" (*xinxihua).* China's communist rulers had watched the collapse of the Soviet Union in 1990 with alarm, attributing it in part to the yawning technological gap that had opened up with the United States. At the beginning of 1994 China had only 27 million phone lines and 640,000 cell phones for a population of 1.2 billion. The early users of cell phones were either government officials or the *getihu* who could afford to shell out $2,000 to buy one, with others making do with pagers.

The Chinese government resolved to change this, seeing an improvement in telecommunications as a tangible improvement they could deliver in the lives of the masses. Just as King Henry IV of France cemented his legitimacy by putting a chicken on every dinner table on a Sunday, with *xinxihua* the Chinese Communist Party began to roll out phone lines, then cell phones, then broadband connections to hundreds of millions of people.

In 1993, Vice Premier Zhu Rongji launched the Golden Bridge Project to create an information and communications network spanning the whole country. In 1994, the government ended the monopoly of telecom services held by the Ministry of Posts and Telecommunications (MPT). To inject some competition into the market, a second carrier, called China Unicom, was established. Other countries, starting with the United Kingdom, had used private capital to finance the competitors taking on state-owned telecom incumbents. China, obsessed with control of information, could not contemplate this—

twenty years on it still hasn't—and opted instead to launch China Unicom as a new state-owned enterprise, backed by three other ministries and a number of other state-owned enterprises, effectively pitting one government department against a coalition of other departments in a uniquely Chinese approach to telecom deregulation.

Spurred into action by the loss of its monopoly, the new minister of MPT, Wu Jichuan, responded with massive new investment in telecom infrastructure.

During a visit by U.S. secretary of commerce Ron Brown to Beijing shortly after the first SLAC-IHEP Internet connection was established, China signed an agreement with Sprint to set up a new Internet connection linking Beijing and Shanghai with the United States. This was the beginning of the "ChinaNet" Internet service provider link that would allow members of the public, including Jack, to dial up to the Internet in China for the first time.

China's First Technology Entrepreneurs

As word spread that China was finally investing in its telecom infrastructure, the country's first technology entrepreneurs began to emerge. Mostly U.S.-educated engineers, they started new ventures to help build out China's communications networks. One of the most prominent was James Ding (Ding Jian), a master's graduate in information science from the University of California, Los Angeles. After the suppression of pro-democracy protests in Tiananmen Square in June 1989, he and many other U.S.-educated Chinese instead shifted their hopes for radical political change in China to a faith in the power of technology to reshape the country. In 1993, James Ding joined forces with Beijing-born Edward Tian (Tian Suning), who had recently completed a Ph.D. at Texas Tech, to cofound AsiaInfo. In 1995, they moved the company's operations to Beijing to work on the data network buildout for China's telcos, including China Telecom's ChinaNet dial-up Internet access network. Edward Tian would go on to become a leading figure in China's telecom market, and both he and James Ding would become high-profile investors in the technology sector.

In 1995, another influential Chinese technology firm, UTStarcom, was formed. Started by Chinese and Taiwanese entrepreneurs in the United States, the company soon set up its China operations in Hangzhou. UTStarcom would play an important role in spurring the growth of China's telecom market by promoting a low-cost mobile system called Little Smart (*xiaolingtong)*. This success helped put Hangzhou on the map for investors as a technology hub.

A key investor in UTStarcom in 1995 was the newly established Japanese investment fund SoftBank, a firm that five years later would start to play a critical role in the success of Alibaba. Founded by Japanese billionaire Masayoshi Son, SoftBank took a 30 percent stake in UTStarcom.

UTStarcom was formed by the merger of Unitech Industries and Starcom Network Systems. Unitech's Taiwanese founder, Lu Hongliang, had studied with Masayoshi Son at the University of California, Berkeley. Starcom's cofounder, Chauncey Shey, went on to head SoftBank China Venture Capital, which led Masayoshi Son's investment in Alibaba in 2000.

By late 1995, with China's telecom and Internet buildout beginning to gain momentum, Jack and his customers were finally able to connect to the Internet from Hangzhou, using the ChinaNet service that had already been rolled out in Beijing, Shanghai, and Guangzhou. Soon after, Jack traveled back to the United States with Li Qi, his newly appointed chief engineer, to visit VBN in Seattle. On returning to China they ended their venture with VBN, setting up their own servers and a new China Pages site.

This helped cut costs, but boosting revenues was proving hard. In

1995, only 1.5 million personal computers were sold in China, mostly to business or government users. Priced at roughly $1,800, the PCs cost a fortune for average Chinese at the time. The costs of getting a fixed line installed and getting online, combined with a lack of awareness about what the Internet actually was, meant that China Pages was having a hard time finding enough customers.

Jack stepped up his efforts to evangelize the Internet. He even enlisted Bill Gates, in a manner of speaking. In late 1995, Gates's book *The Road Ahead* became an instant bestseller in the United States and soon after in China, too. Although the book hardly mentioned[4] the World Wide Web, to convince prospective clients of the importance of the Internet Jack started citing a quote from Bill Gates: "The Internet will change every aspect of human beings' lives." A useful marketing message for China Pages, Jack had in fact made it up, as he later confessed, "In 1995, the world started to know Bill Gates. But if I said, 'Jack Ma says that the Internet will change every aspect of human beings' lives,' who would believe it?" But, he added, "I believed that Bill Gates would definitely say it one day." (Shortly after the book was released, Gates famously did realize the importance of the Internet, dramatically stepping up Microsoft's efforts and releasing a second edition of the book with a much greater emphasis on the Internet.)

Meanwhile, in Beijing, an entrepreneur, Jasmine Zhang (Zhang Shuxin), had started to attract growing media interest after founding in May 1995 one of China's first privately owned Internet service businesses. She called her venture Yinghaiwei, a rough, phonetic equivalent in Chinese of the English term "Information Highway." Other China Internet founders credit her as the source of inspiration for starting their own ventures. One told me: "One day I was driving to work and saw one of their billboard ads saying, 'How far is China away from the Information Highway? Fifteen hundred meters ahead,'" referring to the company's office. Building on a tradition of internal BBS (bulletin board systems), popular in leading academic institutions such as Tsinghua and Peking universities, the company started to serve a few hundred users keen to experience the Internet, then mostly dominated by websites in English, and share comments in Chinese about what they were discovering.

Back in Hangzhou, Jack stepped up his efforts to promote his own venture, scoring a breakthrough when the Zhejiang provincial government invited China Pages to build its website. The government official in charge of commissioning the website, Yang Jianxin, later recalled his dealings with Jack: "The first time he came to my office, frankly speaking, as I understood him to be an Internet guru I didn't expect to meet such a young guy." Jack launched enthusiastically into an explanation of the Internet. Yang recalled Jack talked "nonstop for two hours." Although Yang indicated the government was unable to pay for the project, as its impact was unknown, Jack and his team quickly built the site, hosted by China Pages, in cooperation with a local unit of Zhejiang Telecom called Hangzhou Dife Communications—a partnership that soon after would sour dramatically. The site was one of the first projects in a national initiative[5] to bring the Chinese government online, generating a lot of publicity for Zhejiang. Within a few days Yang received congratulatory emails from overseas, including from members of the U.S. Congress.[6] The coverage also boosted Jack's profile, a local newspaper[7] ran a feature story on his company and his dramatic first visit to the United States.

But the publicity also triggered problems for Jack and the official who had commissioned him. One of Yang's colleagues reported him to the provincial government, accusing him of "hobnobbing with a *getihu*." The disgruntled colleague's report thundered that "government information dissemination was a serious issue, how could it be handled and published via a *getihu*?"

After encountering resistance at the local level, Jack started to spend most of his time in Beijing. There he met up with Jasmine Zhang of Yinghaiwei. The two did not hit it off, Jack later sharing his first impressions: "I though if the Internet's demise comes one day, hers will be earlier than mine. I was already very idealistic, but here was someone who was even more idealistic than me."

Jack and his partner, He Yibing, set about raising the profile of China Pages in Beijing. Jack had brought with him some articles he had written about the Internet, and asked his friends to help publish them. In Beijing, thanks to a relationship with a driver at the publication who was introduced by a friend, he met Sun Yanjun, deputy editor in chief of *China Trade News*. Sun was impressed by China Pages and invited Jack to give a lecture about the Internet to his colleagues. Afterward he published a front-page article on Jack and his company.

While Jack was good at gaining publicity, China Pages still wasn't winning much business, and its efforts to open doors with the central government came to naught. In July 1996, China's national broadcaster, China Central Television, broadcast a documentary called *Ma Yun the Scholar,* which showed Jack being rebuffed by a government official. The documentary was produced by Fan Xinman, married to the famous director Zhang Jizhong, who has brought a number of Jin Yong novels to the screen. Fan was also from Hangzhou and sympathetic to Jack's cause. As she filmed Jack getting shown the cold shoulder, Fan became increasingly concerned for Jack's prospects: "He no longer had his base in Hangzhou, and was crushed in Beijing. He was almost bankrupt." In the documentary, through a window to the Beijing streets outside, Jack made a resolution to himself: "In a few years, you won't treat me like this; in a few years, you will all know what I do. And I won't be in dire straits in Beijing."

The problem for China Pages was that it really was just a directory. The site was pretty rudimentary, merely listings of a company's products for sale. There was no way for prospective customers to make purchases online, so there was a limit on what China Pages could charge for its services.[8]

Squeezed Out

China Pages was running out of cash to meet its payroll. Switching sales staff to commission-based pay relieved the pressure for a while, as did a 10,000-yuan contract from a client in the textile industry. But China Pages was in a vulnerable state. Yet things were about to get much worse. The company that had worked with China Pages to build the Zhejiang government website, Hangzhou Dife Communication, made a bid to take over the company. China Pages was a small, privately owned company, but Hangzhou Dife was a unit of a powerful SOE, Zhejiang Telecom. In February 1996 the two entered into a joint-venture, Dife-Hope. Dife had a 70 percent stake in the venture, investing 1.4 million renminbi ($170,000). Jack would remain the general manager and China Pages would hold the remaining 30 percent, which was valued at 600,000 renminbi ($70,000). At the time, this seemed like a significant achievement for a tiny, cash-strapped company. Zhang Xinjian, then an official with Hangzhou Telecom, termed it the first merger and acquisition transaction in the history of China's Internet; local media[9] provided positive coverage of the joint venture.

But the reality was a lot more sinister. Jack had discovered that when working with China Pages on the Zhejiang government website, Dife had registered the domain name www.chinesepages.com, very similar to his own venture's www.chinapages.com, and a new company called "China Yellow Pages." Yet because Dife was a subsidiary of a powerful SOE, Jack couldn't fight back. Gritting his teeth he had to give interviews with local media lauding the new venture: "The establishment of Dife-Haibo will further strengthen China Pages." He concluded by saying, "We have every reason to believe, with the right policies of the Party and the State, and with the tremendous support from every walk of life in the society, China Pages will surely achieve great success. China's information high-speed train will be faster and faster!"

Years later, after Alibaba had become successful, Jack was free to comment on the experience. China Pages was dwarfed by its new partner, and while Jack was the general manager, the position turned out to be of little value. "When the joint venture was formed, disaster followed. They had five votes on the board, and we had two. Whenever there was a board meeting, whatever ideas I put forward, if one of them voted against it, the rest of them followed suit. During five or six board meetings, none of our ideas were passed."

Jack had lost control of his pioneering venture: "At that time I called myself a blind man riding on the back of blind tigers. Without knowing anything about technology or computers, I started the first company. And after years of terrible experience, we failed."

The China Pages episode provided him with some important lessons, as well as good material for his speeches, such as, "It is difficult for an elephant to trample an ant to death, as long as you can dodge well," and "With good strategies, you will definitely survive. To this day, I've realized one thing: Don't be nervous if you face huge competition in the future." He would later draw on his experiences when taking Alibaba into battle against eBay, in the David versus Goliath struggle that would raise his profile on the global stage.

Jack also points to China Pages as influencing the way he would structure his subsequent ventures: "From then on, I have held a firm belief: When I start businesses in future, I will never hold the controlling stake of a company, making those controlled by me suffer. I will give plenty of understanding and support to lower levels. I have never once had a controlling stake at Alibaba. I am proud of this. I am the

CEO of the company, because I lead it with [my] wisdom, courage, and resourcefulness, not capital."

In November 1997, Jack convened an off-site meeting with the China Pages team in Tonglu, announcing that he was giving up his stake in China Pages and moving to Beijing, leaving his partner He Yibing as CEO.

Jack's invented quote that the Internet would change everything was right. The problem was he had launched his venture too soon. Jack put his dreams on hold, taking a job in Beijing at a unit of the Ministry of Foreign Trade and Economic Cooperation (MOFTEC). There he was like a fish out of water, counting the days until he could jump back into the entrepreneurial sea of China's Internet, which was about to get a whole lot bigger.

Chapter Six

Bubble and Birth

Alibaba might as well be known as "1,001 mistakes." But there were three main reasons why we survived. We didn't have any money, we didn't have any technology, and we didn't have a plan.

—Jack Ma

Third time lucky. After his struggles with Hope Translation and China Pages and an uncomfortable period working for the government in Beijing, Jack went on to found Alibaba at the beginning of 1999. But extricating himself from China Pages and then from his government job cost him two years. Meanwhile, other Internet entrepreneurs in China began to gain traction. Without a venture of his own Jack was running the risk of becoming irrelevant.

Just as Jack had lost control of China Pages to his SOE-linked partner, in Beijing Jasmine Zhang had been forced out of Yinghaiwei by her largest shareholder, rumored to be connected with China's Ministry of State Security. Other entrepreneurs, especially those who had set up Internet service providers (ISPs) to roll out dial-up services to consumers, found themselves squeezed out by large SOEs like China Telecom. Yun Tao from Beijing-based ISP Cenpok summed it up:[1] "It is not yet possible to make money in China on the Internet. . . . I have been at it for the last few years and I tell you, I am bleeding now."

While the telecom SOEs were actively protecting their turf from encroachment by the private sector, China's state-owned media companies proved surprisingly incapable of competing with entrepreneurs building out Internet content businesses. A new generation of Internet entrepreneurs was coming to the fore in China, inspired by Yahoo, the most influential company of the dot-com boom gaining speed in the United States.

Listed in 1996, Yahoo at first commanded little attention from investors. They preferred established technology companies, which they could value with traditional measures such as price/earning ratios (P/E ratios). But Yahoo and its generation of dot-com companies were years from becoming profitable. *Fortune* magazine's Joe Nocera later summed up the valuation challenge: "You can't have a P/E ratio when you have no 'E.'" But all of this started to change in the summer of 1998. Yahoo's shares ran up more than 80 percent in just five weeks, taking the company's valuation to $9 billion and making billionaires of its Stanford cofounders, Jerry Yang (Yang Zhiyuan in Chinese) and David Filo. The dot-coms that had sprouted up in Silicon Valley now suddenly were the center of attention for Wall Street, too.

In China, the Taiwan-born Jerry Yang became a hero. The public was fascinated to learn how an immigrant to the United States had become a billionaire before the age of thirty.

Suddenly there was a flurry of interest in Yahoo's "portal" business model, its directories and search engine connecting users to the rapidly expanding universe of online content. Chinese portals, or *men hu* (literally "gateway") began to appear. A triumvirate soon emerged as the country's "portal pioneers": Wang Zhidong, Charles Zhang, and William Ding. Unlike Jack, they had all excelled at their studies and had strong technical backgrounds. The firms they founded were Sina, Sohu, and NetEase.

Portal Pioneers

Wang Zhidong, the founder of Sina, was already well known, famous for having created several popular Chinese language software applications—BD Win, Chinese Star, and RichWin—that helped people in China use the Microsoft Windows operating system. Born in 1967 to poor but well-educated parents in south China's Guangdong Province, Wang excelled in math and science. He secured a place at Peking University, where he studied radio electronics. In 1997, Wang was the first of the three portal pioneers to raise significant outside investment—nearly $7 million—for his firm, Stone Rich Sight, based on his proven track record as a software developer. In the summer 1998 he launched a dedicated website featuring soccer results in time for the FIFA World Cup held that year in France. This generated a lot of traffic, and the company shifted its focus from software to the Internet, later merging with another company to become Sina.

Charles Zhang (Zhang Chaoyang), the founder of Sohu, was born in Xi'an. One month younger than Jack, he won entry to Tsinghua University to study physics before heading on to the Massachusetts Institute of Technology (MIT). After attaining a Ph.D. in physics, Charles stayed on as a postdoc, working to foster U.S.-China relations through MIT's Industrial Liaison Program. Inspired by the success of Netscape and Yahoo, Charles decided to launch his own Internet company. His original plan was to launch it in the United States, but as a recent Chinese immigrant he felt excluded from the mainstream, including being unable to attract the interest of the media—something unlike the two other media-shy portal founders—he was particularly attached to. "I constantly thought I was an outsider. For example, here [in China] I receive interview invitations, but in the States I would probably never have been able to be on their news shows. So I came back."

Charles returned to Beijing in 1996. He set up his company with the encouragement and financial support of two MIT professors, including Ed Roberts, who at the time of Sohu's IPO four years later held a 5 percent stake. Charles was the sole returning student, known as "sea turtle" (*haigui)* of the three pioneers. His greater exposure to the U.S. technology scene gave Charles a head start. In February 1998 he was the first of the three to launch a Chinese-language search engine and a website directly inspired by Yahoo, even down to the name he chose for his venture: Sohoo.com, later changing the name to Sohu.com.

William Ding (Ding Lei) was born in Ningbo, seven years after Jack. He studied computer science in a technology university in Chengdu. After returning home to Ningbo to work for the local branch of China Telecom, William moved to Guangzhou in southern China to work for the U.S. database company Sybase, then for a local technology firm. In 1997 he launched his own venture, which rolled out the first free, bilingual email service in China. William's venture soon became profitable with the income generated by licensing the email software to other companies. In the summer of 1998 William switched his business from software development to the Internet and launched his website NetEase.com. Initially popular in southern China, NetEase quickly signed up email users all over the country, 1.4 million by the end of 1999.

While Wang Zhidong, Charles, and William were surfing the waves of China's exciting new dot-com sea, Jack was languishing on the dusty dot-gov shore. His job title was general manager of Infoshare Technology, a company set up by the China International Electronic Commerce Center (CIECC),[2] itself a unit of a department of

MOFTEC. At CIECC Jack led the development of MOFTEC's official website, www.moftec.gov.cn, which launched in March 1998. Calling some of his China Pages colleagues to join him in Beijing, Jack then developed another website for MOFTEC, www.chinamarket.com.cn, which launched on July 1, 1998.

The China Market site, which listed more than eight thousand commodities divided into six categories, invited visitors to post supply and demand information and enter into "confidential business negotiations in encrypted Business ChatRooms." The new site attracted the praise of government officials, including MOFTEC minister Shi Guangsheng, who called it a "solid step by China to move into the age of e-commerce." The official Chinese government news agency, Xinhua, commended the site for its "information reliability and orderly operation," with all visitors vetted by the government to ensure that they were valid businesses.

The reality, though, was that all the offline bureaucracy involved in registering on the website made it unappealing to businesses, especially because the website could not facilitate any orders or payments. In other words it was just a bigger and government-backed version of China Pages. Jack fervently believed in the unfolding age of e-commerce, but he also knew that the future belonged to entrepreneurs, later recalling that "it was too tiring doing e-commerce in the government. . . . E-commerce should start with private enterprises." Working for CIECC, Jack was buried by the many layers of government officials above him, including Xing Wei, his fierce boss at CIECC.[3]

Jack became increasingly frustrated as he watched the triumvirate of portal pioneers gain momentum: "Here I was, I had been practicing for five years in the Internet field," Jack recalled. "Everything was changing very quickly. If I stayed in Beijing I couldn't do something really big; I couldn't realize my dreams as a public servant."

But his government perch ended up giving Jack another lucky

break: his first encounter with Jerry Yang, the cofounder of Yahoo. In the coming years, the fates of Jack Ma and Jerry Yang would become ever more closely intertwined.

As the general manager of Infoshare, and a fluent English speaker, Jack was asked to receive Jerry Yang and his colleagues, who in late 1997 came to Beijing to look for opportunities for Yahoo in China. Jack's experience as a self-appointed tour guide in Hangzhou came in handy now in Beijing since Jerry was traveling with his younger brother Ken, and was keen to see some of the sights. Jack introduced him to his wife, Cathy, and they took Jerry, Jerry's brother, and Yahoo vice president Heather Killen to visit Beihai Park, opposite the Forbidden City, and the Great Wall. Here they took a photo that would play an important role in helping separate Jack from the pack,

Jack as Jerry's tour guide at the Great Wall. *Heather Killen*

Jack; his boss, Xing Wei; Jerry Yang; and Heather Killen in front of a photograph of then President Jiang Zemin. *Heather Killen*

illustrating Jack's early meeting with the global king of the Internet at the time.

On the visit Jack also took Jerry and Heather to meet the vice minister of MOFTEC. Jack's charm offensive paid off. In October 1998, Infoshare was appointed the exclusive sales agent for Yahoo in China.

But Jack was already actively planning to slip free of the constraints of government. Back at the Great Wall, Jack organized an off-site meeting with some of his Infoshare colleagues, an outing since feted by the company as the unofficial launch of Alibaba. But Jack was worried about the consequences for him and his planned new venture of walking out of his government job. A friend advised Jack to feign illness, a common ruse in China to escape from such predicaments.

Jack and some of the cofounders of Alibaba at the Great Wall of China in late 1998. The company would be launched a few months later. *Alibaba*

Jack did in fact come down with appendicitis a few months later, but by then he was already back in Hangzhou and his new venture was well under way.

What's in a Name

Jack decided to call his new venture Alibaba, a curious name for a Chinese company.

Jack has been asked many times why he chose an Arabic name for his company rather than something derived from his passion for Chinese martial arts or folklore. Jack was attracted, he said, by the "open sesame" imagery, since he hoped to achieve an opening for the small- and medium-size enterprises he was targeting. He was also looking for a name that traveled well, and Alibaba is a name that is easy to pronounce in many languages. He liked the name since it came at the beginning of the alphabet: "Whatever you talk about, Alibaba is always on top."

In China, a song titled "Alibaba Is a Happy Young Man" was popular at the time, but Jack says the idea came to him[4] for the website on a trip to San Francisco: "I was having lunch, and a waitress came. I asked her: 'Do you know about Alibaba?' She said, 'Yes!' 'What is Alibaba?' And she said, 'Open Sesame.' So I went down to the street and asked about ten to twenty people. They all [knew] about Alibaba, Forty Thieves, and Open Sesame. I think, this is a good name."

But there was a problem. The domain name alibaba.com was registered to a Canadian man who was asking for $4,000 to transfer it over, a transaction that involved some risk if he didn't hold up his side of the bargain. So Jack launched[5] the Alibaba site using alibabaonline.com and alibaba-online.com instead. Alibaba cofounder Lucy Peng recalled how the early team members had joked they were working for "AOL," short for "Alibaba Online."

Jack soon after decided to buy the alibaba.com domain name.[6] Alibaba executive vice chairman Joe Tsai later recounted to me that Jack was nervous about wiring funds to the Canadian owner before he could be assured of gaining control (a problem that the escrow function of Alipay would later solve): "He didn't have that kind of money, so was scrounging around. But Jack is a very savvy businessman, he has that innate ability to say, 'All right, I'm gonna trust this guy.' A lot of entrepreneurs don't trust other people." Jack went ahead with the wire transfer to the Canadian, who (true to national stereotypes) proved honest, and Jack gained control of alibaba.com.

The widespread recognition of the Alibaba name has saved Jack a lot of money in marketing expenses and a ready supply of imagery such as the forty thieves, and 1,001 nights, and other elements he still often incorporates into his speeches.

Lakeside Gardens

Alibaba was launched in Hangzhou by Jack's friends, supporters, and colleagues, including some who joined him from China Pages[7] and Infoshare.

Jack convened a meeting on February 21, 1999, at his Lakeside Gardens (Hupan Huayuan) apartment in Hangzhou. Confident in his future success, he arranged for the meeting to be filmed. With the team seated around him in a semicircle, some wearing coats to fend off the damp cold inside the chilly apartment, Jack asked his converts to ponder the question: "In the next five to ten years, what will Alibaba become?" Answering his own question, he said that "our competitors are not in China, but in Silicon Valley. . . . We should position Alibaba as an international website."

The reality was that Jack, late to the portal game now dominated by Sina, Sohu, and NetEase, had to find his own niche in the China

Jack with other cofounders and supporters of Alibaba in the Lakeside Gardens apartment in Hangzhou, October 30, 1999. *Alibaba*

Internet market. The portals were trying to capture the growing number of individual users coming online, but Jack was going to stick with what he knew best: small businesses. In contrast to the business-to-business sites in the United States that were focused on large companies, Jack decided to focus on the "shrimp." He found inspiration from his favorite movie, *Forrest Gump,* in which Gump makes a fortune from fishing shrimp after a storm: "American B2B [business-to-business] sites are whales. But 85 percent of the fish in the sea are shrimp-sized. I don't know anyone who makes money from whales, but I've seen many making money from shrimp."

When Jack created Alibaba in early 1999 China had only two million Internet users. But this would double in six months, then double again, reaching nine million by the end of the year. By the summer of 2000 there were 17 million online.

Personal computers still cost a hefty $1,500, but prices began to fall as new market entrants like Dell set up shop in competition with homegrown companies Founder, Great Wall, and Legend (later rebranded as Lenovo). Sales of new PCs, still going mostly to businesses or government users, hit five million in 1999.

The government's policy of "informatization" was making the Internet more affordable. Getting a connection from the local phone company still took months and could cost as much as $600. But in March 1999 the government scrapped the installation fee for second phone lines and made it cheaper to surf[8] online, too, cutting the average price from $70 per month in 1997 to only $9 by the end of 1999.

Millions of young, educated people were coming online at their colleges or workplaces, others at the thousands of Internet cafés that were mushrooming across the country. Yahoo's business model in the United States was to make money from the growing market for online advertising. The three China portals in turn planned to grab a piece of a fast-growing online advertising cake,[9] which grew to $12 million in 1999 from only $3 million the year before. But even in the States Yahoo was losing money, and in China the bulk of Internet users had little disposable income to excite advertisers. The potential revenues for the portals were way below their expenditures. Yet in the upside-down logic of the unfolding dot-com boom, losses were not only acceptable but worn as a badge of honor: the bigger the loss, the grander a firm's ambition. Venture capital (VC) firms were there to bridge the gap.

Before Alibaba was even out of the starting gate, Sina, Sohu, and NetEase had started to win the backing of VCs, competing aggressively for new users and investment.

Sina[10] was formed by the December 1998 merger of Wang Zhidong's firm SRS with the U.S. company Sinanet, founded by three Taiwan-born students[11] at Stanford University. Daniel Mao, an early investor in SRS at the Walden International Investment Group, helped broker the merger. Sina.com was launched in April 1999 and the following month raised $25 million in VC from investors, including Goldman Sachs, Walden, and Japan's SoftBank.

Sohu raised $10 million in 1998 and more funding[12] the following year on the back of soaring traffic on its Chinese-language search engine. Founder Charles Zhang was relishing his newfound celebrity status in China, and he brought on Stanford-educated returnee Victor Koo (who later left to found Youku, China's answer to YouTube) to beef up Sohu's management. He also tried, unsuccessfully, to hire Jack as his COO.

NetEase was the last of the three portals to raise VC funding for the simple reason that founder William Ding didn't really need to: He could count on a steady flow of licensing revenues from the webmail software he had personally developed. William Ding had by far the highest equity stake of any portal founder—58.5 percent—when his company went public in 2000.

Watching from the sidelines, Jack realized he would have to hustle if he was to ever catch the attention of VCs or catch up with the portal pioneers who were speeding off into the distance. For Alibaba to thrive he would have to foster a relentless work ethic, ensuring a clean break from the bureaucratic culture that he and some of his colleagues had just left behind in Beijing. Jack exhorted the group assembled in his apartment to "learn the hard working spirit of Silicon Valley . . . If we go to work at 8 A.M. and get off work at 5 P.M., this is not a high-tech company, and Alibaba will never be successful."

Jack likes to put Silicon Valley companies on a pedestal, but he also likes to rally his team by saying Alibaba could knock them off it: "Americans are strong at hardware and systems but in software and information management, Chinese brains are just as good as American. . . . I believe that one of us can be worth ten of them."

Alibaba was formed at a time when the inflating dot-com valuations made even his loyal converts nervous about whether the bubble would soon burst. Speaking to them in his apartment Jack sought to reassure them: "Has the Internet reached its peak? Have we done enough? Is it too late for us to follow? . . . Don't worry. I don't think the dream of the Internet will burst. We will have to pay a very painful price in the next three to five years. It is the only way we can succeed in the future." To rally the troops, Jack set a goal of achieving an IPO within three years. "Once we become a listed company, what each and every one of us will gain . . . is not this apartment, but fifty apartments like this. We are just charging forward. Team spirit is very, very important. When we charge forward, even if we lose, we still have the team. We still have each other to support. What on earth are you afraid of?"

Although Jack and Cathy together were the lead shareholders, Alibaba was cofounded by a total of eighteen people, six of whom were women. None came from privileged backgrounds, prestigious universities,[13] or famous companies. This was a team of "regular people," bound together by Jack's energy and his unconventional management methods. To build team spirit, Jack drew on his love of Jin Yong's novels and gave each of his Alibaba team members nicknames. His own nickname was Feng Qingyang. In Jin Yong's book *Swordsman,*[14] Feng is a reclusive sword and kung fu master, preparing young apprentices to be heroes. As a former teacher, Jack identified with Feng and his "unpredictable yet nurturing"[15] character.

Joe Tsai Comes to Hangzhou

In May 1999, Jack met Joe Tsai,[16] a Taiwanese-born investor then living in Hong Kong. Joe would become Jack's right-hand man, a role he still performs more than seventeen years later. The association between the two would become one of the most profitable and enduring partnerships in Chinese business.

Jack takes pride in being "one hundred percent Made in China." Yet, starting with Joe Tsai, a number of "Born in Taiwan" individuals would make major contributions to Alibaba's success, just as they have to many technology companies in Silicon Valley.

I first met Joe at the beginning of Alibaba's journey in 1999, shortly after he'd joined. In the spring of 2015, I traveled back to Hangzhou to understand what prompted Joe to take such a gamble on Jack. Although the two men were born in the same year, they could hardly be more different. Joe came from a prestigious family[17] and he had a top-tier academic and professional background.

At the age of thirteen, speaking hardly any English, Joe was sent off from Taiwan to the Lawrenceville School, an elite[18] boarding school in New Jersey. There Joe excelled at his studies as well as at lacrosse, which he credits with helping him assimilate into American culture and learn the importance of working in a team: "The sport taught me life lessons about teamwork and perseverance. While I never got past playing on the third midfield line, being part of the team was the best experience of my life."

Joe won entrance to Yale College, where he studied economics and East Asian studies, and proceeded on to Yale Law School. After graduating he began his career in New York with the storied law firm Sullivan & Cromwell and a short stint at a management buyout firm. But Joe wanted to gain investment experience in Asia. He moved to Hong Kong to work for Investor AB, the investment arm of Sweden's powerful Wallenberg family. As the dot-com boom gained momentum, Joe starting looking out for opportunities to team up with an entrepreneur.

I asked Joe how he came to connect with Jack: "I wanted to be more intimately involved in technology start-ups. Because I was making investments for Investor, sitting on boards, I always felt a layer of distance between the board and the management. I said to myself, I should be involved in the operation."

Joe first heard about Jack from family friend Jerry Wu, a Taiwanese businessman who ran a communications start-up. After Jerry came back from Hangzhou he contacted Joe, telling him, "You have to go and meet this guy Jack Ma in Hangzhou. He's kind of crazy. He's got a big vision."

Wu was hoping Alibaba might take over his struggling start-up and asked Joe for his help.

Joe agreed and hopped on a plane from Hong Kong to Hangzhou to meet Jack in the Lakeside Gardens apartment. "I still can remember the first sight of the apartment. It reminded me of my grandmother's apartment in Taipei. When you walked into the building, the stairway was old and narrow. About ten pairs of shoes were in front of the apartment. It was a smelly place. I was in a suit. It was May—hot and humid."

Joe remembers how Jack outlined his ambitious goal for Alibaba: to help millions of Chinese factories find an outlet overseas for their goods. The factory owners lacked the skills to market their products themselves and, Jack explained, had little choice but to sell their goods through state-owned trading companies. Jack was proposing to cut out the middleman, always a compelling idea.

Joe was intrigued by Jack as he talked, "sitting backwards in a chair, clapping, like someone from a kung fu novel." Listening intently as Jack switched effortlessly in and out of fluent English. Joe was impressed. *This guy is good!* he thought to himself.

When Jack spoke Mandarin he did so in an accent that reminded Joe of his own grandfather, whose ancestral home was in Huzhou, near Hangzhou.[19] Speaking in Mandarin, Joe had started the conversation by apologizing to Jack that he couldn't speak the Hangzhou dialect.

Thinking that it might help establish a rapport, Joe added, "I do speak Shanghainese. My parents grew up in Shanghai." Looking back on that first meeting, Joe laughs. "I hadn't realized that Hangzhou people hated Shanghainese. They think they are too sly, too commercial, too money-oriented. Later on Jack told me that there are three kinds of people he doesn't trust: Shanghainese, Taiwanese, and Hong Kong people." But somehow Jack and Joe, a Shanghainese-speaking Taiwanese who lived in Hong Kong, hit it off. "It was fate that the two of us ended up working together."

Joe flew back to Hong Kong and shared his excitement about Jack and Alibaba with his wife, Clara. But trading a well-paying job in Hong Kong for a start-up in Hangzhou was a big risk, especially since Clara[20] was expecting their first child. So Clara suggested she travel with Joe back to Hangzhou.

Jack remembers their visit. Clara told him she wanted to see Alibaba because her husband was crazy about it: "If I agree with him, then I am crazy. But if I don't agree, he will hate me his whole life."

Joe too was thinking carefully before taking the plunge. "I went back a second time because I saw something in Jack. Not just the vision, the sparks in his eyes. But a team of people, his loyal followers. They believed in the vision. I said to myself, If I am going to join a group of people, this is the one. There is a clear leader, the glue to the whole thing. I just felt a real affinity to Jack. I mean who wouldn't?"

Jack struck Joe as being very different from other entrepreneurs he'd met or read about, telling Joe that "[t]o him, friends are as important as family. His definition of friends includes colleagues. When you try to compare [Jack] with, say, Steve Jobs, they are different people, different to the core."

Joe liked the fact that Jack was open about his own shortcomings. "I think me coming into the scene was very novel. I'm the guy who knew finance. I was a lawyer before. I could help incorporate a company and I could help raise capital. So immediately from day one, I think we built a bond."

When I first met Joe, I found him very calm and reserved, in many ways the polar opposite of Jack's exuberance and unpredictability. As I spent more time working with them, I came to appreciate how Joe's professionalism in, say, carefully drafting a contract created the structure for Alibaba to harness Jack's energy and enthusiasm. Another China Internet founder I spoke to agreed, "In the early days, especially, Joe kept Jack in check."

Joe is self-effacing about his role at the company. When I asked him whether he considered himself Jack's "consigliere," he told me he prefers to think of himself as Jack's interpreter: "Jack is very smart. But Jack sometimes says things that people misinterpret, so I am there to explain things."

Jack is effusive in his praise of Joe, often saluting him for the risk he took on joining Alibaba back in 1999. To an audience a few years ago in Taipei, Jack said, "How many would give up a well-paying job like him?" He added, "This is courage. This is action. This is the real dream."

Joe did take a gamble back in 1999, but it wasn't a blind bet. Joe was able to increase his chances of backing a winner by first getting the company ready to raise capital, then taking the lead in finding its first investor.

Joe told his boss at Investor AB, where he would keep his job for now,[21] that he would spend his personal time helping an entrepreneur he had met in China.

Joe got to work sorting out the paperwork at Alibaba. As with many start-ups, it was a bit of a mess. "When I got to Hangzhou Jack didn't even have a company. He hadn't incorporated anything yet. It was just a website."

Joe's first task was to document Alibaba's shareholders: "I called him up and said, 'Jack, I'm incorporating the company. Who are the shareholders?' He faxed me a list of the names. My jaw dropped, because every single one of those kids in the apartment was on the list, as a shareholder. So from day one, he gave away quite a lot [of equity]." But as Joe looked through the eighteen names[22] he realized that "everybody was a crucial part of the team, whether an engineer or in customer service." He laughed as he recalled the nickname Potato for cofounder Lucy Peng, which she used when answering emails sent from Alibaba's Western customers.

Next he wanted to get an understanding of Alibaba's customers. He asked the team how many there were. When told there were twenty-eight thousand, Joe replied, "Wow, that's a big number!" Yet all of the customer information was being stored manually, each one on a piece of paper stuffed into a book with all the others.

Alibaba wasn't generating any revenue and urgently need to raise capital. "Of course at that time no capital was available in China. It was all American." Looking at how Sina, Sohu, and NetEase had done it, Joe registered an offshore company,[23] writing out a personal check for $20,000 to a law firm, Fenwick & West, to ready Alibaba's corporate structure to receive venture capital investment. All they needed now was to find the investors. He set out with Jack for San Francisco.[24]

On arrival, they checked into a cheap hotel off Union Square, then headed down the next morning to Palo Alto to meet some VCs. The meetings did not go well. Joe recalls being peppered with questions: "What are you trying to do? What's your business model?" But they didn't even have a pitch book. "I had tried to prepare something, like a business plan." But Jack said he didn't do business plans, telling Joe, "I just want to go and meet people, and talk to them about it."

The trip was a failure, although they did have one promising lead from a breakfast meeting in Palo Alto with a Singapore-based investor, Thomas Ng, of Venture TDF. The VCs weren't really interested in business-to-business (B2B) e-commerce, which seemed dull compared to the excitement surrounding Yahoo, which Sina, Sohu, and NetEase were all able to tap into. There were a couple of B2B examples that raised venture money—Ariba.com and Commerce One—but they were U.S. based and served a much more mature market than Alibaba.

Other emerging China e-commerce players were beginning to have some success at fund-raising. One was a consumer e-commerce venture called 8848.net.[25] Launched in April 1999 and modeling its business on Amazon, 8848 sold books, software, electronics, and other local items, such as IP phone calling cards that were popular at the time. It had a well-established backer in forty-six-year-old Charles Xue (Xue Biqun). Xue had studied at UC Berkeley at the same time as SoftBank founder Masayoshi Son. The chairman of 8848, Wang Juntao, enjoyed a higher profile in China media circles than Jack. NetEase too was experimenting with consumer e-commerce, holding one of China's first online auctions in July 1999 when the site sold 100 PCs for a total of $150,000. Another new business, modeled on eBay, was also emerging: the Shanghai-based firm EachNet, led by a brilliant young Harvard-educated returnee, Shao Yibo, also known as Bo Shao.

Yet Jack was convinced that as the largest supplier of labor-intensive commodities to the world, China was ready for B2B e-commerce. But other entrepreneurs had come to the same conclusion. A California-based company had launched a B2B website called MeetChina.com and secured the backing of the venture capital firm IDG. In the coming year or so, MeetChina.com would raise more than $40 million in venture capital, significantly more than Alibaba. MeetChina would also excel at courting the support of governments on both sides of the Pacific.

In Beijing, MeetChina.com's founders claimed a special relationship[26] with the powerful Ministry of Information Industry. At its April 1999 launch, the company promoted itself as "China's first major government-sponsored business-to-business Internet portal." Cofounder Kenneth Leonard talked up his ties in Washington, D.C., claiming a business relationship with Neil Bush, the younger brother of George W. and Jeb Bush, and securing an invitation to the White House and publicity for the company's Asia-wide e-commerce push by signing an agreement in Vietnam during Bill and Hillary Clinton's groundbreaking presidential visit to the country the following year.

MeetChina was good at PR in China, too. One of its cofounders, Tom Rosenthal, told the *Wall Street Journal,* "We've got the services to make buying from China as easy as buying from a local hardware store." In the following months, MeetChina opened nine offices and hired more than 250 staff across China, signing impressive-sounding partnerships with a raft of companies including Dun & Bradstreet and Western Union.

B2B websites backed by Chinese government agencies were stepping up their efforts, too, including chinamarket.com, which Jack had helped set up. Watching the traction Alibaba was gaining with companies in Zhejiang Province, neighboring Jiangsu Province launched its own website—Made-in-China.com—as well.

But having just escaped the clutches of government, Jack was convinced that his customer-first approach would prevail over other websites that focused foremost on wining and dining government officials.

None of these sites would end up being Alibaba's main competitor. Instead Jack's biggest rival was not even a "new economy" company at all. It was an old-school publisher of trade magazines.

Global Sources had been around for more than three decades. The company was run by its founder, Merle Hinrichs. A reclusive American whose base of operations was his 160-foot yacht anchored in the Philippines, Hinrichs was a native of Hastings, Nebraska, but had been a resident of Asia since 1965. He had built up his company, originally known as Asian Sources Media Group, by churning out thick trade catalogs stuffed with advertisements from manufacturers in Asia of electronics, computer products, watches, toys, and sporting goods. Sent to buyers such as Walmart, the magazine generated hundreds of millions of dollars of orders per year.

Reluctant to cannibalize its profitable offline business, Global Sources was nervous about building a presence on the Web. Hinrichs was dismissive of B2B sites: "Suppliers and buyers were happy with the fax machine as that was cheap and simple to use."

But as Internet access spread, companies like Alibaba had an opportunity to pitch themselves as the new face of Asian business. Although Alibaba was struggling to convince investors to back it, the company started to have more success with the media, all thanks to Jack's charisma and gift of gab.

On April 17, 1999, *The Economist* ran an article titled "Asia Online." Its lead sentence consisted of the prophetic statement that "America has Jeff Bezos, China has [Jack] Ma Yun." Joe read that article on his flight up to Hangzhou to meet Jack, further piquing his interest in Alibaba.

The article was written by Chris Anderson, then based in Hong Kong. I contacted him to ask him what prompted him to write about Jack in such glowing terms. After more than a decade as editor in chief of *Wired* magazine, Chris lives today in Berkeley, California, where he is the cofounder and CEO of 3D Robotics, a drone manufacturing company.[27] Chris recalled his first meeting with Jack in early 1999 in Hong Kong. "Jack came to see me with what was then an idea for Alibaba. I thought it was a great business but a terrible name. Needless to say, he didn't take my advice, but we've remained friends since."

Chris explained to me that in his *Economist* article he had compared Jack to Jeff Bezos because "[b]oth are clever entrepreneurs who have grown rich by being among the first to exploit the Internet's potential. But there the similarities end." Of course, Jack wouldn't become truly rich for many years yet, but the fact that Chris had been impressed by his infectious enthusiasm is an early example of how "Jack Magic" has played a key role in Alibaba's rise.

Chinadotcom

But unbeknownst to Jack and Joe as they headed empty-handed from Silicon Valley back to Asia, their fortunes were about to be transformed thanks to an event that signaled the beginning of the China Internet gold rush: the Nasdaq IPO of China.com.

China.com, operated by the company Chinadotcom, part of China Internet Corporation (CIC), was led by a deal maker in Hong Kong called Peter Yip. Yip was an unlikely candidate for a China Internet entrepreneur. He wasn't from China—born in Singapore,[28] he was based in Hong Kong—and was a decade or so older than Jack and the portal founders; few people in China had ever heard of him or his website.

But just as dot-com investing began to reach a fever pitch in the United States, CIC found itself sitting on some very important assets:[29] the domain names china.com, hongkong.com, and taiwan.com. Using these as leverage, Yip signed on some influential backers, including the unlikely bedfellows America Online and Xinhua, China's state news agency. To AOL he offered his services as a gatekeeper to the China market. To Xinhua he promised to build a "walled garden" of content, filtering out undesirable content on the Internet.

Yip called his vision the "China Wide Web." In a speech at Harvard University, he argued that much of the content on the Internet was "not relevant to most Chinese." Touting the Xinhua backing, he claimed[30] that the Chinese government had established an Internet strategy and "asked me to help them create a vehicle to allow people to participate." The news area of his china.com website carried the terrifying tagline "We do the surfing for you." But Chinese users wanted access to the full Internet, something that local entrepreneurs such as the three portal pioneers were working hard to enable. Yip's efforts failed to gain traction with Internet users in China. His "know who" approach, based on relationships, was beaten out by the "know how" smarts of China's new generation of tech-savvy Internet entrepreneurs.

But Peter Yip beat out his mainland Chinese rivals in one important aspect: He really knew how to raise money, scoring a $34 million investment in china.com from AOL, then in July 1999 an IPO for the company on the Nasdaq.

People working in China's Internet sector were fiercely critical of the company and its claims. I was one of them, telling the *New York Times* that China.com was "out of step with what Internet users in China are about," and that "companies that make deals with them are actually doing themselves a disservice." In June 1999 I wrote a report warning that if China.com was to IPO before the "real" Chinese portals it would "represent the triumph of form over substance and effectively spoil the market for mainland Chinese Internet companies." How wrong I was. Instead of extinguishing the opportunity for China tech IPOs, China.com lit the market on fire.

On July 13, 1999, China.com listed its shares on the Nasdaq. The stock ticker for the company was as catchy as its website: "CHINA." Listing at $20, the stock closed that day at $67. What's in a name? In the case of China.com, a company that people in China had hardly ever heard of, the answer was $84 million—the amount the company raised in the IPO, to which the company added a then-massive $400 million the following February in a secondary offering, valuing the company at $5 billion. The company raised so much money that it would be eleven years before it finally slipped into bankruptcy.

The shock waves from China.com's July 1999 IPO reverberated across the mainland's nascent tech community. How had a guy with a website that almost no one had heard of raised so much money overnight? The IPO unleashed a frenzy of investments and deal making as entrepreneurs across the country concluded, "If China.com can do it, so can I!"

Chapter Seven

Backers: Goldman and SoftBank

The Internet [is like] beer . . . the good stuff is at the bottom. Without the bubbles, the beer is flat and nobody would want to drink it.

—Jack Ma

On its first day of trading on the Nasdaq, China.com—a company with only $4 million in annual revenues, on which it had lost $9 million—closed the day worth $1.6 billion. Peter Yip had listed only a small number of shares, so investors cast around looking for other China Internet stocks to buy. The problem was, there weren't any.

Seizing the opportunity, venture capitalists and entrepreneurs leapt into action. In Hong Kong there was a sudden explosion of tech gatherings, speed-dating exercises between young entrepreneurs and the investors that wanted to back them. One of the largest meet-ups was called "I&I," short for "Internet & Information Asia." The event had been around for a while, typically with a few people gathering around a table in one of the tiny bars of Lan Kwai Fong, just up the hill from the city's main central business district. But the China.com IPO changed all that. Suddenly hundreds of people showed up at I&I, the venues switching to five-star hotels like the Ritz-Carlton as banks and law firms tripped over one another for the right to sponsor the champagne and hors d'oeuvres. Hong Kong was ready to package the deals, but the market and the entrepreneurs to build the companies were across the border in mainland China. Suddenly Beijing and Shanghai were awash in deal makers. The China Internet bubble had officially begun and new dot-com ventures started to sprout up like weeds. Alibaba would have to fight for its share of sunlight.

Media Coverage

Before even the VCs had showed up, foreign media arrived to cover the China Internet story. Jack became a regular fixture at tech and investor conferences around the country, his comments so quotable that the *Los Angeles Times* called him a "sound-bite machine."

Soon after the China.com IPO, a *BusinessWeek* magazine cover story named Jack one of "China's Web Masters." Alibaba had yet to generate meaningful revenues but *BusinessWeek* predicted that investing in B2B e-commerce could mean an even bigger payoff than investing in China's three portals.

On August 31, 1999, an article written by my colleague Ted Dean appeared in Hong Kong's leading English-language daily, the *South China Morning Post*.[1] Ted had first met Jack a year or so earlier when Jack was still working for the government. In the article, Ted predicted that Alibaba "may turn out to be a global powerhouse" in B2B e-commerce. Jack laid out his ambition: "We don't want to be number one in China. We want to be number one in the world."

In our small investment consultancy, we were hearing a lot of those kinds of statements and were already becoming a bit cynical about the dot-com boom. But after interviewing Jack for the article in Hangzhou a few days earlier, Ted told me there was something about Jack that was different. I knew I had to meet him.

When Jack invited me to visit, I hopped on a train from Shanghai to Hangzhou. I booked myself back into the Shangri-La Hotel, the same hotel where Jack as a boy had first approached David Morley to practice his English. After checking in I took a taxi over to the Lakeside Gardens apartment.

I was immediately struck by Jack's infectious enthusiasm and capacity to charm, influenced no doubt by growing up in a household where both his parents practiced *pingtan,* the traditional art form that includes comedic routines.

In his article, Ted had quoted Jack saying, "If you plan, you lose. If you don't plan, you win." After working in Beijing, the land of the five-year plan, I found Jack's spontaneity refreshing. Foreign professionals[2] began to enter Jack's orbit, giving Alibaba an international flavor within months of its founding. Alibaba also had a strong component of female executives,[3] adding to the achievement of women making up one third of its founding team—in contrast to many Silicon Valley–based companies.

Goldman Invests

Meanwhile, in Hong Kong, shortly after their unsuccessful fund-raising trip to Silicon Valley, Joe had started negotiations with Transpac, a Singapore-based fund, about investing in Alibaba. Soon they had agreed to a term sheet that would value Alibaba at $7 million.[4] But Transpac insisted on an onerous provision[5] and Joe wanted to walk away.

He then called up a friend at Goldman Sachs. Like Joe, Shirley Lin was born in Taiwan and educated in the United States. The two had met a decade earlier. For Alibaba it would prove to have been a fateful encounter.

In the summer of 2015, I met up with Shirley in New York to talk about Goldman Sachs's transformative investment in Alibaba in 1999. Shirley and I have known each other since 1999. We had been classmates at Morgan Stanley, the investment bank we joined fresh out of college. While I stayed on at Morgan Stanley, Shirley had left after a few years for Goldman Sachs to start making investments in technology and Internet companies across Asia.

Ten years before the Alibaba deal, Shirley and Joe had met by chance on a long plane ride from Taipei to New York. "I was going back to Harvard, he was going back to Yale. We were seated adjacent to each other." She remembers Joe's face was buried for most of the trip in a book on constitutional law. He remembers Shirley intently reading the *Wall Street Journal,* cover to cover. After a while they struck up a conversation. Contemplating the books and exams that awaited them back at college, "pretty soon we were both lamenting each other's fate," Shirley told me.

As Jack and Joe had already discovered, there weren't many investment firms in Asia with much experience in technology companies. In 1999, Shirley was already busily placing bets[6] on China Internet companies, ultimately investing in all three portals. Goldman invested directly in Sina and NetEase, and indirectly in Sohu.[7]

Goldman had given Shirley and her team a lot of leeway, provided she kept the investments below $5 million. This was peanuts to Goldman, whose Principal Investment Area (PIA) unit would make $1 billion in investments in tech companies from 1995 to 2000, one-quarter in companies based in Asia.

With so few funds already on the ground in Asia, Shirley was bombarded with requests for investment from her Harvard classmates and other friends pursuing the new wave of dot-com riches. The quality of the business plans was pretty low, often simple copy-and-paste jobs.

Shirley and her team worked around the clock, wading through stacks of pitch documents, investing, she estimates, in less than one in a thousand.

While the easy route was to invest in companies with at least one known quantity—founders who were classmates or friends—for the China Internet story Shirley had a strong preference in finding homegrown talent. "I really thought that to invest in China, you have to know the local market."

But scouring through China start-ups had its drawbacks. Traveling on unpaved roads in provincial cities, Shirley felt more like a loan officer with the Asian Development Bank than an investment banker. She also had a hard time being taken seriously: "Even though we were at Goldman, people in China didn't know who we were. They asked, 'Are you Mrs. Goldman? Are you married to the owner of this business?' They thought Goldman and Sachs were two people who owned the company, and I must be married to one of them."

So when Joe Tsai approached her about a start-up run by a local entrepreneur in Hangzhou, she was interested, particularly when he told her he planned to join the company. Shirley decided to fly up from Hong Kong to Hangzhou to meet Jack in late September 1999.

Jack, she recalled, was "as local as it gets."

"I went up to the apartment, where they were all working twenty-four/seven. . . . The whole place stank. Jack's ideas were not entirely original—they had been tried in other countries. But he was completely dedicated to making them work in China. I was moved by what I saw."

As with Joe before her, Shirley was less impressed by the business itself than by the team, the real reason she would decide to invest: Who were they? What was their history? Knowing Joe checked one box. Seeing Jack and the team in action checked another. "Really, it was all about Jack and his people." Shirley remembers being impressed by how hard Jack's wife, Cathy, was working. She and Jack toiled away, she recalled, like "revolutionary comrades."

Alibaba had been approached by other investors, but Shirley knew that the backing of Goldman would make all the difference for an unknown start-up in China. They discussed the investment over tea. If Goldman invested, she told Jack and Joe, she would personally ensure Alibaba was known to the world. With B2B competitors like MeetChina waiting in the wings and actively fund-raising, the offer proved too tempting to resist. Shirley negotiated to acquire a majority stake in Alibaba for $5 million. She headed back to Hong Kong, where her colleagues Paul Yang and Oliver Weisberg[8] drew up the term sheet for the investment.

The following weekend Shirley was swimming with her family at the Repulse Bay beach on the south side of Hong Kong Island when her cell phone rang. It was Jack. He really wanted to do the deal but asked Shirley to leave him more equity. If Goldman took a controlling stake in his company, he explained, he couldn't feel like a true entrepreneur. Jack told her how he'd put everything into the venture. "This is my life," he said. Shirley replied, "What do you mean this is your life, you've only just started?" Jack explained, "But this is my third venture already." Jack finally convinced her. The term sheet for the investment had been drawn up, but there were brackets around the numbers so it would be an easy change. Goldman would invest the $5 million for 500,000 shares, half the company, while retaining veto rights over key decisions.

Just after she had agreed to the new terms, mid-conversation with Jack, she accidentally dropped her cell phone into the sea. Oops, she thought to herself. Well, I guess there goes $5 million.

Jack had succeeded in securing a big-name investor in what would prove a critical step in Alibaba's story. But he would also come to regret selling such a large stake in the company, 50 percent, which he would never recoup. In reality, though, Jack had little choice. He was an unproven entrepreneur based in a provincial city in China who was negotiating with a huge, global financial institution. But having already given out a lot of equity to his cofounders and now 50 percent to investors, he ended up with a much lower share of his company than many of his peers. Jack would later joke, only half-kidding, that it was the "worst deal I ever made."

When Shirley took the deal to her investment committee, which oversaw all the fund's investments, she encountered an unexpected snag. They pushed back. If Goldman invested the full $5 million, the fund would need to gain the approval of their investors. "Please get rid of some," they told her. So, Shirley reduced Goldman's stake to 33 percent. Now she quickly had to find investors for the other 17 percent.

Today the thought of having to cast urgently around for buyers willing to pay $1.7 million for a 17 percent stake in Alibaba, now worth tens of billions of dollars, is laughable. In the end she brought in Thomas Ng of Venture TDF, who had met Jack and Joe that summer in Palo Alto, for half a million dollars. Fidelity Growth Partners Asia came in for another half a million. Joe had already told his employer that he was going to join a start-up in China. When Joe informed his boss, Galeazzo Scarampi, that he had found investors and was going to leave to join Alibaba, Investor AB also came in for a slice. Transpac rounded out the balance of the $1.7 million investment alongside Goldman's $3.3 million.

Some of the investors, including Venture TDF and Fidelity, held on to their stakes all the way through Alibaba's 2014 IPO, generating returns of billions of dollars.

When the Goldman-led round was finalized on October 27, 1999, the investment cemented Joe's authority as Jack's right-hand man.

The $5 million round led by Goldman was a start, but peanuts compared to the war chest of the three China portals, who were besieged by eager investors as the Nasdaq began its vertiginous climb, gaining 80 percent in eight months, valuing its component companies at $6.7 trillion in early 2000.

All eyes were on the companies who positioned themselves as the Yahoo of China, as well as the moves of Yahoo itself in China. In September 1999, Yahoo, then valued at $36 billion, announced a partnership with Founder, the largest local PC manufacturer at the time, targeting the mainland.[9] At the same time, Sohu, Sina, and NetEase ramped up their fund-raising.

Sina would raise the most, including $60 million in November 1999 from investors, including Goldman Sachs and SoftBank, putting the company in pole position for an IPO in the United States. Sohu raised $30 million, its founder Charles Zhang capturing the mood of the day: "This is a game of spending money and how fast you can spend money." Even William Ding at NetEase relented, raising in two rounds $20 million from investors, including Goldman Sachs, but not without venting his frustration that now "people never ask you about your new products. . . . They only ask you, 'When is your IPO?' "

On October 7 Alibaba tried to grab some of the limelight with a press conference in Hong Kong to announce a new version of its website and disclosing that it was open to an IPO in the United States or on the planned "second board" of the Hong Kong Stock Exchange, the Growth Enterprise Market.

Caught up in the excitement of Hong Kong, Alibaba also announced that it would move its headquarters there from Hangzhou. Jack had been spending most of his time in Hong Kong, working with Joe and some new recruits out of a conference room in Goldman's office. The contrast couldn't have been greater between Alibaba's humble, second-floor Lakeside Gardens apartment in Hangzhou and its new perch atop the gleaming Citibank Plaza skyscraper with breathtaking views over Victoria Harbor.

To support Goldman's newest portfolio company, Shirley Lin conducted a series of interviews with media in Hong Kong, even going on local television stations to spread the word about Alibaba. "My Cantonese was so bad back then they had to subtitle me," she recalls.

When Goldman moved to even shinier new offices atop billionaire Li Ka-shing's brand-new Cheung Kong Center, Alibaba signed a lease on its own impressive (and expensive) new space, the first major outlay from Goldman's $5 million that had hit the bank. Alibaba could get down to business.

Its business was simple: to become the leading website in China for business-to-business leads. To match buyers with sellers, Alibaba organized its members' postings into twenty-seven industry sectors, such as "Apparel & Fashion," "Electronics and Electrical," and "Industrial Supplies." Users could sign up for free to receive notification of trade deals, and search for offers to buy or sell within a sector or a geographical area. By October 1999, Alibaba had signed up more than forty thousand users. Now it had to go for a much higher quantity of users, while maintaining the quality of the messages tacked onto its virtual bulletin board.

Most of the sellers on its site were export or trading companies in China, including a strong representation of firms led by Zhejiang entrepreneurs. The Internet was still new for many of these firms, but they quickly became loyal users of Alibaba.com. Many lacked the scale or connections needed to trade through the state-owned trading companies, and some were located in remote areas that made traveling to trade shows like the Canton Fair too expensive. Having grown up among them and served them as clients of Hope Translation and China Pages, Jack had a keen sense of what these small firms needed: "Most SMEs [small and medium enterprises] have a very changeable dynamic. Today they might sell T-shirts, tomorrow it could be chemicals."

To attract buyers, Alibaba needed to ensure vendors' listings were translated accurately into English. Drawing on the talent pool of university graduates in Hangzhou, Alibaba started to hire English-speaking editors to ensure that the posts on the bulletin board were complete, intelligible, and properly categorized. Leveraging his contacts from MOFTEC in Beijing, Jack also hired recruits with trade know-how to make the website attractive to foreign buyers.

Posting on the site, for buyers and sellers, was free—a central tenet of Jack's approach throughout his career. His "if you build it, they will come" approach helped him pull clear of any rivals. If visitors to Alibaba.com were able to make new trade leads, he figured, they would demonstrate increasing loyalty, or "stickiness" to the website.

But while free was great for users, it was a tough business model. Alibaba was vulnerable to any downtime in the Internet funding frenzy. Also, as traffic grew dramatically on Alibaba's website, maintaining the quality of postings was a big job. If Alibaba wasn't careful it could be overwhelmed. Another challenge was the increasing competition for talent. In the dot-com boom, skilled employees constantly jumped ship to rival ventures or, tapping the growing pool of venture funding, tried their luck at their own start-ups. The cost of talent started to spiral upward, including for the software developers, Web designers, and project managers that Alibaba would need to build out its offerings.

Here Alibaba had two important things going for it: Hangzhou and Jack Ma. Unlike Beijing and Shanghai, where turnover of qualified employees was a major headache for entrepreneurs, Hangzhou had a deep pool of fresh graduates and very few local employers. In addition, Alibaba benefited from Hangzhou's relative isolation. There weren't really any rivals to poach his employees. A few other technology firms were located in the town, such as UTStarcom or Eastcom, but in the dot-com craze these were fast becoming "old economy" ventures. Alibaba also benefited from Hangzhou's distance from Shanghai—then some two hours away. For young talented engineers in Hangzhou who wanted to work for a fast-growing Internet venture, Alibaba was it.

This helped keep costs low, too. For the price of one engineer in Beijing or Shanghai, Alibaba could hire two. The comparison with Silicon Valley was even more dramatic, as Jack pointed out: "[To] keep one programmer happy [in Silicon Valley] takes $50,000 to $100,000. For that much money in China, I can keep ten very smart people happy all the time."

As a "second tier" city real estate was cheaper in Hangzhou, too. Even after Alibaba moved into a 200,000-square-foot office in early 2000, its total rental bill was just $80,000 a year, a fraction of what it would have been in Beijing or Shanghai. Jack liked the distance from Beijing: "Even though the infrastructure is not as good as in Shanghai, it's better to be as far away from the central government as possible."

Ali People

When building up his team Jack preferred hiring people a notch or two below the top performers in their schools. The college elite, Jack explained, would easily get frustrated when they encountered the difficulties of the real world. For those who came aboard, working for Alibaba would be no picnic. The pay was low: The earliest hires earned barely $50 per month. They worked seven days a week, often sixteen hours a day. Jack even required them to find a place to live no more than ten minutes from the office so they wouldn't waste precious time commuting.

From the outset, Alibaba has been driven by a Silicon Valley–style work ethic, with every employee issued share options in the company, vesting over a four-year period. This is still a rarity in China, where the traditional setup in private companies was an emperor-like boss who treated employees as disposable and salaries as discretionary.

As the Alibaba.com website grew in popularity—aided by offering its services for free—the team in Hangzhou struggled to keep up with the volume of incoming emails. Alibaba's customer service team found themselves at times acting as free tech support to clients, responding to questions about how to reboot a computer. But wedded to its "customer first" tenet, Alibaba resolved to respond to every email within two hours.

Keeping the team focused, cofounder Simon Xie recalled, Jack was "a culture, a nucleus." Jack greeted new recruits with a sobering message, and a promise:[10] Then trotting out one of his favorite sayings: "Today is brutal, tomorrow is more brutal, but the day after tomorrow is beautiful. However, the majority of people will die tomorrow night. They won't be able to see the sunshine the day after tomorrow. Aliren[11] must see the sunshine the day after tomorrow."

Cofounder Lucy Peng, Alibaba's first human resources director and later its "chief people officer," also played an important role in the hiring process and in shaping the company's culture. In a 2000 Harvard Business School case study on the company, she commented that "Alibaba employees don't need experience. They need good health, a good heart, and a good head."

As the website's members grew, companies in China began to use the site to connect with one another as well as to the outside world, prompting the launch of a Chinese-language marketplace[12] for wholesalers in China seeking domestic trade leads.

Yet Alibaba still encountered difficulties winning converts to the e-commerce cause. Some balked at the high costs of buying computers;

others lacked personnel with a sufficient understanding of IT. An even bigger obstacle was a pervasive lack of trust. Suppliers worried that customers they had never met might never pay for their orders. Buyers overseas were concerned about fake or defective goods, or shipments that never arrived.

Alibaba couldn't wave a magic wand to make these risks go away, as Jack emphasized to the media: "We are just a platform for businesspeople to meet, but we do not take legal responsibility." Alibaba kept its focus as a bulletin board for businesses. But others, such as MeetChina, were talking up their plans to expand into areas like market research, credit checks on suppliers, quality inspections, shipping, insurance, and payments.

Jack argued this was premature: "Small- and medium-sized companies do not trust transactions online yet. And we believe the current banking system is good enough for small business. As long as our members feel it's easy, they'd prefer to do their transactions offline."

Alibaba was struggling to define itself in ways that investors could understand: "We don't really have a clearly defined business model yet," Jack admitted. "If you consider Yahoo a search engine, Amazon a bookstore, eBay an auction center, Alibaba is an electronic market. Yahoo and Amazon are not perfect models and we're still trying to figure out what's best."

Goldman's cash had helped, but the commitment to free listings meant that Alibaba had to raise more capital soon, something made more pressing by the opening of the new Hong Kong office and another in Shanghai, which Alibaba announced would serve as its new China headquarters. To sign up more customers, Alibaba started to host gatherings of SMEs in hotel ballrooms, arranging tables to group together companies from similar industries.

Despite the hectic pace during the Internet bubble, and the growing sense of inevitability that it would soon pop, Jack betrayed few signs of anxiety. I visited Hangzhou several times in late 1999 and 2000 and witnessed Alibaba sprout from the Lakeside apartment through a series of ever-larger offices.

I never witnessed Jack lose his cool, even when he dinged the fender of his car one day on a concrete column when we were parking at a restaurant where he'd invited me to lunch. I always found my visits to Hangzhou enjoyable. Spending time with Jack was invariably good fun. Like many visits before and since, I enjoyed seeing the city's sites. On one visit Jack's wife, Cathy, took me to visit the famous Long Jing (Dragon Well) tea plantations, including a walk through the bamboo forest nearby—a breath of fresh air (literally) after Beijing.

Jack was now spending much of his time away from Hangzhou, speaking at industry and investor conferences. In January 2000 we were both invited to speak at a student-organized event[13] at Harvard. I met up with Jack before the conference. As we walked along an icy pathway on the banks of the Charles River I noticed one of his entourage was filming the scene, something I later discovered she had been doing for years already.

The conference featured a number of other China Internet entrepreneurs, most with much stronger academic pedigrees than Jack. Some were recent returnees to China like Shao Yibo of EachNet, who had actually studied at Harvard. Peter Yip from China.com was also there.

But Jack quickly emerged as the star of the show, especially when he confessed to the audience that he really had no idea what Alibaba's business model was, adding "and yet I got investment from Goldman Sachs!"

Jack reveled in the attention he received at Harvard, including the moniker "Crazy Jack" that *Time* magazine gave him shortly after. He particularly enjoyed talking about the reversal of fortune of being once rejected[14] by Harvard but later being invited there to give a talk. "I did not get an education from Harvard . . . I went to Harvard to educate them."

Jack has always been dismissive of business schools: "It is not necessary to study an MBA. Most MBA graduates are not useful. . . . Unless they come back from their MBA studies and forget what they've learned at school, then they will be useful. Because schools teach knowledge, while starting businesses requires wisdom. Wisdom is acquired through experience. Knowledge can be acquired through hard work."

SoftBank Invests

One of the reasons that Jack was on such a high at Harvard was that he was on the verge of announcing another important milestone for Alibaba: $20 million in fresh funding from the Japanese investment firm SoftBank.

With this, and a subsequent investment, SoftBank became Alibaba's largest shareholder. The deal was teed up by Alibaba's investor, Goldman Sachs. SoftBank was on the lookout for tech investment opportunities in China when Mark Schwartz, then president of Goldman Sachs Japan, told Masayoshi Son, SoftBank's founder, about the bank's growing portfolio of tech investments in China.

In October 1999, Jack was one of several entrepreneurs invited to meet Masayoshi Son in one of a series of "speed dating" sessions between the Chinese start-ups and the Japanese billionaire arranged by Chauncey Shey, president of SoftBank China Venture Capital. The two men met at the wedding cake–styled Fuhua Mansion in Beijing. The venue turned out to be a fitting one, their meeting the start of an enduring partnership that would eventually make Son the richest man in Japan. Son's backing of Jack, coming just months before the dot-com crash, transformed Alibaba's fortunes.

Masayoshi Son

Masayoshi Son, known to his friends as "Masa," shares some similarities with Jack. Both are short in stature and known for their outsize ambitions.

Son grew up in circumstances even more difficult than Jack's. Born on Japan's southernmost main island of Kyushu, the Sons lived in a shack that didn't even have an official address. His father was a pig farmer who brewed moonshine on the side. Son was bullied for being ethnically Korean and was forced to adopt the Japanese surname Yasumoto. At the age of sixteen, Son moved to Northern California in search of a brighter future. Staying with friends and family, he attended Serramonte High School in Daly City, just south of San Francisco, before gaining acceptance to the University of California, Berkeley, where he started his entrepreneurial career. His most successful venture was building a voice-operated translation device to be sold at airport kiosks. Son designed, built, and then licensed the technology to Sharp Electronics for half a million dollars. In the United States, Son started to import early models of the Pac-Man and Space Invaders game consoles that were becoming popular at the time, leasing them to local bars and restaurants, including Yoshi's, a North Berkeley sushi bar (now a famous Bay Area jazz venue). At Berkeley, he also met and hired Lu Hongliang, whose venture, Unitech Industries (renamed Unitech Telecom in 1994), later became part of the technology venture UTStarcom, the Hangzhou-based company in which SoftBank invested in 1995.

After moving back to Japan in the early 1980s, Son started a software distribution company. At the launch of the venture, in a scene echoing Jack's own irrepressible optimism, he famously climbed on top of a shipping box in front of his employees—just two at the time, both working part-time—and vowed that their new venture would make 50 billion yen ($3 billion) in revenues within ten years.

By the time he first met Jack, Son had become a billionaire many times over. He was known for making quick decisions. One of his best was the prescient investment he made in Yahoo in 1995. When Yahoo went public in 1996, Son topped up SoftBank's stake in the portal to 37 percent, becoming its largest investor. Son also negotiated the right for SoftBank to become Yahoo's exclusive partner in Japan, a deal that would yield him tens of billions more.

Meeting Son, Jack knew he had found a kindred spirit. "We didn't talk about revenues; we didn't even talk about a business model. . . . We just talked about a shared vision. Both of us make quick decisions," Jack recalled.

"When I went to see Masayoshi Son, I didn't even wear a suit that day. . . . After five or six minutes, he began to like me and I began to like him. . . . People around him have said that we are soul mates."

At their first meeting, after Jack had finished describing Alibaba, by now some 100,000 members strong, Son immediately turned the conversation to how much SoftBank could invest. "I listened to Mr. Ma's speech for five minutes and decided on the spot that I was ready to invest in Alibaba," Son recalled. Son interrupted Jack's presentation to tell him he should take SoftBank's money because he "should spend money more quickly." Around the time of Alibaba's 2014 IPO, Son was asked what it was that prompted him to bet on Jack back in 2000: "It was the look in his eye, it was an 'animal smell.' . . . It was the same when we invested in Yahoo . . . when they were still only five to six people. I invested based on my sense of smell."

This impulsiveness was typical for Son. "Masa is Masa. He has ADD [attention deficit disorder] and can't sit still. He just wants to give you money now, now!" commented a former business associate.

A few weeks after their first meeting in Beijing, Son invited Jack to Tokyo to finalize terms. Joe Tsai joined him on the trip.

As soon as they entered Son's office, the negotiations began. Jack would later infuse his description of their meeting with martial art imagery: "Masters of negotiation always listen, don't talk. Those who talk a lot only have second-rate negotiation skills. A true master listens, and as soon as he moves his sword, you pretty much collapse."

Joe, who had met up with SoftBank China's Chauncey Shey before the trip, told me the details of their meeting. "Goldman and the other funds had just invested $5 million for half of the company, valuing Alibaba at $10 million. Masa opened the negotiations by offering $20 million for 40 percent of the company. This valued Alibaba at $50 million 'post-money,' and $30 million 'pre-money.' In just weeks, Goldman's investment had increased in value by three times."

Joe and Jack looked at each other, Joe recalled, thinking, "Woohoo, that's three-times! But then we thought, we didn't want to give up too much equity. So Jack said, 'Masa, that doesn't work for us.' Masa had a calculator; he was literally doing the math right there. But Masa wanted 40 percent, so he said, 'How about double the amount. I put $40 million for 40 percent.' That means $60 million pre-money."

Jack and Joe offered to think it over. Upon their return to China, Jack wrote Son an email turning down the $40 million investment. Instead he offered to take in $20 million for 30 percent, adding, "If you agree, we will go ahead; if not, that's it." Jack later explained why he turned down the larger amount: "Why would I need to take so much money? I didn't know how to use it, and there would definitely be problems." Jack didn't have to wait long for his reply from Son, which came in the form of two words: "Go ahead."

Jack credits fortune with playing a hand in connecting him with Son, conceding that "[i]t is quite difficult to find such an investor." Commenting on the dynamics of their relationship, Jack said, "I think Masa is definitely one of the world's best [businessmen], very sharp on investment." But he adds Son is also a good operator of business, too: "It's not easy to shift from investor to operator and meanwhile still be a good investor. For me, I'm just an operator. I love to be an entrepreneur. I'm not a good investor."

Jack also liked to joke about their appearances: "The difference between me and him is that I may look very smart, [but] in fact I am not; that guy seriously doesn't look very smart, but he is a very wise person."

An early Alibaba employee, Shou Yuan, has an interesting take on the relationship between the two founder-CEOs: "Son has a lot of self-confidence, he's even conceited, but his appearance is always one of modesty. He's crazy, but Ma's also crazy. It's very common for crazy people to like each other."

Announcing the deal, Son himself drew a comparison with his wildly successful investment in Yahoo.

"We would like to make Alibaba the next Yahoo. . . . I think this will probably be the first Chinese Internet company which will become a global brand, a global success in a big way. I am very excited to make that happen."

The two firms also announced a joint venture for Alibaba Korea, which would launch in June 2000, to fend off the growth of a local player there, and drew up plans for a site in Japan as well.

The deal was clearly a transformative one for Alibaba, and cause for celebration. In less than a year after the company's founding, Jack and Joe had reeled in $25 million from two of the largest and most prestigious investors in the world.

The deal was not without a price: The sale of 30 percent of Alibaba to SoftBank came on the heels of the sale of 50 percent of the company to Goldman Sachs, meaning a hefty dilution of Jack's stake.

Yet the SoftBank investment provided Alibaba with serious street cred in China, just as the three Chinese Internet portals geared up for their U.S. IPOs. The deal also gave Alibaba insurance. No one could predict with any certainty how long the tech investment boom would last. SoftBank's $20 million allowed it to build out a much longer "runway" on which to achieve takeoff and future profitability.

Jack wanted to be noticed in Silicon Valley, too. Soon after he secured the $20 million investment from SoftBank, Jack headed to Santa Clara, California, the home of Yahoo. He traveled there to offer John Wu[15]—a Yahoo executive whom Jack had first met when working at China Pages—the post of chief technology officer of Alibaba. It was an ambitious pitch. Jack was proposing that John take a 50 percent pay cut and leave the hottest company in Silicon Valley for a risky start-up in Hangzhou.

John expressed his misgivings to Jack, as he later recalled, "Yahoo was doing well, my parents were immigrating to the U.S., I wasn't seriously considering this possibility." He was particularly keen to avoid moving his family back to China. Instead Jack proposed he run Alibaba's R&D team from Fremont, California. John accepted.

Jack, with a background as an English teacher, was keen to ensure that his own ignorance of technology was not replicated in Alibaba. "For a first-class company, we need first-class technology. When John comes, I can sleep soundly." Hiring John Wu also gave Jack the opportunity to sprinkle some more Yahoo stardust on his venture. Sitting next to Jack in a press conference, John described Alibaba as a new form of Yahoo: "Yahoo's search engine has shaped the way millions of people surf the Internet. Now Alibaba's e-commerce platform will fundamentally change the way people conduct business online." The *Los Angeles Times* commented that the "ability of a Chinese start-up to poach one of Silicon Valley's key players could bolster China's claim as the ultimate Internet frontier for the best minds in the industry."

John jumped from Yahoo to Alibaba, he explained, because Alibaba's idea was an original one. "If you compare the other leading Internet companies in China," he said, "almost all of them are copying business models already existing in the U.S." Shirley Lin at Goldman Sachs had been attracted to Alibaba for its "localness." John Wu saw the same merits: "There are a lot of Internet companies started by people who studied in the U.S. and came back to China. . . . Jack Ma is different. He has been in China all his life."

With fresh capital, new recruits, and more than 150,000 members in 188 countries signed up on the website, things were looking up for Alibaba. But the bubble was about to pop.

Chapter Eight

Burst and Back to China

Be the last man standing.

—Jack Ma

By the spring of 2000, Alibaba was signing up more than a thousand new members a day.

Connecting suppliers in China with global buyers was clearly a good idea. But other companies with the same idea were proliferating, and some actively raising capital, too. MeetChina raised another $11 million, some of which came from a SoftBank fund, and announced a sales target of $10 million that year and planning for an IPO. Global Sources, the veteran publisher of trade magazines, announced it had hired Goldman Sachs to prepare for a Nasdaq IPO and stepped up its hiring in China.

Other contenders entered the fray as well, including entrepreneurs[1] who pivoted to business-to-business e-commerce after seeing Alibaba's success in raising capital.

Faced with increasing competition, and flush with cash, Alibaba accelerated its expansion. In the months following SoftBank's investment, the company went on a hiring spree in mainland China, Hong Kong, and Fremont, California, where incoming CTO John Wu set up their U.S. outpost.

Government on the Fence

Speculation grew about an IPO. Yet the most likely companies to go public, the three Chinese portals, had hit a roadblock. Their success was helping popularize the consumer Internet faster than the government had expected. Four million Internet users was a drop in the ocean in a population of 1.3 billion. Yet the things that made the portals popular, especially email and news, made a government bent on control increasingly nervous.

Within China's ruling Communist Party a debate was raging over how to handle the Internet. Conservatives pointed out that the Internet had originated as the project of a U.S. defense agency. They argued that just because it was new, there was no reason to exclude Internet companies from the same restrictions that prevented or severely constrained foreign investment in the telecom sector or in print, radio, film, and TV. There was no "Ministry of Internet," but the Internet touched so many areas that it set off bitter turf battles between existing regulators. To demonstrate their relevance, China's regulators regulate regularly, manifested in the "Great Firewall of China," under construction ever since the Internet came to China's shore, an unceasing effort to filter content they deemed a threat to the country or to Communist Party rule.

At the same time, with its huge investments in telecom infrastructure the government had been actually pushing *xinxihua*—informatization—as essential for developing China's economy. There was consensus among the all-powerful politburo standing committee—

nearly all trained as engineers—that China needed a "knowledge economy."

An inability to adapt to new technology could spell disaster. The fall of the Qing dynasty is popularly attributed in part to its failure to adapt to modern military and industrial technologies, leaving it vulnerable to domination by Western powers. Some in China also blamed the fall of the Soviet Union on a failure to keep up with waves of technological advances in Silicon Valley, such as the semiconductor, computer, and software industries.

But the government rejected any notion that the Internet would usher in the Western concept of an "information society," something they believed could pose an existential threat to the Communist Party.

Yet without foreign investment, how could China's Internet entrepreneurs finance their ventures? Restricting them to domestic financing channels was impractical. China's own venture capital market was in its infancy, and its stock markets were dominated by SOEs. In any case, the Shanghai and Shenzhen exchanges required companies to have been in business for at least three years, and to be profitable. All of China's Internet companies were new, and operating unashamedly at a loss.

China wanted a Silicon Valley, but one that it could control, built on its terms. Yet the distributed, bottom-up nature of the Internet was inimical to China's traditions, both imperial and Leninist, of top-down control of information. For those coming online, this was the Internet's central appeal.

Professor Xu Rongsheng, who had helped establish the first connection between the Institute of High Energy Physics in Beijing and Stanford University, describes the impact of the Internet as an "information bomb" exploding over China. Another popular description was that the Internet was "God's gift to the Chinese," something echoed by investors and dissidents[2] alike.

Unable to stop the Internet, but nervous about facilitating its rise, how was the government to proceed?

How could Chinese Internet entrepreneurs raise money overseas without their companies being classified as foreign companies and walled off from businesses in China? To resolve the contradiction the three portals attempted all manner of contortions to secure government approval for their IPOs, arguing they weren't even Internet companies.

After months of debate, an accommodation was finally reached: the "VIE." The VIE, or "variable interest entity," is much loved by corporate lawyers in China for its rich, fee-producing complexity. Still in use today, it allows the Chinese government effectively to have its cake and eat it, too—in this case allowing a thriving entrepreneurial Internet, while maintaining control. The VIE is the subject of ongoing debate for investors in Alibaba—how much protection does it really give them? The structure allows foreign investors a degree of control over the revenues generated by a Chinese company (through a complicated arrangement of interlocking contracts) that, thanks to the personal engagement of Chinese entrepreneur founders, continues to treat that company as Chinese.

The compromise was brokered by Sina (and its lawyers) with the Ministry of Information Industry (MII), amongst other agencies. MII minister Wu Jichuan had earlier stood in the way of any portal IPOs, but the VIE broke the logjam. His voice carried weight, as he was the architect of the drive for "informatization," the investment in infrastructure without which the country's Internet boom would not have been possible. The VIE has its origins in another complicated investment structure[3] that a few years earlier Wu, ironically, had taken the lead in dismantling.

On April 13, 2000, the first of the three Chinese portals finally got its IPO. Sina raised $68 million on the Nasdaq. NetEase and Sohu soon followed.

But the portals were to have a very difficult birth as public companies. The reason? The bubble had burst.

Bubble Ball and Burst

From its peak in March 2000, the Nasdaq began a two-year losing streak, wiping out trillions of dollars of market capitalization and taking down many technology firms with it. NetEase's shares dropped 20 percent on the first day of trading after its IPO in June. Sohu limped to an IPO in July but after that there would be no more issuances for Chinese Internet companies for more than three years. The IPO door was now firmly shut to the other Chinese Internet companies, including Alibaba, as investors once again cared about revenues and profits.

Just as the markets started to tank, and on the fringes of the Internet World conference in Beijing, I hosted a party at a business club called the Capital Club. I titled the party, as a joke, "The Bubble Ball." They say you never know you're in a bubble until it pops. But in the spring of 2000 there was a growing sense that everything was about to come to a crashing halt.

For me the trigger was an event a few weeks after *Time* magazine ran a cover story, on February 28, 2000, on the Chinese Internet market, entitled "struggle.com." The opening paragraph was a story I had told to *Time* journalist Terry McCarthy about my first meeting with one of the portal pioneers:

> William Ding, founder of Netease, one of China's top Internet portals, was uneasy. As he talked to a friend in a Beijing restaurant last summer, something was irritating him. The air-

conditioning. It was too cold. Without interrupting the conversation, the self-taught techie took out his Palm Pilot electronic organizer, pointed the infrared port at the aircon unit and adjusted the temperature from across the room. His friend's jaw dropped.

At an extravagant dinner party hosted in Shanghai on the grounds of a colonial-era mansion a few weeks after the *Time* article ran, an investor came up to introduce herself and told me excitedly about how our host, a senior investment banker, had confided that she, not I, was the "friend" featured in the article. Wounded ego aside, I started to realize that, as the bankers began to invent stories of their closeness to the entrepreneur, the days of the Internet boom were numbered.

The Bubble Ball name proved more apt than I could have imagined. Jack came along and danced until the small hours, along with Charles Zhang from Sohu—in a unique style that reminded me of Elaine Benes in *Seinfeld*—William Ding from NetEase, and four hundred others, in what turned out to be the last party of a short-lived but Gatsbyesque era. CNN and the Australian broadcaster ABC were there to videotape the scene. Viewed today, the graininess of the videos conveys how long ago it was but also the unbridled exuberance of that time.

For Jack, the bursting of the bubble represented a great opportunity for Alibaba. "I made a call to our Hangzhou team and said, 'Have you heard the exciting news about the Nasdaq?' . . . I'd like to have had a bottle of champagne on hand," adding, "This is healthy for the market, and it's very healthy for companies like us."

He felt confident that now the IPO gate had closed, venture capitalists would stop funding Alibaba's competitors. "In the next three months more than sixty percent of the Internet companies in China will close their doors," he said, adding that Alibaba had spent only

$5 million of the $25 million it had raised. "We haven't touched our second-round funding. We have lots of gasoline in our tank."

With the field opening up, Alibaba increased its hiring of foreign employees to market the company to buyers overseas. Jack started to travel intensively around the world to attend trade shows and meet chambers of commerce. Jack was by this time quite familiar with the United States. On his first trips to Europe, though, he experienced some culture shock. I advised Alibaba on its expansion strategy there, recommending a Swiss friend of mine, Abir Oreibi, who would oversee the company's European operations for the next eight years. On his first visit to London, Jack was booked into the city's prestigious Connaught Hotel but couldn't understand why he had to stay in such an old building. In Zurich, Jack and Cathy were perplexed by the fact that all the shops were closed. Abir explained that it was a Sunday, prompting Cathy to exclaim, "Oh, I see, they're all working second jobs today." Coming from the nonstop business culture of China, the concept of shopkeepers taking a whole day off to rest was unimaginable.

Alibaba stepped up its advertising, too. Suddenly the company's signature orange blanketed print and online media in the mainland, including on the Chinese portals. Alibaba commissioned a glossy television ad that ran on CNBC and CNN, a first for a China-based tech start-up. Todd Daum, an American executive who had recently joined Alibaba in Hong Kong, oversaw the production of the video, which Jack described to him jokingly as "my second favorite video, after *Forrest Gump*."

TV ad campaigns aside, Jack continued to be Alibaba's most effective marketing tool. Despite the dot-com downturn, people came in droves to hear his speeches. When he spoke in Hong Kong in May 2000 at an I&I (Internet & Information Asia) event in the Furama Hotel, more than five hundred people turned up. Jack was gaining profile overseas, too, invited as a global Internet luminary to an Internet event in Barcelona, Spain. As Alibaba surpassed the 300,000-member mark, Jack was featured on the cover of *Forbes Global* magazine, which named the company—along with Global Sources—as "Best of the Web" for B2B e-commerce. That was followed by a full-page profile in *The Economist* titled "The Jack Who Would Be King."

But as the stock market continued its downward slide, enthusiasm for Internet companies of any description began to dwindle. In August 2000, NetEase's shares sank below a third of their IPO price, and Sohu's under half. In late July, only five months after a blockbuster Hong Kong IPO, the local portal Tom.com, backed by billionaire Li Ka-shing, laid off eighty employees. China.com followed suit soon after.

The Internet conferences started to thin out. I&I even dropped the word *Internet* and then faded into oblivion along with many of the companies that had once presented at its events. Dot-com had become dot-bomb.

At a venture capital investor conference in Hong Kong that fall, Jack was one of the featured speakers. In a dramatic reversal from the crowds that Jack had drawn just a few months earlier, Goldman Sachs had to scramble to find people to fill an empty conference room to hear his pitch. Standing at the podium in front of a skeptical audience, an investor recounted to me, Jack cupped his hands in front of his face, squinted his eyes, and declared, "I can see the end of the tunnel." But in the face of growing investor cynicism about the sector, Jack Magic was wearing off.

Meanwhile, in California, Alibaba's efforts to build an R&D center under John Wu's leadership were running into problems. In an effort to overhaul the company's disparate software platforms, Alibaba had hired more than thirty engineers in its new Fremont office, but coordinating with their colleagues in China across a fifteen-hour time difference was proving a headache. Forced to use English for the benefit of non-Chinese-speaking colleagues in California, Chinese engineers in both offices struggled to communicate among themselves. The team started to fracture and tempers frayed as Hangzhou pushed to develop one product and Fremont another. After an infrastructure upgrade, the whole Alibaba.com site went down. Jack was visiting Fremont at the time and had to step in personally to force better cooperation between the two teams so that the problem could be fixed. It was clear that splitting the technology team across the Pacific had failed. Alibaba started to move core functions back to Hangzhou. Alibaba was about to embark on a new, defensive strategy: "B2C," or "Back to China."

Pressures were mounting on Jack, including from his first investor Goldman Sachs, to prove that Alibaba could actually make money. "Alibaba.com has a revenue plan for today, tomorrow, and the day after tomorrow," Jack commented. "Today we are focused on revenues from online marketing services. Tomorrow, we will add revenue sharing with third-party service providers. And the day after tomorrow, we will add transaction-based revenues."

To reassure investors and his team, Alibaba agreed to look at offering third-party services such as credit, transport, and insurance services. Together these accounted for as much as $300 billion in annual revenues on total global trade of $7 trillion. Grabbing even a small slice of this pie could be extremely lucrative.

This was the strategy already touted by MeetChina. The company claimed that more than 70,000 Chinese suppliers and 15,000 prospective purchasers had joined its site. Although few transactions had been facilitated online, it disclosed it planned to take 2 to 6 percent of all transactions on its site. Bucking the investment downturn, MeetChina surprised the market with a fresh venture capital infusion of $30 million, taking its total haul to over $40 million, some $15 million more than Alibaba. Cofounder Thomas Rosenthal told reporters, "The volatility of the Nasdaq actually made it relatively easier to get private financing. You have a large amount of money chasing fewer deals." Recently appointed CEO Len Cordiner pursued a vision for the site as a place where "you cannot only find buyers but also negotiate online." But MeetChina would never make much headway in China. Talking up partnerships with third parties was much easier than making them work, and many of the tie-ups ending up being nothing more than links to its partners' websites. A former employee[4] later summed up MeetChina's experience as spending $30 million to "train Chinese enterprises to use the Internet." Eventually the company switched focus to Southeast Asia, launching MeetPhilippines.com and MeetVietnam.com (in the presence of President Clinton) and inking partnerships in India, Indonesia, South Korea, and Thailand, before it folded.[5]

Jack had long been dismissive of MeetChina, and as it fell to the wayside he turned his guns on Global Sources, now Alibaba's main rival, and its founder, Merle Hinrichs. Jack dismissed Global Sources as an "old economy" company that had misunderstood the nature of online trade: "They are a company pushing a publication." Merle Hinrichs in turn dismissed Alibaba as "a mile wide and half an inch deep." Although Global Sources' (recently listed) shares[6] had tanked along with the Nasdaq, it was buoyed by substantial profits generated from its offline print business.

Later in 2000, Jack and Hinrichs were both keynote speakers at an Internet conference in Hong Kong. Although he never referred to Hinrichs by name, Jack later told a story about a rival (who owned "a beautiful yacht") who after paying a $50,000 fee to be a keynote speaker was incensed to find that Jack had been invited to give a keynote speech without having to pay a fee. The conference organizers explained to his rival, so Jack's story goes, that "it is because you want to be a keynote speaker, but the audience wants Jack Ma to speak," to which his rival vowed, "I will sail the yacht to Hong Kong and will invite all the keynote speakers and speakers of the conference to have a party on my yacht, but I have one condition: that Jack Ma is not allowed." Merle Hinrichs's office declined to comment on the spat, but the rivalry is something that Jack, the philosopher CEO, invested with a deeper meaning: "If you can't tolerate your opponents, you will be definitely beaten by your opponent. . . . If you treat your opponents as enemies, you have already lost at the beginning of the game. If you hang your opponent as a target, and practice throwing darts at him every day, you are only able to fight this one enemy, not others. . . . Competition is the greatest joy. When you compete with others, and find that it brings you more and more agony, there must be something wrong with your competition strategy."

But in the latter half of 2000, it looked like there was something wrong with Alibaba's strategy. Although it had raised $25 million and signed up more than half a million users, its revenues that year wouldn't even hit the $1 million mark. Alibaba did start to charge some fees—helping build and host websites for some of its members—but expenses were increasing far more rapidly than revenues. Alibaba's hiring spree was creating more problems than it solved, as new recruits arrived before reporting and budgeting systems had been put in place. The international nature of its business was also a challenge, both in dealing with clients and in managing human resources. Trying to market a Chinese company with an Arabic name to clients in the United States and Europe wasn't proving easy, and Jack admitted that "managing a multinational organization is no easy task with the language and cultural gaps."

As the tech downturn continued into 2001, Jack and Joe recognized that things needed to change. In January 2001 they brought on board as chief operating officer Savio Kwan, a fifty-two-year-old veteran of GE,[7] who gave a frank assessment of the company: "We need to ground [Alibaba] in reality and make it into a business."

Back to China

Kwan's arrival heralded a new management structure that became known internally as the "Four O's": Jack as CEO, Joe Tsai as CFO, John Wu as CTO, and Savio Kwan as COO. To signal to the company how serious he was about change, Jack divided his own office in Hangzhou in two, giving the other half to Kwan.

Kwan slashed monthly expenses by as much as half, stepping up the "Back to China" retrenchment. A joint venture in South Korea was scrapped and Alibaba's Silicon Valley presence drastically scaled back. Many of the higher-paid foreign employees were let go. Expensive advertising campaigns were abandoned and replaced with word-of-mouth marketing. Reducing expenses overseas allowed Alibaba to increase its hiring at home, leveraging Hangzhou's deep pool of lower-cost talent. It rapidly expanded its sales team to focus on promoting fee-paying services such as TrustPass, which provided credit information and authentication services, and Gold Supplier, which gave exporters in China their own presence on Alibaba's English-language website. For $3,600 they could use this to display their products and prices and be linked to Alibaba's search engine. Gold Supplier was explicitly designed to undercut the $10,000–$12,000 in annual fees that Global Sources charged for its online listings.

Despite the early promise from these new revenue sources, Alibaba was taking a beating. Since it was still a private company the negative sentiment couldn't be measured in dollars and cents, unlike the three portals, whose shares had by now been reduced to penny stocks.

BusinessWeek ran an article in April 2001 titled "Alibaba's Magic Carpet Is Losing Altitude," which concluded that the "former professor will have to work hard to ensure his company doesn't flunk out." The company had initiated a restructuring that it hoped would turn things around, but in the years following the dot-com crash Alibaba was resigned to a very uncertain future. Jack even floated the prospect of quitting, so he could return to teaching before he turned forty.

In his darker moments, he took to comparing his struggles to those of the revolutionary Mao Zedong after the Long March, even calling for a "rectification movement" to set Alibaba on a new course: "Once many well-known managers in America came to Alibaba to be vice presidents. Each of them had their own opinions. . . . It was like a zoo at the time. Some were good at talking while others were quiet. Therefore, we think the most important purpose of a rectification movement is to decide a shared purpose of Alibaba, and determine our value."

Alibaba's reversal of fortunes had been dramatic, but it didn't break the bond between Jack and Joe Tsai. I asked Joe what kept him at Alibaba when everything seemed so bleak. "Alibaba," he explained, "was my fourth job. I wanted this job to work." Unlike the three portals, Joe also saw the advantages for Alibaba of not having had an IPO. "I knew all of this was a bubble, and even if we had gone public in 2000 we would have to live with the consequences, the delivery. You would have had to grow into your valuation; it was a quick-buck kind of thing."

The dark days of 2001 and 2002 would later become part of Alibaba lore. Jack later referred to the period in one of his pep talks to the team: "At that time, my slogan was 'Be the last man standing.' Be the last person to fall down. Even on my knees, I had to be the last man collapsing. I also believed firmly at that time [that] if I had difficulties, there must be someone who had worse difficulties; if I had a hard time, my opponents had an even harder time. Those who can stand and manage will win eventually."

In the years that followed the dot-com crash, Alibaba slashed costs and found a way to steadily increase its revenues. Even though the venture capital market had dried up completely, Alibaba was able to stand on its own two feet. And thanks to a new business launched in the spring of 2003, it was about to succeed on a scale that even Jack could never have imagined.

Chapter Nine

Born Again: Taobao and the Humiliation of eBay

Among China's leading businessmen, Ma is known for his bombastic comments. He routinely uses eBay as a dartboard while simultaneously praising it as one of the companies he most admires.

—*San Francisco Chronicle*

"The pioneers take the arrows, settlers take the land" is a phrase often used to describe the conquering of the American West. As a new frontier known as the Internet unfolded in China, Jack was determined to become one of the settlers. He'd already been a pioneer with his early experience of going online in Seattle in 1995. But with his first Internet venture, China Pages, he'd taken an arrow from his state-owned partner, leaving the portal pioneers (Wang Zhidong of Sina, Charles Zhang of Sohu, and William Ding of NetEase) to become the settlers, the first Internet entrepreneurs in China to lead their companies to an IPO. To close the gap, in September 2000, Jack invited the three portal founders plus Wang Juntao—the chairman of consumer e-commerce venture 8848—to a martial arts themed business conference entitled

"Sword Discussion by the West Lake" (*xihu lunjian*)[1] that he hosted in Hangzhou. I chaired a roundtable discussion at the event, held to promote the city as a "Silicon Paradise." Jack announced that Alibaba would move its China headquarters from Shanghai back to Hangzhou. This was designed no doubt to please the governor of Zhejiang and mayor of Hangzhou, who were among the local dignitaries in attendance. But I quickly understood that the event, in particular the participation of the four leading Internet figures of the day, was convened to demonstrate Alibaba's continued relevance in China's Internet sector. Even though the company had not yet secured an IPO, Jack wanted to stay in the limelight. Jack pulled this off with a clever idea: inviting VIP guest Jin Yong, the Hong Kong author who had been an inspiration to Jack since his childhood. He knew Jin Yong would be a big draw to the other Internet founders, too.

Shortly after Jack's Hangzhou gathering, two of the four China Internet pioneers were felled. Wang Juntao, the chairman of consumer e-commerce pioneer 8848, was forced out by investors nervous about the mounting costs incurred to overcome payment and logistics hurdles. Wang Zhidong, the founder of Sina, was deposed in a palace coup,[2] victim of the company's fractured and fractious shareholder base.

Now only Jack, William Ding, and Charles Zhang remained at the helm of the companies they had founded. Alibaba was surviving, but the business-to-business e-commerce model he had chosen to follow was proving a struggle. In the closing months of 2002, as Alibaba edged toward profitability, Jack started to look at a new direction for the company: targeting China's consumer e-commerce market. Two models from the United States stood out: Amazon and eBay.

Mimicking Amazon, 8848 had already folded. But two other domestic "e-tailers," both set up in 1999 when they had successfully raised venture capital,[3] had survived, selling books and other products at fixed prices:[4] Dangdang.com, run by cofounder Peggy Yu (Yu Yu), who had started her career as an interpreter and secretary at a boiler manufacturer before studying for an MBA at New York University, and Joyo.com, founded by Kingsoft's Lei Jun (later of handset vendor Xiaomi fame) and run by Diane Wang (Wang Shutong).

Shao Yibo

eBay had proved an instant investor hit with its September 1998 IPO, its valuation growing from $2 billion to $30 billion by March 2000. Numerous entrepreneurs in China launched ventures that aspired to be the eBay of China. Most prominent among them was a charismatic wunderkind from Shanghai called Shao Yibo, who had founded his firm EachNet[5] after returning to China in June 1999 from Harvard Business School. EachNet quickly pulled ahead of the other China clones.

To launch his consumer e-commerce attack, Jack opted to go the eBay route, setting up a contest with EachNet. But in Shao Yibo, known as Bo to his friends, Jack could very easily have met his match.

Bo came from a modest background. His parents were teachers. His father sparked Bo's interest in mathematics with a deck of cards. Bo recalled, "With fifty-two cards, and scoring a king as thirteen etc., the deck adds up to three hundred and sixty-four. My father hid one card and asked me to add up the rest. If I did it right, I would know what the hidden card was."

Bo practiced relentlessly. By the age of twelve he could add up a deck in twelve seconds. After winning more than a dozen high school mathematics competitions across the country, Bo became one of the first students from mainland China[6] to be admitted directly to Harvard College on a full scholarship. After graduating he worked for two years at Boston Consulting Group before returning to Harvard and enrolling at the business school. While Jack had already settled on business-to-business e-commerce, Bo looked at a range of U.S. Internet businesses that might work in China and found that "The only business model that got me excited was eBay."

Before leaving Boston, Bo auctioned off his unwanted possessions—on eBay—and in June 1999, then twenty-six years old, returned to Shanghai to build the eBay of China.

Before he even landed he had raised almost half a million dollars in funding.[7] Nonetheless, "my parents thought I was nuts, to turn down very lucrative job offers and a green card and become self-employed," Bo recalled. "I was very naïve and totally unprepared for business in general and the huge challenges of bootstrapping a start-up company in particular."

Bo rented a cheap apartment in Shanghai and hired a high school classmate as his first employee—unemployed, his friend was the only person he could afford. Unable to shell out on expensive engineers, he arranged for two employees of the Shanghai Electricity Bureau, who had some IT experience but had never built a website, to moonlight for him. After 5 P.M., when they got off their shift at the electricity utility, they came to the EachNet apartment and worked until 1 A.M., sleeping there before they clocked in back at their day job. Soon after, Bo convinced a fellow Shanghai-born Harvard Business School classmate, Tan Haiyin, to come on board as cofounder. Before business school Tan had been one of the earliest employees of McKinsey in Shanghai. After Harvard she had taken a job at Merrill Lynch in New York. She was traveling on a business trip in China when Bo called her up to ask her if she wanted to join him, and stay in China. She agreed.[8]

Bo attracted the attention of foreign media early on. The *Washington Post* quoted him vowing that EachNet would gain "even greater dominance in China than eBay has achieved in the U.S." Bo quickly commanded the attention of investors, too. The angel investment was followed swiftly by a $6.5 million venture round.[9]

I got to know Bo soon after he returned to Shanghai. We were neighbors on Hengshan Road in the city's former French concession district. Despite his impeccable résumé, Bo lived modestly, moving in with his parents. This was seized upon as a sign of his humility—although greater attention was given in local media to the fact that this handsome, Harvard Business School returnee was still single.

Although a relative latecomer to the China Internet scene, he made an instant splash and moved to quickly outmaneuver his rivals.[10] Bo doesn't suffer fools gladly. In 2000, onstage at an Internet conference in Shanghai at which we were both speakers, Bo demolished a rival who had just given a presentation stuffed with inflated website traffic and exaggerated transaction data. Bo calmly but methodically exposed all of the flaws in the other presenter's math and logic, demolishing him so effectively that the audience almost felt sorry for the hapless competitor, who did not ride out the dot-com bust.

EachNet, by contrast, bucked the downturn and surprised everyone by securing a massive $20.5 million investment in October 2000. The lead financier was Bernard Arnault, the French luxury baron of LVMH, via his dot-com investment vehicle Europatweb. But as the market crashed the fund got cold feet and tried to pull out entirely; it finally ponied up $5 million. Bo demonstrated his considerable powers of persuasion by cobbling the remaining $15 million from existing investors and others even as the public equity markets continued their downward slide. China was entering its "Internet winter," but EachNet had gathered a large stack of acorns.

Yet making a viable business of EachNet would be no picnic for Bo. Could the eBay model really work in China? In the United States, eBay became popular for offering goods through online auctions, with the transactions often taking place between consumers themselves. In

China, although people loved to haggle, the trading of secondhand goods, even offline, wasn't common. Shoppers were just beginning to exercise their newfound freedoms. Few people had many possessions to sell.

In the United States, eBay served an online population of more than 100 million and could count on a well-developed credit card market and reliable nationwide courier services. In China, the much-vaunted online consumer market of 10 million was a mirage. In 2000, it was too early to build an "iron triangle." Few people could pay online or access reliable delivery services. More fundamentally there was a complete absence of trust in online shopping. Banking regulations restricted the development of credit cards, which were only allowed in 1999, their use restricted to customers who kept money on deposit in their banks. Debit cards were beginning to gain popularity but each bank issued its own card and there was no central processing network for merchants. Forget about online payment—even buying offline with cards was a mess: Checkout counters at the time were a tangle of cables, connecting or powering a half-dozen individual point-of-sale (POS) machines. Online payment was years away from becoming widely accepted. Courier networks were restricted to individual cities: There was no "China market" to speak of, just a loose collection of local markets. The absence of trust, though, was the biggest hurdle to greater consumer e-commerce adoption, as Bo described: "In the U.S., if you place a bid, it's a contract, and by law you need to fulfill that bid if you win the auction. That's very clear. People would be afraid of getting sued if they did not abide by that contract. In China people don't care. 'I place a bid, I don't want it anymore, tough luck.' "

In response, EachNet limited its initial auction offerings to the city of Shanghai, where it had set up physical trading booths for customers to meet. Having first connected online, they would come to meet one another in person to evaluate the goods on sale, ever mindful of being defrauded, then pay for the goods face-to-face. EachNet had to lease and operate multiple trading booths across Shanghai, clearly not a sustainable strategy for a supposed Internet venture. By early 2001 they were all shut down.

EachNet had to find new ways of making money, and so acquired a distributor of mobile phones and launched auction platforms on NetEase and Sina. To broaden its appeal, EachNet started selling stamps and baby clothes.

But with no new VC funding at hand, Bo had no alternative but to find a way to get around the roadblocks to online shopping: the problems of payment, package delivery, product quality, and people's confidence.

Combining payment and package delivery was one popular method. Cash on delivery allowed consumers to see before they paid. EachNet set up a system for courier companies to act as collecting agents. Cash was a stopgap solution but by 2002 bank cards were finally becoming a viable payment option. China still had very low credit card penetration but the use of debit cards was exploding. Bank cards grew from 150 million when EachNet was launched to almost half a billion cards by the end of 2002. The banks' IT systems also started to talk to one another, too, because in 2002 China's banking regulator rolled out a unified card processing system called China UnionPay (*zhongguo yinlian*). UnionPay's red, blue, and green logo is today a common sight in shop windows and on ATMs around the world. UnionPay solved a major headache for merchants in China, both offline and online, in making sure they could accept a customer's card no matter which domestic bank had issued it. The process didn't happen overnight, though, and for years EachNet encouraged its most active customers to apply for credit cards from one of the big four commercial banks to ensure that they could complete their purchases online.

As Bo had pointed out, China's legal system offered few protections for merchants, who worried that customers wouldn't pay for goods already shipped, nor for customers, who were worried that the goods they purchased might never arrive. To address this, EachNet set up its own escrow service, where it would collect funds from customers and release them only after delivery had been confirmed, charging a 3 percent commission as a service fee. Few customers signed up, however, and with an eye on the success of PayPal in the United States, EachNet drew up plans for its own local equivalent.

Product quality issues were also tricky to overcome. In the States, eBay had pioneered a system that allowed consumers to rate vendors, but in China unscrupulous vendors quickly figured out they could game the system by using masses of fake accounts to drive up their positive ratings, or dilute their negatives. EachNet tried to limit the number of ratings one user could post, and set up a team to investigate consumer complaints of fraud. But both efforts were rapidly overwhelmed. A key challenge was how to identify the buyers and sellers on its platform, never mind implementing any sanctions.

EachNet clearly was in for a long haul, not projecting any profits until 2005. EachNet's prospects of raising new venture capital investment dimmed further. Bo and his investors realized that their best shot at making EachNet the eBay of China was to sell out to eBay itself.

eBay Comes to China

In the fall of 2001, eBay CEO Meg Whitman made a trip to Shanghai to meet Bo. In March 2002, EachNet once again surprised the market with a landmark deal, announcing it was selling a 33 percent stake to eBay for $30 million.

Despite EachNet's challenges, eBay had been impressed by what it saw. The EachNet website had more than three million registered users, of which over 100,000 visited the site each day. The company had expanded from Shanghai to Beijing and Guangzhou. More than half of its business involved a party outside one of these cities. The site featured more than 50,000 items at any time, ranging from clothing to real estate, and offered by fixed prices or via auctions. Transactions exceeded $2 million a month.

EachNet was tiny compared to eBay. But the allure of China was of critical importance to Whitman. She badly needed some good news to reassure investors after announcing just one month earlier the loss of the Japanese market to Yahoo Japan, backed by Masayoshi Son's SoftBank, a blow to Whitman's ambition to build eBay as a "truly global marketplace." From $750 million in 2001, eBay was targeting $3 billion global revenue by 2005. Japan would have been a big step in achieving this, with more than $1.6 billion in goods traded, but eBay was late[11] to the party there, launching only in February 2000, five months after Yahoo Japan. eBay's strategy was a mess from the start. In Japan, eBay charged commissions but its competitor Yahoo Japan did not. Credit cards were still a rarity in Japan but eBay required customers to use them to register on its site. eBay chose a Japanese CEO and a local partner (NEC) with little experience of the Internet, charting a rapid course for irrelevance in the country. By the summer of 2001 it had garnered a measly 3 percent of the market. When in February 2002 eBay pulled the plug, its site offered just 25,000 products, compared to the 3.5 million on offer from its rival Yahoo Japan. In the Land of the Rising Sun, the sun had already set on eBay's ambitions and the company laid off its staff.

Where next? eBay had more success in South Korea[12] and Taiwan,[13] but only China could really move the needle. By 2002, China's Internet population had grown to over 27 million, the world's fifth largest.[14] Whitman was earlier than many in Silicon Valley to recognize the importance of China: "With the demographics and incredible changes in China, our hypothesis is this could be one of the largest e-commerce markets in the world," she told the media, projecting $16 billion in e-commerce revenue by 2006.

eBay had failed to understand the needs of local customers in Japan but Whitman was determined not to repeat the experience in China. They wanted to back a leading player in the local market. EachNet was an obvious target. eBay senior vice president Bill Cobb later commented, "[Bo] had studied eBay up one side and down the other and had really tried to adapt a lot of the eBay principles to the market." It didn't hurt of course that Bo (and his cofounder, Tan Haiyin) had both attended Harvard Business School, Meg Whitman's alma mater.

Yet eBay didn't just want to back EachNet; it wanted to buy it. The initial deal[15] gave eBay one-third of the company but also an option to take full control, which it did just fifteen months later, taking its total outlay to $180 million. Rebranded eBay EachNet, the company became a vessel for eBay's China aspirations. The decision to own EachNet outright set the stage for Alibaba's triumph, and eBay's humiliation.[16]

Things looked good at the outset. With EachNet, eBay gained a 90 percent share of China's consumer e-commerce market. But within two years eBay was reduced to irrelevance in China and forced to beat another embarrassing retreat from Asia.

Why did things go so wrong so fast? Even though Whitman had granted Bo a generous allocation of options, making EachNet a subsidiary inevitably changed the dynamics with managers at eBay. Soon after the acquisition, for family reasons Bo had to move to California, which Meg Whitman was very generous in facilitating, as Bo had recounted to me in 2015. He stayed involved in the business, but the long distance between San Jose and Shanghai started to show. With Bo no longer in Shanghai, the head of marketing in the United States began to tell marketing in China what to do, and the head of technology did the same.

With the acquisition, eBay had dented EachNet's entrepreneurial culture. The damage was revealed when another entrepreneurial company arrived on the scene: Alibaba. Worse still, Alibaba had the backing of SoftBank, the author of eBay's defeat at the hands of Yahoo Japan.

One senior EachNet engineer, who would soldier on for several years after the acquisition, summed up the critical problem: "eBay thought it was a done deal, but it turned out it was not." eBay had a leading position at the outset, but the market was growing so fast that all that really mattered was grabbing the dominant share of the millions of new online shoppers. Incremental users, not incumbency, was the name of the game.

In his B2B business Alibaba.com, Jack had trained his firepower on Merle Hinrichs at Global Sources. For his new consumer e-commerce venture, Jack set his sights on a much bigger target, an icon of Silicon Valley: eBay and its CEO Meg Whitman.

Squaring Off

Alibaba launched its preparations to enter China's consumer e-commerce market in 2002, initially as a defensive move sparked by eBay's entry. As Jack later explained, "I needed to stop eBay to protect Alibaba." Although EachNet was targeting consumers, not the businesses served by Alibaba, Jack was concerned that some of the larger merchants active on EachNet could encroach on Alibaba's turf: "At that time, there were only two companies in China that understood online marketplaces, eBay and Alibaba. I was particularly concerned that eBay's power sellers would grow their business to compete in the B2B space."

Jack's plans to target consumers encountered resistance within Alibaba. The B2B business wasn't yet profitable, and the VC market was closed for the time being. Could the company really afford to open a new front when they were still fighting the B2B battle? Was Jack just being paranoid?

CTO John Wu adamantly opposed the idea, visiting Jack the night before the new project was kicked off. John warned Jack that the move would harm Alibaba: "How on earth could you fight against eBay?" Jack replied that the market was still open: "There are one hundred million Internet users today, but only five million people are doing online shopping." Jack's ambitious plans for Alibaba also gave him a different perspective: "eBay wants to buy the Chinese market, but we want to create China's Internet trading market."

With his firsthand experience as a small-business owner in Zhejiang, Jack was adamant that the threat from eBay was real: "In China, there are so many small businesses that people don't make a clear distinction between business and consumer. Small business and consumer behavior are very similar. One person makes the decisions for the whole organization." Jack also understood the temptation for eBay, later reflecting, "We launched Taobao not to make money, but because in the U.S. eBay gets a lot of its revenue from small businesses. We knew that someday eBay would come in our direction."

So it was decided. Alibaba would target the consumer e-commerce market. Jack was emboldened after a trip at the end of 2002 to Tokyo, where he found Masayoshi Son in a buoyant mood. Yahoo Japan had just repelled eBay from its shores, boosting SoftBank's standing after several painful years of dot-com write-downs. SoftBank signed up to commit $80 million[17] to Alibaba's new venture.

The project was kept highly confidential. Few within Alibaba were even aware that the idea of targeting consumers in China had been contemplated, let alone that a team had actually been formed to code a new website. Secrecy, and some useful Alibaba folklore, was achieved by sequestering a handful of employees, including Alibaba cofounder Toto Sun, in the original Lakeside apartment where Alibaba had been founded.

Two years later Jack recalled the scene as he invited a half-dozen, handpicked employees to his office: "Our COO, CFO, the vice president of HR, and I were all there. We talked to them one by one: 'The company has decided to send you to do a project, but you are required to leave your home, and you must not tell your parents or your boyfriend or your girlfriend. Do you agree?' " Holed up in the small apartment, the team got to work.

In taking on eBay, Jack wanted to preserve the element of surprise. Explaining his strategy, he dipped into his reservoir of martial arts stories: "I've seen lots of people yelling 'Fight the Shaolin Temple!' at the foot of the Shaolin Temple; that's complete nonsense. However, if I reach your doorstep to challenge you, I pretty much know that I will defeat you. In the future there will be no need to yell; as soon as you stand on the doorstep, people will be scared."

Throughout the project, Jack emphasized that their target was not EachNet but eBay itself. Once the project became public knowledge, he wanted to ensure the fight was seen as a David versus Goliath struggle. One team member[18] recalled the mood: "We were just a group of country bumpkins, and our competitor was eBay." Reuters later summed up the culture as "kung fu commerce with a dash of theater."

To keep up morale the small group of software engineers took breaks between coding to play video games or do exercises. Jack encouraged the team to do handstands. As a child, he explained, looking at the world upside down had given him a different perspective on life.

The new business was to be named[19] "hunting for treasure," or *taobao* in Chinese. Taobao.com's tagline was "There is no treasure that cannot be hunted out, and there is no treasure that cannot be sold."

Taobao was officially launched on May 10, 2003, celebrated each year as "Aliday," a "take your family to work" day and the date of the company's famous group wedding celebration. Aliday celebrates the team spirit that helped Alibaba overcome an unexpected challenge that tested its employees as never before.

SARS Attacks

The SARS (severe acute respiratory syndrome) virus outbreak started in southern China in 2002, spreading to create clusters of infection around the world that caused eight thousand people to fall sick as well as almost eight hundred deaths. Seven thousand of those infected, and most of those who died, were located in mainland China and Hong Kong.

In Hangzhou, four hundred employees in Alibaba's head office underwent voluntary isolation at home after one of their colleagues, Kitty Song (Song Jie), fell ill with a suspected case of SARS. She had traveled to Guangzhou, the epicenter of the outbreak, as part of an Alibaba team participating in the biannual Canton Fair.

SARS bound an already close company even closer. Because its origins and full impact were unknown, SARS was a frightening experience—as I experienced myself in Beijing at the time. The outbreak also bound people together.

In early May, Jack donned one of the face masks that the company had distributed to all its employees and initiated a plan that confined all of its employees at home for one week. Soon after they were sent home, Alibaba's office was sealed off to avoid any risk of infections from exposure to the suspected case. In a letter to employees distributed that day, Jack's ability to inspire the troops, and to keep them focused on the company's goals, was on full display: "We care for each other and we support each other. We never forget the mission and obligation of Alibaba, in face of the challenge from SARS. Tragedy will pass, but life will continue. Fighting with catastrophe cannot prevent us from fighting for the enterprise we love."

Although it sickened thousands and killed almost eight hundred people, the outbreak had a curiously beneficial impact on the Chinese Internet sector, including Alibaba. SARS validated digital mobile telephony and the Internet, and so came to represent the turning point when the Internet emerged as a truly mass medium in China.

The virus gave a major boost to texting, which increased business for cellular companies like China Mobile. However, SARS also boosted the three Chinese Internet portals thanks to revenue-sharing agreements with the telecom company. As the shares in Sina, Sohu, and NetEase began to climb, investor interest in Chinese technology companies was suddenly reignited. Cell phone usage wasn't the only thing to benefit; broadband Internet access got a huge lift, too, as millions of people, confined to their homes or dormitories for days or weeks on end, looked to the Internet for information or entertainment.

Within days of home confinement, Alibaba employees had Internet connections installed at home. While the Hangzhou authorities supplied food and twice-daily disinfection visits, employees continued their work, holding virtual meetings in online chat rooms.

Reliable information about SARS was hard to come by, especially in the early months of the outbreak, when China's official media, including state broadcaster China Central Television, stayed mute. Instead people looked to their cell phones and PCs to learn about the virus and the best ways to protect themselves. Crucially for Alibaba, SARS convinced millions of people, afraid to go outside, to try shopping online instead.

The suspected case of SARS within the company turned out not to be infected by the virus after all, and so for Alibaba, SARS ended up a blessing in disguise. Because the Taobao stealth team had relocated to

During the SARS outbreak, Alibaba employees self-quarantined and worked from home, 2003. *Alibaba*

work in the Lakeside apartment, they were not affected by the quarantine of the main office. Jack was still confined at home and unable to join the Taobao team for the May 10 launch, as he later recalled, "A few of us agreed to talk on the phone at eight P.M. and raised our glasses in the air and said 'Wishing Taobao a safe journey.' The day that Taobao was launched there was a line on the website that declared, 'Remembering those who worked hard during SARS.' "

Taobao

Although Taobao was launched on May 10, visitors to the website could not discern any connection with Alibaba. Taobao made a virtue of its start-up status by relying on word-of-mouth marketing to popularize the site, including postings on the many free bulletin board systems and other online forums popular in China at the time.

Taobao's association with Alibaba was kept so well hidden that a number of Alibaba employees even voiced concerns to management about a potential new rival on the scene. Jack recalled, "We have a very active intranet. In late June, someone posted a message asking the company's senior management to pay attention to one website, which might become our competitor in the future." Soon the Alibaba intranet was alive with discussions about who was behind Taobao, and employees commenting on the disappearance of some of their colleagues. Finally, on July 10, 2003, Alibaba announced that Taobao was part of the company. "There was a resounding cheer within the company," Jack recalled.

The cat was out of the bag, and with the full resources of Alibaba at its disposal Taobao was now free to take on eBay. Yet Jack wanted Taobao to maintain an innovative, start-up culture, something aided by a preemptive move by eBay to try to sew up the market. eBay signed exclusive advertising contracts to promote its site on all the major China Internet portals, preventing them from displaying ads promoting rival sites. This forced Alibaba to adopt a series of guerrilla marketing techniques, including reaching out to hundreds of small but fast-growing sites and online communities that eBay had deemed unimportant.

With the backing of SoftBank, Jack took a move from Yahoo Japan's playbook. In 1999, when it launched its e-commerce business, CEO Masahiro Inoue asked his 120 employees to list items for sale on his new site to make it look active and popular. Four years later in China, Jack did the same: "We had all together seven, eight people [in the Taobao team]. . . . Everyone had to find four items. I rummaged through my chests and cupboards. I barely had anything at home. . . . We pooled about thirty items, and I bought yours and you bought mine, that's how it started. . . . I even listed my watch online."

Jack also insisted that Taobao maintain a distinctively local culture, including choosing nicknames[20] from Jin Yong's novels or other popular tales. Taobao was successful at developing a whimsical culture and instilling a strong sense of teamwork. Yet it would be years before Taobao would make any money. Fortunately, Alibaba could count on SoftBank's support once again. In February 2004, SoftBank led a new $82 million investment to replenish Alibaba's coffers, in preparation for Taobao's long battle with eBay.

This transaction also was the end of the road for Goldman Sachs. Shirley Lin had left the bank in May 2003. With no one to oversee the stake, Goldman had written down the value of its stake to zero. The following year, just before the new investment led by SoftBank, Goldman sold off its entire 33 percent stake. The bank had paid $3.3 million for it in 1999 and sold it for more than seven times that amount five years later. This seemed like a good result at the time, although no one involved with the deal still remained at Goldman to take any credit. The investors who bought out the stake saw an immediate appreciation once SoftBank anted up more funds for Taobao. Worse was to come for Goldman, though, when in 2014 the full extent of the mistake sank in. The stake the investment bank had paid $3.3 million for in 1999 would rise in value to more than $12.5 billion at the IPO had they held on to it. Worse still, the partners at the bank could calculate how much they personally had forgone. Some calculated their missed windfall at more than $400 million, quite a few mansions in the Hamptons.

Along with SoftBank, other investors committing fresh funding to Alibaba included Fidelity Investments, Venture TDF, and new investor Granite Global Ventures (later known as GGV Capital), backed by Rockefeller affiliate Venrock. The deal was announced as part of a move to "aggressively expand" Taobao to make it the "most popular online marketplace for Chinese retailers and individuals to list their products on the Internet."

Masayoshi Son publicly endorsed Alibaba's strategy. Four years after SoftBank's initial investment in Alibaba, he declared himself "extremely pleased" and predicted that "Alibaba has the potential to become another extraordinary success like Yahoo." Meanwhile, Alibaba disclosed that revenues from its Alibaba.com B2B site had grown threefold in the previous year, propelling that business at last to profitability.

Despite the fresh backing for Taobao, eBay itself remained oblivious to the rising threat, considering itself far superior to this quirky, local rival. When asked by *BusinessWeek* in the spring of 2004 about rivals in China, eBay's senior vice president Bill Cobb mentioned only one: 1Pai, a joint venture between Yahoo and Sina.

Jack reveled in being ignored. "During the first year, eBay didn't consider us their rival. They didn't even think that we could be their rival. They thought, We haven't even heard about Alibaba. Such a strange name. Chinese all know what *tao bao* means, foreigners don't."

eBay was confident that its global network and experience would ensure EachNet pulled well clear of any competitors. But corporate bureaucracy, worsened by the extended and dysfunctional reporting lines all the way to San Jose, were to smother whatever embers of entrepreneurialism still burned within EachNet in Shanghai. eBay's China adventure, lasting from 2003 to 2006, is today a case study in how not to go about managing a business in a distant market.

eBay's first big mistake was to tell the market that China was already an ace in the hole. Meg Whitman deserves credit for recognizing China's potential as an Internet market before that was popular. Her early interest in business opportunities in China was sparked by a family connection to the country: "In the 1970s my mom was invited to be part of group of women, led by actress Shirley MacLaine, to visit China. There were lots of reasons not to go: China was then an undeveloped country that had been closed to outsiders for many years. And my mom had just ten days to get ready. But instead of worrying about her safety, she seized the chance to have an adventure. Over four weeks, the group covered two thousand miles in China, mostly by train, visiting schools, farms, and villages."

Whitman recalled that the trip "changed my mother's life and, indirectly, mine, too. My mom learned Mandarin in subsequent years and returned to China eighty times. And after her first trip, she told my sister and me, 'I've seen women doing all sorts of marvelous things—so realize you have the opportunity to do and be anything you want.'"

Mary Meeker, then an Internet analyst at Morgan Stanley, where she was dubbed the "Queen of the Internet,"[21] was one of Meg Whitman's lead cheerleaders. The dot-com bust had dented the reputation of nearly the entire Wall Street tech research community, but China played a big role in Meeker's redemption. In April 2004, Morgan Stanley released a 217-page report under her name that profiled the Chinese Internet sector. It would be reprinted more than twenty-five thousand times. Meeker had a reputation for being a contrarian: "One of the greatest investments of our lifetime has been New York City real estate," she said, "and investors made the highest returns when they bought stuff during the 1970s and 1980s when people were getting mugged. . . . The lesson is that you make the most money when you buy stuff that's out of consensus."

Whoever Wins China, Wins the World

Meeker now saw China as the Next Big Thing. Picking the right Chinese company to bet on wasn't easy, Meeker said, so she recommended instead that investors leverage Silicon Valley companies with exposure to China: "Both Yahoo and eBay have interesting plays in the Chinese market. So our simplistic point of view is that one way to play the Chinese market is by owning Yahoo or eBay." The report quoted

Whitman, raising the stakes, as predicting, "Whoever wins China, will win the world."

Meeker's vocal support for Whitman, including cheering on her China strategy, helped boost eBay's share price by 80 percent in 2004. But the climbing valuation obscured growing challenges for the company. A series of hikes in commissions sparked protests from its virtual store merchants, tens of thousands clubbing together to denounce "FeeBay" or "GreedBay." Complaints reached a crescendo in February 2005 when eBay increased commissions by almost 3 percent (to 8 percent) on its worldwide mall. Whitman remained sanguine. "The thing to know about the eBay community . . . is that it's been vocal from Day One." She did concede, however, that the dissatisfied merchants had "perhaps been a tad more vocal than in the past."

China became a useful way of distracting eBay's investors from problems at home. Worse, before the company had even secured its position there, a "we're winning in China" attitude, at both eBay and its newly acquired business, PayPal, ensured a form of collective denial even when confronted with signs that things were not going to plan. China was considered so important that managers, keen to present a positive story to Whitman and other senior executives, made sure that everything looked great on PowerPoint and sounded smooth on conference calls. But thanks to its own missteps as well as Alibaba's competitive moves, this was increasingly at odds with the facts on the ground.

eBay's biggest mistake was in getting the culture wrong. A "leave it to the experts" attitude demoralized the original EachNet team in Shanghai, as eBay executives were parachuted in from headquarters in San Jose or other parts of the eBay empire. No matter how skilled the new arrivals, most spoke no Chinese. They faced a steep learning curve to understand the local market. Key EachNet team members started to leave, their exit interviews revealing concerns that San Jose no longer involved them in key decisions. eBay had sent over a number of China-born executives, but most had studied or worked in the United States for many years, sparking misunderstandings or friction with the local team. EachNet found itself at a serious disadvantage to the 100 percent local Taobao.

This gap was reflected in the design of the two rivals' websites. eBay moved quickly to align the EachNet site with its global site, revamping how products were categorized and altering the design and functionality of the website. This not only confused customers, but also alienated a number of important merchants who saw their previously valuable China account names had been deleted. This invalidated their trading history and forced them to scramble to reapply for new names on an unfamiliar global platform. Worse still, the Chinese website lacked a customer service telephone number. eBay's China site, modeled closely on eBay in the States, looked foreign to local users, who found it "empty" when compared to local sites.

In website design, culture matters. In the West, websites like Google had become popular for their clean lines and uncluttered "negative space." But to the mass market of Chinese Web users, accustomed to pop-ups and floating banner ads, they seemed static and dull. As you can see for yourself by opening taobao.com, successful Chinese websites are typically packed with information and multimedia graphics, requiring many scroll-downs to see the whole page. From its outset Taobao has been a website built by Chinese for Chinese. And it worked.

It's not just the graphics that helped Taobao connect with consumers. Taobao structured its website like a local bazaar, even featuring innovative ideas such as allowing male or female shoppers to click on a button to display products most suited to their interests. The design of the site makes it the virtual descendant of the Yiwu wholesale market, where Jack and many other Zhejiang entrepreneurs draw their inspiration. The founder of another, niche e-commerce venture explained, "If you go to Yiwu, you can order as little as three pairs of shoes. One factory specializes in soles, another in the uppers, another factory—or perhaps a small village—specializes in the laces. Taobao tapped the motivation of those small merchants to make money."

For companies like eBay and Amazon, their experience in the United States and other Western markets proved to be of little use. "E-commerce in China is very strange," the rival e-commerce founder continued. "It started with C2C (consumer-to-consumer) and with nonstandardized products. This was unlike Amazon, unlike the conventional wisdom where you need to start with standardized products, like books. The more standardized the supply chain, the higher the barriers for e-tailers. All the smaller, mom-and-pop stores selling nonstandardized products are more accommodating, more flexible in supplying goods. That's unique to China. The lack of national supply chains removed the barriers to entry that exist in the West, making it possible for individuals to make money.[22] By starting with C2C, it made the price factor very appealing. Individuals[23] can be happy to make even five *mao* (less than 1 U.S. cent) on a sale."

Again aided by its roots in Zhejiang, Taobao outsmarted eBay by having a better understanding of the country's merchants, for whom membership has been free of charge from the outset. Just as free listings was a core principle for the B2B Alibaba.com, it became a key competitive weapon for Taobao.com, too. Buyers pay nothing to register or transact; sellers pay nothing to register, list their products, or sell online.

EachNet had started out with free listings, but faced with spiraling costs in August 2001, it started to charge listing fees to sellers, adding commissions on all transactions the following year. These resulted in a sharp reduction in the number of auctions on the site, but given the state of the VC markets, EachNet management felt they had no choice. The decision to start charging fees, core to eBay's model, ironically fueled its interest in buying EachNet. But once eBay was in charge in China, it pushed the fee culture much more aggressively than Bo and his team. eBay's vice president for global marketing, Bill Cobb, summed it up:[24] "We're mainly interested in making sure that we structure this to have long-term sustainability. We have the essential eBay format—the insertion fees, final-value fees, and features fees—though at a lower level."

Meanwhile, Taobao's decision to forgo charging fees was not without risk, since it forced it to look to other ways of generating revenues, especially if the site became popular and drove up operating costs. But making the site free for both shoppers and merchants turned out to be the key factor in ensuring Taobao's triumph over eBay. A research paper[25] that analyzed more than a decade's worth of transaction data on Taobao concludes[26] that in the early phase of the company's history, attracting merchants, who in China are especially allergic to paying fees, was more important than attracting shoppers. Taobao's popularity was fueled by a "virtuous circle": More merchants and product listings meant more shoppers were attracted to the site, which meant more merchants and products, etc.

In addition to being popular with consumers, offering free services ensured that Taobao was not distracted by a persistent problem that plagued EachNet from the beginning: worrying about how to prevent vendors and consumers from figuring out ways to use the website simply as a place to connect with one another, then conducting their transactions offline or through other means. As Taobao charged no fees, they had no incentive to police this behavior. On the contrary, Taobao actively encouraged communications between the transacting parties by setting up bulletin boards and, beginning in June 2004, launching an embedded, proprietary chat window with the unfortunately in English named AliWangwang.[27] Buyers on the site use the service to haggle with sellers, which resonates well with the vibrant marketplace culture in China. Communication is a key underpinning of commerce, but eBay users struggled to communicate with vendors.

Designed with input from Taobao users, AliWangwang is an early example of the type of "consumer-driven innovation" that drives successful technology firms in China today, such as the role that cell phone vendor Xiaomi's fan club plays in suggesting new product features.

To this day, AliWangwang remains a popular feature on Taobao, allowing consumers to maintain their own list of personal purveyors—one, say, for cosmetics, another for baby formula—who are at their beck and call around the clock. Customer service on Taobao is so good that it can be overwhelming. A purchase on Taobao is often accompanied by a flurry of messages on AliWangwang, a series of virtual bows and scrapes from merchant to customer, who may have a hard time exiting the conversation.

But whatever the "pull" of Taobao, a decision by eBay in September 2004 would serve to "push" many of EachNet's customers away. eBay executives in San Jose decided to "migrate" the China website to the United States. Instead of hosting the website close to customers in China, it was shifted to the States. In a borderless Internet, where a website is hosted shouldn't matter. But China's is not a borderless Internet. Today the Chinese government is actively promoting its vision of "Internet sovereignty" around the world: a rejection of the idea that a nation-state's virtual borders should be less meaningful than its actual frontiers. In China, the effects of the government's longstanding efforts to build and extend the "Great Firewall of China" often means websites hosted overseas are much slower to load than those hosted in China itself. All Web traffic accessing sites hosted outside the mainland has to go through a series of chokepoints where the request is screened. This is to ensure that a foreign website does not display material the Chinese government deems "sensitive," including the "three T's" (Tibet, Taiwan, and Tiananmen Square). These and other sensitive topics, such as unrest in Xinjiang, are widely thought to have been the reason that China has blocked some of the world's leading websites, from Twitter to YouTube to Facebook and, increasingly, Google.

While e-commerce and online shopping typically don't touch on these sensitive areas, the Great Firewall can often ensnare or seemingly block even anodyne activities or requests. For example, once eBay had moved its servers outside China, a user who happened to have a "64" or an "89" as part of his or her username might see their account blocked or be unable to access the Internet—the reason being that both numbers automatically trigger the censors in China as part of the effort to block any mentions of the events in Tiananmen Square on June 4, 1989 (6/4/89).

eBay had its reasons for the migration. As the business grew in China, the engineers in San Jose worried whether the platform built by a Shanghai-based start-up could cope. It turned out that EachNet had built robust technology, capable of scaling up by even a hundred times. But after a series of site outages that had damaged its reputation at home, eBay had become obsessed with the stability of its platform. eBay pushed ahead with the China migration anyway. The attraction of a unified worldwide site with a consistent set of features was just too hard to resist.

Some senior executives within eBay already knew that migration would be a mistake—the company had already seen the damaging impact in Taiwan—but bizarrely eBay managers in Taipei were blocked by migration-obsessed managers in San Jose from sharing their experience with the team in Shanghai.

As predicted, as soon as the China site was migrated and integrated into the global site, the impact on EachNet's traffic was disastrous: It dropped off precipitously. Customers in China started to experience long delays and time-outs on the site. Why would they bother to wait for eBay in China—a site that charged fees—when Taobao was available instantly and for free?

Migration was also costly for eBay because the company typically carried out maintenance of its servers every Thursday at midnight on the West Coast, ahead of the peak traffic of Friday. But this meant the disruption happened at the peak of China traffic, fifteen hours ahead of San Jose. EachNet tried to adjust the maintenance schedule but with no success.

Meg Whitman had made China a key priority for eBay. But when migration caused traffic in China to plummet, no one told her. She found out only a month later on a visit to Shanghai, and she was furious at not having been kept informed.

Things quickly spiraled out of control for the company in China. Once the website had been migrated to the United States, all modification requests from engineers in China were stacked up in what the company called a "train seat" system. Departments would submit their requests for changes, and like an assembly-line process these were then lined up and consolidated into a "train of needs." Changing one word on the site would take nine weeks. Changing one feature would take one year.

How could eBay be so inefficient? There are two explanations. First, eBay had an effective monopoly in the States, and this bred complacency. Second, despite its Silicon Valley aura, eBay was never very strong at technology. One eBay executive famously once said, in public, "Even a monkey could run this business." After the embarrassing site outages, stability and process trumped technology.

Once Taobao appeared on the scene, eBay's "train seat" system quickly became a train wreck. EachNet executives desperately tried to signal the danger to senior executives in San Jose, but to no avail.

Although Taobao had its merits, Alibaba could hardly believe its luck as the ineptness of this supposedly world-renowned company became apparent. Jack compared eBay's lumbering approach to a jumbo jet: "A global technology platform sounds great, like a Boeing 747 flying is great. But if the airport is a school yard, you cannot land. Even if you want to change a button, you have to report to, like, fourteen guys."

Looking back on the fiasco eight years later in her new role as CEO of Hewlett-Packard, Meg Whitman was contrite about eBay's missteps in China. "You've got to have a set of products uniquely designed for this market by Chinese. It is not a market where you can take a product or a system that works in Europe or the United States and export to China."

She also concedes that migration was the fatal blow to eBay's China ambitions. "We made one big mistake. We should have left EachNet on their own platform in China. Instead what we did was put EachNet onto the global eBay platform because it had worked everywhere. It had worked in Western Europe, it had worked all over. . . . We had bought all these baby eBays and basically migrated them to one common platform, which had a lot of advantages. One is cost. Second is speed to market, because when you roll 'buy it now' you could roll it to thirty countries as opposed to do it incrementally. But we made a mistake in China."

She gives credit to Alibaba's achievements in designing Taobao to suit the local market: "They had a uniquely Chinese platform—and by the way they didn't charge anything for years and years and years and years—and they just outexecuted us."

After Bo stepped down, eBay struggled to find a replacement, going through a series of executives, from James Zheng to a Taiwanese-born American, Martin Wu, newly hired from Microsoft China, who would last only twelve months.

Whitman today rues the loss of the entrepreneur who had founded EachNet: "What I would have done is left Bo Shao in charge and owned the thirty percent of China that we originally owned and let him do his own thing."

Sensing eBay's disarray in China, Jack pushed ahead. At a four-hour session in a stadium in Hangzhou in September 2004 to celebrate Alibaba's fifth birthday, Jack rallied all two thousand employees of Alibaba, including the fast-growing Taobao team, who held aloft flags emblazoned with worker ants, the mascot of Taobao. The ant was chosen to symbolize how even the smallest creatures can prevail over their enemies provided they work closely together. The assembled masses then held hands and chanted a song, "True Heroes," whose lyric "You have to go through a thunderstorm to see a rainbow, and no one can succeed easily" was a reference to the challenge of SARS that they had overcome. This was followed by "The ants that unite can beat an elephant," after which everyone headed off to a disco, where Jack danced on the bar into the wee hours.

The elephant in the room was, of course, eBay. From the moment he conceived of Taobao, Jack maintained a relentless focus on the company. In a much-quoted analogy, Jack commented to *Forbes* magazine in 2005, "eBay may be a shark in the ocean, but I am a crocodile in the Yangtze River. If we fight in the ocean, we lose, but if we fight in the river, we win."

The tide was turning against eBay. From a market share of more than 90 percent in 2003, eBay's market share fell by half the following year—barely ahead of Taobao.

And there was another problem for eBay: online payment.

On October 18, 2003, just five months after the launch of Taobao, Alibaba rolled out Alipay, its own payment solution. Although it was rudimentary, reminiscent of the early days of Alibaba's customer log three years earlier, it proved an instant hit with customers.

Lucy Peng, a cofounder of Alibaba, is today CEO of Ant Financial, the Alibaba affiliate that controls Alipay. In 2012, at a talk I moderated for her at Stanford University, she reflected on the launch of the service: "The simple [escrow] model established a trust system in online shopping during its early stages. This was a very primitive model. . . . During Alipay's initial operations one department had a fax machine, after clients wired monies via banks or post offices, they had to fax bank slips to Taobao. We would then double-check and confirm."

It would be three months before eBay woke up to the threat of Alipay. In January 2004, PayPal assembled a task force in San Jose to pick up on EachNet's earlier unsuccessful efforts to devise an escrow solution.

In the United States, eBay had shelled out $1.4 billion to buy PayPal in 2002. But it was slow to integrate the company and roll it out to China. To be fair to PayPal, regulatory obstacles in China were an important factor in the delay: The country's banking sector is closely guarded by the government. Also, China's currency is not freely convertible, meaning that foreign payment providers are banned from facilitating international transactions or offering credit. PayPal struggled to come up with workarounds to these challenges, including local partnerships.

PayPal had started out in the United States as a huge risk taker, legendary for its swashbuckling founders and early executives, today often referred to as the "PayPal mafia": Peter Thiel, Reid Hoffman (cofounder of LinkedIn), and, after they bought his payments company, Elon Musk (Tesla Motors, SpaceX, SolarCity). But within eBay, and far from home, PayPal would struggle in China from the outset.

Attempts to figure out a way forward for the company in China were complicated when PayPal was sued for alleged patent infringement in the United States by AT&T, causing new work on escrow solutions to grind to a halt. To keep momentum on solving the China problem, eBay's newly established China Development Center initiated its own proposed escrow product, called An Fu Tong (AFT). The idea was that while PayPal was tied up with the lawsuit in the States, AFT could be deployed as a stopgap solution. Finally, in December 2004, eBay could provide an answer to Alipay and deployed AFT in China. But by then PayPal had resolved the AT&T lawsuit and wanted to deploy its own solution, not AFT. Meanwhile, Alibaba hadn't been standing still, rolling out a steady stream of improvements to Alipay including popular text message notifications to inform customers of successful payments and, working with domestic logistics companies, shipments as well. Alibaba's "iron triangle" was beginning to take shape.

For Alan Tien, a Stanford-educated engineer working on PayPal's China efforts since 2004, the AFT/PayPal infighting and the disastrous migration of servers to the United States were the beginning of the end for eBay in China. In a series of internal memos to the head office, he tried to raise attention to the seriousness of the threat from Alibaba and Alipay. In January 2005 he wrote, "Current situation isn't good. Momentum has shifted away from us. Must execute on get well plan to stay in the fight," adding, "We cannot afford to deceive ourselves anymore."

eBay just wouldn't take Alibaba seriously, questioning the reliability of mounting data that showed Taobao was selling more goods than eBay in China. Taobao now had more listings, but eBay convinced itself that because those listings were free they must be inferior. Jack vigorously rejected that thesis: "The survival and growth of Taobao are not because of free service. 1Pai [the joint venture of Yahoo and Sina] is also free but it is nowhere close to Taobao. Taobao is more eBay than eBay China [because] Taobao pays more attention to user experiences."

Sensing it was game over, Alan Tien concluded, "Taobao's product development cycle is much faster. Jack Ma's right. We cannot fight on his terms."

Whitman had reached the same conclusion and secretly began to look for a way out of the China morass. The most obvious route was to make an offer to buy Alibaba, and so she sent three senior executives[28] from San Jose to Hangzhou, where they met Jack and Joe. The meeting got off to a bad start when eBay senior vice president Bill Cobb talked down Taobao's achievements and CFO Rajiv Dutta offered a lowball number of $150 million to buy the company. After Jack told the eBay delegation that he was just getting started with Taobao, Joe countered with a sales price of $900 million, at which point the two sides parted company.

Having failed to buy its rival, Meg Whitman announced[29] an infusion of an additional $100 million into its China operations. This was prompted out of fear of Taobao, but Whitman spun it to investors as a positive: "The China Internet market is developing more rapidly than anticipated. . . . We see even greater opportunities in China today than we did six months ago." The $100 million was to be spent upgrading the credit system, hiring personnel, and splashing out a new advertising campaign that soon blanketed billboards in China's major cities.

This was music to Jack's ears. He joked to *Forbes* magazine that eBay had "deep pockets, but we will cut a hole in their pocket." Talking to Chinese media, he ridiculed the new investment: "When I heard that eBay would spend one hundred million dollars to break into this market, I didn't think they had any technical skills. If you use money to solve problems, why on earth would the world need businessmen anymore. Businessmen understand how to use the smallest resources to expand." Even with SoftBank's backing, Jack didn't have the resources that eBay could bring to China if it wanted. Dismissing eBay's approach, he added, "Some say that the power of capital is enormous. Capital does have its power. But the real power is the power of people controlling the capital. People's power is enormous. Businessmen's power is inexhaustible."

Having earlier ignored them, eBay was now paying a lot of attention to Alibaba. Jack later commented that he saw this as a decisive moment: "The moment she [Meg Whitman] wanted to use money as her strategy we knew she would lose. First they didn't consider us as a rival. Then they treated us too seriously as a rival. Neither of them was the right [strategy]. When we say, 'If you have no enemy in your heart, you will be invincible in the world,' we mean you have different strategies and tactics. In terms of strategies, you must pay attention—whenever there is a rival emerging you have to study whether it could become your rival, and if so what to do. Whatever is stronger than you, you have to learn not to hate it. . . . When you treat it too seriously as a rival, and intend to kill it, your techniques are completely exposed. . . . Hatred only makes you a shortsighted person."

In May 2005, Meg Whitman and a number of other key Silicon Valley executives, including Jerry Yang, traveled to Beijing to attend the Fortune Global Forum. There Whitman met up with Jack and Joe. But further talks, which included a proposal for eBay to invest in Taobao, came to nothing.

At PayPal China, the mood was darkening, with Alan Tien writing to colleagues: "I think it's absolutely frightening that eBay doesn't take these threats more seriously. . . . Taobao/Alipay has grabbed the mantle as the auctions/payments leader in China. We are caught on our heels every time. Yet instead of developing a leapfrog, or even a flanking, strategy we try to match feature-for-feature, six to nine months later."

While eBay was trying to put on a good face, Whitman was growing increasingly frustrated at the AFT/ PayPal infighting, warning that PayPal China "is coming to a town near you, whether you like it or not. Although this may be suboptimal for marketplace, it's good for eBay Inc. to have two horses in this race."

Instead of picking AFT or PayPal, eBay had decided to go with both—meaning customers in China would have to navigate not one but two websites when buying online.

Not surprisingly, running two payment systems in parallel in China proved to be a disaster.

Customer complaints flooded in, such as, "My experience on eBay was painful. Can't fill order information. I'm a 100 percent good feedback user, I was never delinquent, and never broke the rules. The payment systems used to be pretty good." Another customer vented, "I can't stand it anymore. Does EachNet call this customer service? They can only scare away more users. Did my two payments totaling 5,000 [yuan] disappear? My confidence in EachNet is once again severely blown."

One customer even complained that his PayPal check was impounded by the Bank of China in Nanjing under a law to "prevent overseas criminals from money laundering through this method." By the middle of 2005, Taobao had facilitated online payments for 80 percent of the products on its sites, but eBay barely 20 percent.

In a last-ditch attempt to turn things around, Whitman and a number of key executives relocated temporarily from San Jose to Shanghai for a couple of months. With the concentration of senior executives, Shanghai was quickly dubbed "Shang Jose" within eBay. But its China business was looking increasingly like a lost cause.

eBay shifted its focus to new horizons, including the landmark $2.6 billion acquisition in September 2005 of Skype.[30] In China, things went from bad to worse when Taobao reaffirmed its commitment to a no-fee model. Extending its pledge of free services for a further three years, Taobao vowed to create one million jobs in China. eBay's PR executive, Henry Gomez, fired off a terse press release titled a "Statement from eBay Regarding Taobao's Pricing Challenge," which consisted of the following three sentences:

> "Free" is not a business model. It speaks volumes about the strength of eBay's business in China that Taobao today announced that it is unable to charge for its products for the next three years.
>
> We're very proud that eBay is creating a sustainable business in China, while providing Chinese consumers and entrepreneurs with the safest, most professional, and most exciting global trading environment available today.

Whitman and her COO, Maynard Webb, already knew that the global product wasn't working in China, so they initiated a new project to launch the best e-commerce site in China from scratch. They called the initiative *de nuevo* (which means "from scratch" or "anew" in Spanish). After all the talk about being more sensitive to local culture in China, adopting a Spanish name for the project hardly inspired confidence.

By the end of 2005, eBay's market share had slipped to barely one-third of the market and Taobao was closing in on 60 percent. Just two months after eBay publicly defended its fee-based business model, eBay stopped charging fees altogether. Having talked up China so much to investors, eBay's struggles there started to weigh on its share price, which dropped dramatically from a high of over $46 in early 2006 to only $24 by August.

Jack didn't pull any punches: "In China, they're gone. . . . They have made so many mistakes in China—we're lucky."

Having failed to team up with Taobao, Whitman launched discussions to sell eBay's China business to the Li Ka-shing–backed venture Tom Online, finally abandoning its troubled business by leaving it in a minority-owned joint venture, along with $40 to 50 million in cash. It left a note, in the form of a press release, that, true to form, attempted to spin an obvious negative as a positive. The joint venture, it read, left eBay "even better positioned to participate in this growing market. This agreement is a sign of our continued commitment to delivering the best online buying and selling experiences in China." The venture quickly faded into obscurity.[31]

eBay had lost China. But in Jack, China had gained a folk hero. When asked today about the experience, Whitman can only tip her hat to Jack's achievements.

"If you look at Japan and China, two important markets, it's where we didn't strategically, actually do the right thing. But it was not obvious at the time, honestly. So more power to Jack Ma, what a powerful franchise he has built—and it is really in some ways the combination . . . of eBay, PayPal, and Amazon. He's done a remarkable, remarkable job."

eBay had lost a few hundred million dollars on its China folly. But this would soon look like small change to Alibaba, thanks to a one-billion-dollar deal that Jack pulled off thanks to another Silicon Valley giant: Yahoo.

Chapter Ten

Yahoo's Billion-Dollar Bet

Nobody knows the future. You can only create the future.

—Jack Ma

Alibaba put paid to eBay's ambitions in China. But eBay was not the first Silicon Valley company to run into problems there, nor would it be the last. Despite being one of the most popular sites in China when people first logged on to the Internet, Yahoo would quickly fall behind—until a billion-dollar deal with Alibaba changed everything.

Jerry Yang

Yahoo's early success in the United States and Jerry Yang's ethnicity set up high expectations for the company in China. Known in mainland China as Yang Zhiyuan (Yang Chih-yuan in his native Taiwan), Jerry and the company he cofounded[1] served as an inspiration for the founders of Sohu, Sina, and NetEase. His appeal went far beyond the tech community. People in China were fascinated with how a young software engineer born in Taiwan came to found such an iconic American company and become so wealthy at such a young age.

Born in Taiwan in 1968, Yang took the name Jerry after he moved to the United States in 1978 with his mother, Lily, and younger brother, Ken. His father, born in mainland China, had died from a pulmonary disease when Jerry was just two years old. In Taiwan his mother had been a teacher, of English and drama, and in California she took a job teaching English to other immigrants. The family settled in a modest one-story home off Hostetter Road in a suburb of San Jose. Jerry's longtime neighbor Bill Otto remembers him as a "very congenial" young boy, playing with his husky dog Bodie in the front yard and lugging a large backpack off to Sierramont Middle School.

Jerry came to the United States with just one word of English—"shoe": "We got made fun of a lot at first. I didn't even know who the faces were on the paper money."

Struggling at first with English, he spent his first two years in the United States in remedial classes. But Jerry excelled in math and science. At Piedmont Hills High School he played on the Pirates tennis team and was elected student council president, finishing his senior year as valedictorian and winning a full scholarship to Stanford. A member of the class of 1990, Jerry completed both his bachelor's and master's degrees in electrical engineering, and between rounds of golf continued his studies in pursuit of a Ph.D. For one of his classes, Jerry's teaching assistant at Stanford was David Filo, two years his elder. David, known for his shyness and reserve, had come to Stanford after an undergraduate degree in computer engineering at Tulane University in New Orleans. Born in Wisconsin, his family moved to Louisiana when he was six and he grew up on a commune in Moss Bluff. Jerry and David had worked in the same design automation software research group, and while teaching at the Stanford campus in Kyoto,

Japan, had become close friends, sharing an interest in watching sumo wrestling.

Returning to Stanford, they took adjacent cubicles in a Stanford trailer, where they launched what would become Yahoo on two servers: "Akebono" and "Konishiki," both names of Hawaii-born sumo wrestlers who had excelled in Japan.

Like the messy Lakeside apartment in Hangzhou where Jack launched Alibaba five years later, the trailer where Jerry and David launched Yahoo was not a pretty site. The company's first investor, Michael Moritz of Sequoia Capital, recalled, "With the shades drawn tight, the Sun servers generating a ferocious amount of heat, the answering machine going on and off every couple of minutes, golf clubs stashed against the walls, pizza cartons on the floor, and unwashed clothes strewn around . . . it was every mother's idea of the bedroom she wished her sons never had."

Yahoo began as a list of other sites that Jerry and David had bookmarked using Marc Andreessen's recently launched Mosaic browser. Known initially as Jerry's Guide to the World Wide Web, then Jerry and David's Guide to the World Wide Web, the list consisted at first of a hundred sites categorized manually into relevant headings. At first, traffic on the site was a thousand or so visitors each week. But by early 1995, traffic had grown to millions of hits a day. Stanford told them to move the site to their own servers. Jerry and David needed to raise funds to pay for them. Registered as Yahoo.com in January 1995, the company was incorporated in March 1995, and the following month, Sequoia invested $2 million, taking a 25 percent share of the company. The two engineers never finished their Ph.D.s. Jerry recalled, "When I first told my mom what we were doing, the best way I could talk about it was like a librarian. And she said you know you went through nine years of school to become a librarian. She was kind of shocked to say the least."

In the fall of 1995, Jerry, David, and Yahoo CEO Tim Koogle initiated discussions with new investors, including Eric Hippeau, the CEO of Ziff-Davis Publishing Company, a large publisher of PC and technology magazines. In November, SoftBank acquired Ziff-Davis, and Hippeau introduced Masayoshi Son to Jerry and David. Son and a colleague flew to meet Yahoo's founders, in their small office in Mountain View, California, just south of Palo Alto. Meeting over a lunch of takeout pizza and sodas, Son and the two founders hit it off. Son agreed to invest $2 million for a 5 percent stake in Yahoo. In March, Son doubled down. In a gutsy move, Son agreed to pay more than $100 million to top up his stake, ending up with over 41 percent of Yahoo, more than Jerry and David, who together held just under 35 percent.

Jerry recalled, "Most of us thought he was crazy. . . . Putting $100 million into a start-up in March 1996 was very aggressive, but I don't think it was luck."

SoftBank saw the potential for Yahoo in Japan, and the two companies launched their joint venture. Jerry flew to Japan in January 1996 to oversee preparations. The site, run by Son's deputy, Masahiro Inoue, launched three months later and was an instant success, racking up five million page views per day in January 1997, and hitting 100 million by July 2000.

On April 12, 1996, Yahoo went public on the Nasdaq, raising $33 million. After a healthy first-day 154 percent gain, investors valued the company at almost $850 million. Yahoo had just $1.4 million in revenues[2] and losses of over $600,000. Only a year after incorporating the company, Jerry Yang and David Filo were each worth more than $165 million on paper. Within three years they were billionaires. Their success propelled SoftBank to list in January 1998 on the primary board of the Tokyo Stock Exchange, making Son a billionaire, too.

Yahoo's popularity spread quickly around the world. The company rolled out localized sites where the business case was strongest. China was not a high priority, as Jerry indicated on a visit to Hong Kong in 1997: "China is probably the last market we want to address right now. It may be the most important one, but the last sequentially. There's not enough people using the Internet for us to be spending money over there."

Instead, Yahoo started to reach out to other parts of Asia, launching a regional site in Singapore in 1997 targeting Internet users in Southeast Asia. The following year it launched regional sites targeting overseas Chinese users and then users in China itself.[3] Consisting of links to ten thousand sites, the Chinese Yahoo was the thirteenth of its "mirror" sites around the world, hosted on servers in the United States and run from its headquarters in Santa Clara, California. Visitors could download free Chinese software to help with different character sets. The site was instantly popular on the mainland. Several hundred thousand visitors a day came to the site, impressive given that China then had less than a million Internet users.

As the Internet gained in popularity in China, Yahoo started to look at getting more deeply involved in the country. Jerry, who spoke fluent Mandarin, had yet to visit mainland China. In a fateful meeting, in 1997, Jack was his tour guide, assigned to the task while working for the government trade ministry in Beijing. In addition to the business meetings with MOFTEC and others, the trip was an opportunity for Jerry to see the sights. Jack's skills as a self-appointed tour guide on the shores of West Lake in Hangzhou came in handy when he and Cathy took Jerry, his younger brother Ken, and Yahoo vice president Heather Killen on a trip outside Beijing to see the Great Wall.

The image of Jerry sitting on the Great Wall is an appropriate metaphor for Yahoo's China dilemma. The market was growing rapidly, now home to millions and soon tens of millions of Internet users. Yahoo had already managed to become a dominant player in Japan, so why not in China, too? But China presented a quandary: how to deal with a government intent on control at all costs.

In 1996, speaking in Singapore, Jerry had shared his views: "Why the Internet has grown so fast is because it is not regulated." There were limits to how much Jerry's Chinese ethnicity would translate into an inside track for Yahoo in China: "The First Amendment safeguards freedom of speech. I'm more American in terms of my upbringing now."

Yahoo from the outset was about content, and that would be tricky in China, where all forms of media were tightly controlled. When Yahoo opened its office in Hong Kong, Jerry was asked about the issue of censorship. He replied that Yahoo would "stay within the boundaries of the law and try to stay as free as possible." He disclosed that Yahoo was in touch with the authorities in China but "to be honest, the policy is not very clear as to what is politically sensitive," adding that they had been informed that "as long as we're just listing content and not hosting it then we can just go right ahead."

Although Yahoo was initially just a directory of links to websites run by third parties, even the choice of which links to present to the public was a sensitive matter. Furthermore, Yahoo was no longer just about links. Following an early partnership with Reuters the company added news content to its site, then chat rooms and, following an acquisition, Yahoo Mail.

The expanding scope of Yahoo's business invited growing scrutiny from regulators on the mainland, who also harbored reservations about the company's links to Taiwan. On a visit to the island in 1997, Jerry had been treated as a conquering hero, mobbed by the media and received by Vice President Lien Chan. His trip came just after Taiwan's relations with Beijing had hit a new low. How could Yahoo comfortably serve users both in Taiwan and the mainland? Jerry Yang admitted it was a challenge: "We may or may not be able to get around it, because they [the Chinese government] can shut us off. . . . The point there is to take a very neutral stand. I don't know if we can get away with it. We are already running into problems."

Could Yahoo go it alone in China? Or would it be better to pick a local partner, perhaps buying out one of the portal pioneers, such as Charles Zhang's Sohu, the original name of which, Sohoo, left no doubt as to its plans to become the "Yahoo of China"?

Build or buy? Either course had its complications. There were simply no precedents for Yahoo to look to. AOL opted in the summer of 1999 to invest in Hong Kong–based China.com. Even after it returned to Chinese sovereignty in 1997, Hong Kong was exempted[4] from the draconian media restrictions that made investing in China so fraught with risk for foreign companies. But China.com was a bit player in China, and even AOL's Steve Case admitted that Hong Kong was just "a logical staging area for China. We want to launch Hong Kong, and then we'll see what happens." (AOL's subsequent partnership in mainland China, with the computer manufacturer Legend Holdings, never gained traction.)

In September 1999, Jerry announced in Beijing that Yahoo was going into the mainland in a joint venture with Founder, a Chinese manufacturer of personal computers and software. The choice of partner was uninspiring but safe: The company was a spin-off from Peking University and retained strong ties to the Chinese government. Yahoo was finally in China itself, adding the coveted ".cn" suffix to become www.yahoo.com.cn. The site started as a directory of links to twenty thousand Chinese websites, plus additional content translated from its U.S. website, and Yahoo Mail and instant messenger. COO Jeffrey Mallett acknowledged that China wouldn't be easy: "We are walking into this with our eyes wide open. The site significantly expands the existing features of a Chinese Yahoo website already online, and it is being hosted in China by government-owned Beijing Telecom."

Yahoo's launch in China came just as the country's own portal pioneers had been dealt a blow in their efforts to launch an IPO. The announcement from Wu Jichuan, the powerful minister of information industry, appeared to ban all foreign investment in the Internet: "Whether or not it is an ICP [Internet content provider] or ISP [Internet service provider], it is about value-added services. In China, the service area is not open."

Yet, in an illustration of the gray area in which the Internet was operating, Minister Wu's own deputy[5] was onstage with Jerry Yang at the launch of Yahoo China, her presence as good a sign as any that Wu had given his tacit blessing to the venture. But an MII official described Yahoo's business as still being offshore, with Founder merely acting as a trustee: "No company was set up inside China's border." This admission revealed that, as with many deals in China, the negotiations only began once an agreement had been signed.

After the launch ceremony in Beijing, Jerry flew down to Shanghai to attend the Fortune Global Forum. He was one of sixty Fortune 500 CEOs—including AOL's Steve Case, GE's Jack Welch, and Viacom's Sumner Redstone—along with other dignitaries, including Henry Kissinger, who gathered at the new, $100 million international convention center built in the city's Pudong district, on the right bank of the Huangpu River, directly opposite the city's iconic Bund. China's president Jiang Zemin inaugurated the Global Forum: "Set your eyes on China. China welcomes you. China's modernization needs your participation, and China's economic development will offer you tremendous opportunities."

The American host for the event was Gerald M. "Jerry" Levin, CEO of Time Warner, the publisher of *Fortune* magazine. Burnishing his credentials as an insider in China, Levin introduced the president of China onstage as "my good friend Jiang Zemin." The forum was a frenzy of China and Internet-infused deal making that soon swept up Jerry Levin himself. Soon afterward he inked Time Warner's $165 billion merger with AOL, a deal that became notorious as "the worst merger in history."

Unlike that deal, Yahoo's partnership with Founder in China ended up having little consequence. Founder was not the gatekeeper to China that Jerry Yang had hoped. The company's links to the Chinese government, which Yahoo had looked to as a shield from regulatory uncertainty, also prevented an entrepreneurial culture from ever taking root. Yahoo China's content was boring, and Chinese Internet users noticed, being drawn instead to the more compelling offerings of Sina, NetEase, and Sohu. Yahoo was losing the battle to stay relevant in China just as the country's Internet population was taking off.

Victor Koo, then COO of Sohu,[6] recalled that "Yahoo China could not match us in scale, localization, or investment. That was why it lost the China market." Their IPOs in 2000, facilitated by the VIE investment structure, allowed the three portals to survive the dot-com crash. Within a few years they had become profitable companies for the first time.

But, unbeknownst to them, the era of the China Internet portals was coming to an end, replaced by a new era of the "Three Kingdoms" of the "BAT": Baidu, Alibaba, and Tencent.

Yahoo's struggles, and backing, were to provide Alibaba its entry ticket to this exclusive club. Here's how.

Tencent

Tencent harnessed two trends that would transform the Chinese Internet sector: content delivered to cell phones, and online games played on PCs. Founded a few months before Alibaba, Tencent (*tengxun* in

Chinese) was launched in late 1998 by two twenty-seven-year-old computer scientists who had met at Shenzhen University. Pony Ma (Ma Huateng) later became chairman and CEO of the company and is today one of China's richest men. Although no relation to Jack, Pony's last name, Ma, is the same as Jack's, his English name chosen as a joke since "Ma" means horse in Chinese.

Like Jack, Pony came from a modest background, and although he is much shyer than Jack he could also claim to be "one hundred percent Made in China." He was born in the coastal city of Shantou, Guangdong Province. His father worked as a port manager in Shenzhen, adjacent to Hong Kong.

After graduation, Pony took a job developing software for mobile pagers, a key entry point to the exploding market for cellular communications that would make his fortune. *Time* magazine anointed him as "China's Mobile Mogul." Pony named his company Tencent because the cost of sending a mobile text message at the time was ten Chinese cents (about 1.2 U.S. cents). Tencent's breakthrough product was its OICQ instant messaging client, installed on desktop computers, which was essentially a clone of the ICQ ("I seek you") product developed by Israeli company Mirabilis.[7] Facing the threat of a lawsuit, Tencent rebranded its service as "QQ," the letters chosen to approximate "cute" in Chinese. With a cuddly penguin in a red scarf for a mascot, the service became a big hit with young Chinese Internet users, initially on PCs, then on cell phones. When China's telecom operators began offering revenue-sharing partnerships with Internet players, Tencent's mobile business really took off. The partnerships, modeled on NTT DoCoMo's iMode in Japan, offered up to 85 percent of the new revenues generated. As mentioned earlier, when SARS hit the country many Chinese turned to mobile text messaging to gather or spread information about the outbreak.

Tencent has been the leading player in China's mobile social networking market ever since. But mobile messaging alone doesn't explain its meteoric rise. The company's biggest business today is online games.[8] Tencent's success in offering MMORPG (massively multiplayer online role playing games) titles such as The Legend of Mir 2 and Lineage, pioneered in South Korea, unlocked the largest revenue streams in China's Internet sector.[9] Tencent's success in QQ, games, and later with WeChat would propel its market capitalization in 2015 to exceed $200 billion, surpassing at times Alibaba, and generating a gold mine of tens of billions of dollars for the South African media company Naspers. In 2001, Naspers made one of the best investments in China, in any sector, ever—acquiring a 46.5 percent stake, three times that of founder Pony Ma, in the company for a mere $32 million from investors, including Richard Li, the son of Hong Kong tycoon Li Ka-shing.

Baidu

Baidu was founded in Beijing in 2000 by Robin Li (Li Yanhong) and his friend Dr. Eric Xu (Xu Yong). Born in November 1968, Robin was one of five children of factory workers in Shanxi, a gritty province in central China. His smarts won him entry to Peking University to study information science. After June 4, 1989, he was keen to head overseas: "China was a depressing place. . . . I thought there was no hope."

Rejected from the top three U.S. schools he had applied to, Robin won a full scholarship in 1991 for a master's degree in computer science at the State University of New York (SUNY) at Buffalo. There he joined a computer lab focused on designing automation technologies, funded by a grant from the U.S. Postal Service. His professor, Sargur N. Srihari, recalled that "he started doing information retrieval here at Buffalo, and we were well ahead of the game in terms of the importance of search engines."

After SUNY, Robin worked for a subsidiary of Dow Jones in New

York. Visitors today to Baidu's one-million-square-foot campus in Beijing are shown a copy of Robin's patent filing from February 5, 1997—when he still worked for Dow Jones—for a search mechanism he called "hypertext document retrieval" that determined the popularity of a website based on the number of other websites that had linked to it. Robin then moved to California to work for the search company Infoseek, before raising $1.2 million in start-up funding and returning to China in January 2000 to found Baidu. The company first operated out of a hotel room near his alma mater, Peking University, its business starting as a third-party supplier of Chinese language search engines to other websites.[10] Although it quickly gained the bulk of the market, Baidu wasn't profitable.

Robin Li, CEO, recalled, "I wanted to continue to improve the search experience, but the portals didn't want to pay for it. . . . That's when I knew we needed our own branded service." Baidu's stand-alone search website was launched in October 2001.

Robin Li has remained closely involved in Baidu's technology development. To ensure that its search engine was cutting-edge, in late 2001, Li temporarily set aside his role as CEO to drive a new development project called "Project Blitzen," recalled by the company's engineering team as a "Great Leap Forward" effort. Li would often sleep in the office, and meetings doubled in frequency until the project was completed.

Looking back, Li said, "Once you find out what you should do, then you need to stay focused. That's what we did during the difficult times back in year 2000, 2001, 2002. Many people think search was a done deal. It's boring. Everyone has figured that out in terms of technology and product, but we thought we could do a better job. We resisted all kinds of temptations from being a portal, being an SMS player, online games, developing all kinds of things that could make money in the short term. We really, really focused on Chinese search. That's how we got here."

In 2002, Baidu's Chinese index of searchable sites was 50 percent greater than its nearest rival's. By 2003 it had become the number one search engine in China. Prior to Baidu's August 2005 IPO on Nasdaq, even Google invested $5 million in it. Baidu's shares rose more than 350 percent on the first day of trading. As it became apparent that Baidu was now its chief rival in China, Google sold its stake the following summer for $60 million.

Baidu would emerge as China's largest search engine.[11] Although worth around $70 billion, it remains a much smaller company than Alibaba and Tencent, two companies that, interestingly, enjoy a better relationship with each other than they do with Baidu.

Yahoo and "AK47"

But back in 2003, there was little sign of the emergence of the "BAT." Yahoo thought it still had a shot at cracking the China market. In search, Yahoo partnered with Baidu. To take on eBay, Yahoo launched an online auction venture with Sina. But, like the Founder partnership, neither deal made a difference.

Becoming increasingly desperate for a fix for its China business, in November 2003, Yahoo announced a deal it hoped would transform its fortunes, buying a company called 3721 Network Software.

Founded five years earlier by a feisty entrepreneur called Zhou Hongyi, 3721 had spotted a niche in the market. Domain names in the Internet were available only in alphanumeric characters (one reason it had chosen numbers rather than a name in the Roman alphabet, for its own website, since "3721" was a saying for something easy, as "easy as 3 times 7 equals 21").

The company 3721 allowed the millions of new users coming online in China to search using Chinese characters thanks to a special toolbar that would then link the Chinese characters input to the corresponding website. The software was downloaded, although not always with the user's knowledge, and was hard to remove. Competitors criticized 3721's technology, arguing it supplanted existing browsers. In 2002, Baidu took 3721 to court, one of many Internet companies to tussle with Zhou Hongyi; 3721 raised several rounds of venture capital and by 2001 had broken even. By assembling a large sales force to market the most valuable Chinese names in the tool bar, 3721 started to make a lot of money, generating $17 million in revenues in 2002.

Born in 1970 in southern China's Hubei Province, Zhou Hongyi grew up in the agricultural province of Henan before attending Xi'an Jiaotong University. He tried his hand as an entrepreneur twice, but both ventures failed before Zhou signed on as an employee of Founder, China's largest university-run enterprise. Three years later, he launched 3721 in partnership with his wife, Helen Hu (Hu Huan), and four others.

Zhou felt his earlier failures cost him his rightful place as a true pioneer of the Internet industry, and he was constantly spoiling for a fight with his rivals. He relished the publicity of the lawsuits or public spats he engaged in with Jack, Robin Li, Pony Ma, William Ding, and Lei Jun (Kingsoft and Xiaomi), among others.

Jerry Yang was known for his affable and approachable manner, but Zhou was the polar opposite: a self-styled bad boy of the Internet in China. He had a passion for guns. After 3721 was acquired by Yahoo, Zhou's new colleagues in Sunnyvale, California, were aghast when they saw his photo in the Yahoo internal directory, in which he toted an AK-47. The team immediately adopted it as his nickname. Zhou even liked to adorn the walls of his office with bullet-hole ridden sheets from target practice. His main investor, Wang Gongquan from

IDG, described Zhou as a "frenzied idealist," an "aggressive and wild child."

Whatever their differences in personality, Jerry Yang saw in Zhou Hongyi's firm the opportunity to boost Yahoo China's revenues. In 2003, Yahoo China made only a few million dollars in revenue, but 3721 raked in an estimated $25 million from its clients. It was the fourth-most-visited Chinese website after Sina, Sohu, and NetEase.

In November 2003, Yahoo acquired 3721 for $120 million (with $50 million paid up front, and $70 million to follow based on performance in the following two years). The deal boosted Yahoo's China team, from 100 to nearly 300. But just as eBay botched its acquisition of local partner EachNet, Yahoo's efforts to integrate 3721 rapidly fell apart.

The culture clash was immediate. Former Yahoo CFO Sue Decker recalls, "Zhou reportedly felt that the original Yahoos were overpaid and lazy, whereas the Yahoo team felt bullied and believed Zhou wasn't focused on the Yahoo operations." Yahoo had carefully courted relations with the Chinese government. But just a couple of months after Yahoo acquired his company 3721, Zhou Hongyi was sued by none other than the Chinese government, whose Internet domain name agency, the China Internet Network Information Center (CNNIC) accused 3721 of damaging its reputation.[12]

Next, Zhou dumped Baidu, which he was in the process of suing, as Yahoo's search partner in China, and launched a new search offering instead.[13] But Zhou hadn't consulted first with Yahoo executives in Sunnyvale. Zhou recalled, "I believed that with an annual investment of only several millions of dollars, it would be entirely possible for us to overtake Baidu." Zhou became frustrated by the managers at Yahoo headquarters: "They were unwilling to invest in the company's future. It is like farming. If you only care about harvesting, but not fertilizing or cultivating, eventually the land will lose its vitality."

China was the least of Yahoo's worries. In the United States, the company was being eclipsed by Google, whose algorithmic search engine was outgunning Yahoo's directory-based design. Yahoo was slow to recognize the threat posed by Google, a company like Yahoo founded by two Stanford Ph.D. candidates. Yahoo had missed an opportunity in 1997 to buy Google from Larry Page and Sergey Brin, but its biggest mistake of all was the June 2000 decision to make Google its search partner. With Google's logo featured on its home page, millions of customers discovered a superior search product and gateway to the broader Internet that made Yahoo increasingly irrelevant.[14]

In July 2005, six months before the end of his two-year earn-out, Zhou announced he was quitting Yahoo China. Within two months he had set up his own company, Qihoo 360 Technology. Here he would adopt the same aggressive tactics[15] that he'd used at 3721.

It wasn't long before Zhou took to the media to criticize Yahoo, telling journalists that selling 3721 to Yahoo was his biggest regret, that Yahoo's corporate culture stifled innovation, and that the firm was poorly managed: "Yahoo's leaders have unshakable responsibility for its decline. Whether it is spiritual leader Jerry Yang or former CEO [Terry] Semel, they are good people, but [they] are not geniuses. They lack true leadership qualities. When facing competition from Google and Microsoft, they didn't know what to do, and had no sense of direction."

Yahoo had struck out twice in China: first Founder, then 3721. After years of frustration, Jerry Yang made a bold decision. He handed Jack $1 billion, and the keys to Yahoo China's business, in exchange for a 40 percent stake in Alibaba.

Project Pebble

Although it took some time for them to realize it, the deal was transformative for Alibaba and Yahoo. Alibaba gained the ammunition to finish off eBay in China, and to build Taobao and Alipay into the behemoths that they are today. The rising value of its stake[16] gave Yahoo leverage in dealing with its increasingly frustrated investors, concerned about its deteriorating market position versus Google and its subsequent controversial decision to rebuff Microsoft's offer to buy the company.

The deal originated in a May 2005 meeting[17] between Jack and Jerry at the Pebble Beach golf course in California. Before a steak-and-seafood dinner with other tech luminaries from the United States and China, the two founders, who had a common shareholder in Masayoshi Son, took a stroll[18] outside. Jack recalled, "It was extremely cold that day, and after ten minutes I couldn't bear it anymore. I ran back indoors. [But] in those ten minutes we exchanged some ideas. I told him clearly that I wanted to enter the search business, and my opinion was that search engines would play a very important role in e-commerce in the future."

From this initial discussion, the outlines of a deal—which Yahoo called Project Pebble—started to take shape two weeks later when Jerry[19] held further meetings with Jack and Joe on the sidelines of the Fortune Global Forum, hosted that year in Beijing.

Yahoo had known for some time that 3721 was not going to be the silver bullet to solve its China woes. But after a thorough screening of which company might be the answer, Alibaba had not been Yahoo's first choice.

Sina was the most logical target. The company had started as an Internet portal and was positioning itself as the "undisputed online media leader in China." Guided by CEO Terry Semel,[20] Yahoo was increasingly trying to become a media and entertainment company. Yahoo and Sina had already signed a memorandum of understanding for Yahoo to invest in Sina, subject to Chinese government approval. Sina's executives and investors were ready to pop the champagne corks when Sina CEO Wang Yan went to meet China's propaganda chief, Li Changchun.[21] Li rejected the deal. Sina would not be allowed to align itself with a foreign strategic investor.

David Chao, a partner at the investment firm DCM, related a conversation in 2004 with Hurst Lin, then COO of Sina: "When their stock was about three dollars Hurst called me up and said, 'I just met Jerry and I think I can finally get rid of my stock. We have a deal.' He was really happy. But, of course, as you know 'the forces above' were uncomfortable."

Yahoo's second choice of partner was Shanda, the Shanghai-based online games specialist.[22] But Shanda's founder and CEO, the Zhejiang-born Timothy Chen (Chen Tianqiao), wasn't interested.[23] Baidu wasn't an option for Yahoo, either; it was already on its way to an IPO.

A deal with Alibaba was attractive on a number of levels. It was a private company, and this meant a deal could be struck quickly. Yahoo and Alibaba had a common shareholder. SoftBank owned 42 percent of Yahoo and 27 percent of Alibaba.[24]

Another positive was good chemistry. Jerry and Jack had known each other for seven years, since their first meeting in Beijing, when Jack played tour guide. The two men hadn't stayed in regular contact, but they had established a rapport.

For Jerry, dealing with Jack was a breath of fresh air after the cantankerous Zhou Hongyi. Jerry also got on well with Joe Tsai. Both were born in Taiwan and educated in the United States. Yahoo CFO Sue Decker recalled that the two companies "immediately felt a strong cultural alignment."

Yet the logic of the combination was not immediately obvious. Yahoo, a consumer content company, was to hand over its China assets to a company that was essentially a B2B business information company with two newer businesses, Taobao and Alipay, tacked on. Taobao was gaining traction in consumer e-commerce, but Alibaba had recently committed not to charge fees for the next three years. How do you value free? Sue Decker recalled Yahoo's concerns: "At the time this seemed like a big leap of faith: More than half the value of the venture—more than two billion dollars—was attributed to Taobao and Alipay, both of which were losing money." The decision to hand over Yahoo's China business was a gutsy move, as Decker recalled, "We realized we needed to be willing to give up all operating control. Practically speaking, this meant forgoing our previous desire to own more than fifty percent of the local operations. It also meant we would leave all employee issues to our partner and allow our code to be used by people with no previous connection to the company. Scary."

A decade later, Jerry Yang reflected[25] on the deal, pointing out that in 2005, when Yahoo made the investment: "The balance sheet at Yahoo was around $3 billion, so it wasn't as though there were huge amounts of cash at Yahoo." Putting a billion dollars into Alibaba, he added "probably raised a lot of eyebrows." Although Yahoo conducted extensive analysis on the underlying business, Jack's charisma and vision for Alibaba also played an important role, as Jerry recalled, "It was probably in retrospect a big bet, but if you met Jack, and having got to know him and seeing what his vision was, you certainly thought it was worth it. And he really had an inside track on being a very dominant commerce platform in China, so that really gave us a lot of comfort." Asked about which company got the better side of the deal, he answered, "If you look at that partnership over ten years, clearly Alibaba was a beneficiary of a very strong vote of confidence back in 2005, and now Yahoo as a company is a beneficiary of that investment."

For Alibaba, the deal immediately delivered the cash it needed to support Taobao, still unprofitable, in its fights with eBay. Yahoo and SoftBank already had a profitable relationship stretching back almost a decade. The Yahoo investment in Alibaba added a new dimension, creating a "Golden Triangle" that has linked Jack, Jerry, and Masayoshi Son for a decade more. With the deal, the *New York Times* crowned Jack as "China's New Internet King." Jack couldn't resist taking yet another shot at eBay: "Thank you, eBay. . . . You made all of this possible."

With the sale, Alibaba was also able to reward its employees, by allowing them to cash out a quarter of their shares, and its early investors, who sold about 40 percent of their stakes in the company to Yahoo at a valuation of about $4 billion. Although they had made an impressive return, the investors then saw Alibaba sell a stake in itself to Yahoo at a valuation some four times higher.[26]

Jack later emphasized that the impact of the transaction went beyond the funding and market recognition provided by Yahoo. Although Alibaba had demonstrated its ability to build start-ups—Alibaba.com, Taobao, and Alipay—the deal brought much-needed experience in mergers and acquisitions, something that would become increasingly important in the future.

The final ownership of Alibaba would be Yahoo, 40 percent; SoftBank, 30 percent; and existing management, 30 percent. In 1999, Jack had sold a 50 percent stake in Alibaba to Goldman Sachs and other investors—something he had joked was the worst deal he ever made. Did he feel any seller's remorse about parting with this 40 percent stake? A decade later he again looked back on the deal: "I asked for one billion dollars, and they gave us one billion dollars. I thought the war between Taobao and eBay would last for a long time, so we needed enough cash to fight." In the end, $1 billion was enough to scare off eBay.[27] "We asked a lot. But we did not know when we got the money eBay would run away. So the money [wasn't used]." Jack said he would do the Yahoo deal again but "in a better, smarter way," adding, "Nobody knows the future. You can only create the future."

The deal left Jack and Joe in charge of Alibaba, although the agreement also included a little-noticed clause that gave Yahoo the right, in October 2010, to appoint an additional board member. If that board member aligned with SoftBank, then Yahoo could then enjoy a majority and the ability, in theory, to take control of Alibaba.

The key terms decided, Alibaba and Yahoo prepared to position the deal to the public. Jerry Yang told *BusinessWeek* that Alibaba was now "the only company in China that has commerce, search, communications, and a very, very strong local management team. This is going to be a very valuable franchise going forward." The media reaction was mixed. Andreas Kluth at *The Economist* was unconvinced: "Yahoo can't keep on being all things to all people. It seems to me that Yahoo has to decide what it is, which means deciding what it's not. Does Yahoo think that it's a search and a media and an e-commerce company now? So why not manufacturing, retailing, banking, health care? So I'm confused."

Yahoo was keen to reassure the market, and its employees, that Alibaba was a safe pair of hands to manage its China business. Yahoo China staffers in particular were unhappy about the change in ownership. Former Yahoo China employee Liu Jie, who quit the company for Qihoo soon after, remembered the jarring change in management style under Alibaba: "At noon the sales-oriented departments at Alibaba would jog and sing. I felt a bit low at that time."

The reception in Yahoo's headquarters was more positive. Former executive vice president Rich Riley[28] recalled, "Markets like China had proven challenging for Western companies," adding that, "this seemed like a smart way to go."

But other than the financial return, did Yahoo achieve its other objectives?

When the deal was announced, Jerry Yang told the media that although Alibaba was taking over Yahoo in China, this didn't mean the end of the Yahoo brand in the country: "All of the consumer Internet products will be branded Yahoo—search, mail, and anything new they decide to come up with. They definitely feel that the Yahoo brand in China has not only global implications but a lot of resonance."

Yet under Alibaba's management the Yahoo brand would rapidly fade and indeed eventually disappear entirely from China. Within a year of the deal, local media started to refer to Yahoo China as the unwanted "orphaned child," with Alibaba more focused on nurturing its own baby, Taobao. In May 2007, Alibaba changed the name of the business from Yahoo China to China Yahoo, an apt reflection of who was in charge.

Alibaba did invest heavily in the Yahoo China brand at first, pouring in 30 million yuan (over $4 million) to make TV ads to promote Yahoo Search. Jack spared no expense for the ads, partnering with the Huayi Brothers film studios, in which he would later invest, and hiring three of China's most famous directors, Chen Kaige, Feng Xiaogang (who directed Alibaba's Singles' Day TV special in 2015), and Zhang Jizhong. Zhang was known for his flamboyant, big-budget TV adaptations of Jack's favorite author Jin Yong.

But in the core area of search, the superior algorithmic search of Google and Baidu was winning out. China Yahoo was in trouble. After the deal, Jack became exasperated at how slow Yahoo was in delivering on the search and other technology it had committed to provide. The pressure was so great that in 2006 Jack made the decision to remodel Yahoo's home page in the uncluttered, clean style popularized by

Google, which Baidu had already mimicked. But Jerry Yang was very unhappy with the move and asked Jack to change the China Yahoo site back to its original portal look and feel, which he did. Not surprisingly, Yahoo's users were confused by the changes, and the company's market share slid further. From a 21 percent share of search revenue in 2005, driven largely by the 3721 tool bar, Yahoo's share fell to only 6 percent in 2009 as Baidu's soared to take almost two-thirds of the market, leaving Google with just 29 percent.

Messy Exit

But had Yahoo soldiered on without selling its China business to Alibaba, the company would still have had to contend with two major challenges: 3721 founder Zhou Hongyi, and an ethical and public relations catastrophe involving Chinese journalist Shi Tao.

Zhou Hongyi, on learning of the Yahoo-Alibaba deal, immediately announced his resignation and became a disgruntled former employee. He began to brief journalists that he would be starting his own venture and started to hire people away from Yahoo. In the coming years Zhou and his new firm, Qihoo 360, caused a lot of headaches[29] for Alibaba, China Yahoo's new owner.

But even after it sold its China business to Alibaba, Yahoo's image would be tarnished in the United States by the case of imprisoned Chinese journalist Shi Tao. The source of intense personal anguish for Jerry Yang, the affair would illustrate the unpredictable risks that awaited any foreign company planning to build a business in China's Internet sector.

Shi Tao was an editor and reporter at a newspaper in Changsha, the capital of Hunan Province, called *Contemporary Trade News* (*Dangdai Shang Bao*). He was also a customer of Yahoo Mail. On April 20, 2004, Shi participated in an internal editorial meeting, convened by the newspaper's deputy general editor, to discuss a classified document sent from Beijing with instructions on how to avoid social unrest in the run-up to the fifteenth anniversary of the June 4 Tiananmen Square crackdown. Although copies of the document were not handed out, Shi Tao took notes during the meeting later that evening using a Yahoo China email account,[30] then emailed them to a Chinese, pro-democracy website based in New York. Two days later, Yahoo China was requested by the government to hand over details of the account owner,[31] which they provided that day.

On November 23, 2004, Shi was detained by the State Security Bureau in Changsha. On December 15 he was arrested and charged with revealing state secrets. After a trial lasting two hours in March 2005, Shi was found guilty and sentenced to ten years' imprisonment.

Shi's case was quickly taken up by activist groups[32] who accused Yahoo of being a "police informant." The publicity and appeals, launched by Shi's journalist friends and his mother, Gao Qinsheng, were unsuccessful in reversing the verdict. After what Amnesty International alleged was intense harassment from the Chinese government, Shi's wife divorced him.

It was a nightmare for Shi and his family. For Yahoo it was a black eye. For Alibaba, although it now ran the China business, the case had happened on Yahoo's watch. Jack was asked to comment on the case and said, "As a business, if you cannot change the law, follow the law. . . . Respect the local government. We're not interested in politics. We're just focused on e-commerce."

On September 10, 2005, I attended Alibaba's Alifest in Hangzhou. The partylike atmosphere was heightened that year by the newly minted $1 billion deal with Yahoo and the growing sense that Taobao would prevail over eBay. Jerry Yang was to appear onstage with Jack as part of the celebrations. The icing on the cake was Jack's invited keynote speaker that year: former U.S. president Bill Clinton.

Clinton had accepted the invitation to speak in July, but news of the Yahoo connection to Shi Tao's case emerged only days before the summit, putting Clinton[33] in an awkward position. Clinton did not refer to Shi's case but discussed more generally the economic cost of censorship and the need for China to develop greater tolerance for dissent.

After Clinton left the room with his Secret Service and Chinese government security detail, Jerry Yang took the stage for a Q&A session to talk about the deal with Alibaba. *Washington Post* reporter Peter S. Goodman asked Jerry Yang directly about Yahoo's role in handing over the information that led to Shi Tao's incarceration.

Yang answered, "To be doing business in China, or anywhere else in the world, we have to comply with local law. . . . We don't know what they want that information for, we're not told what they look for. If they give us the proper documentation and court orders, we give them things that satisfy both our privacy policy and the local rules." He added, "I do not like the outcome of what happens with these things. . . . But we have to follow the law."

The audience, made up mostly of Chinese Internet executives and investors, erupted into applause, what seemed like an inappropriate response given the seriousness of the case, but thanks to the Great Firewall few in the audience had even heard of Shi Tao. Things would get much worse for Jerry Yang after that, culminating in a public skewering in Washington, D.C., in 2007 when he was summoned to appear before Congress[34] to answer questions about the case. The committee chairman, California congressman Tom Lantos, opened the session by introducing Shi Tao's mother. Jerry Yang, wearing a dark suit and tie, bowed solemnly to her three times as she sat behind him sobbing. Lantos lambasted Yahoo for its "inexcusably negligent behavior at best and deliberately deceptive behavior at worst" and concluded, "While technologically and financially you are giants, morally you are pygmies."

Yahoo later settled out of court a lawsuit filed by Shi's family, paying an undisclosed amount. Shi Tao was released in September 2013 after serving eight and a half years in prison, his ten-year sentence having been earlier reduced by fifteen months.

Yahoo's travails proved that for companies dealing with Internet content, China was a highly risky market, as Google would later experience itself before it closed up most of its operations in 2010. Google had launched its search engine on servers hosted in China (as google.cn) in 2006, keeping servers for Gmail and other products that involved personal and confidential information offshore. But in early 2010, in response to an attempt to hack its servers and the cumulative pressure of growing need to censor its search results, Google announced its withdrawal from China. In March 2010, Google stopped censoring search results in China, rerouting traffic to its site in Hong Kong—the other side of the "Great Firewall of China"—and signaling its exit from the market.[35]

eBay, Yahoo, and Google had all recognized that China's Internet market would become massive. But as the market grew, so did regulatory barriers and the competitive challenge from entrepreneurial and well-financed companies like Alibaba, Baidu, and Tencent.

Speaking in 2015, Jerry Yang took stock of the China Internet market: "Maybe in the next ten years some American or Western brands will be successful in China. But in that 2000–2010 time frame there just weren't any."

Western Internet companies trying to crack the China market came to experience firsthand the old adage that in China "it is better to be a merchant than a missionary." And the biggest merchant of all was Alibaba.

Chapter Eleven

Growing Pains

If you own a hundred percent of the business that cannot operate, you own a hundred percent of zero.

—Joe Tsai

When eBay exited the China market in 2006, Taobao's users were 30 million. Within three years they were 170 million, and sales on the Taobao's platform had grown from $2 billion to $30 billion. With no obvious competitor on the horizon, the outlook for Alibaba looked rosy. The Chinese economy was growing at an unprecedented rate, topping 14 percent in 2007. Anticipation about the 2008 Olympic Games in Beijing set off a massive stock market rally at home. Western capital poured into China and the share prices of the country's leading Internet players took off. Baidu's stock trebled in 2007, valuing the company at over $13 billion. Tencent, with more than 740 million QQ instant messaging users and a growing games business, climbed to $13.5 billion. A new wave of China Internet companies prepared to go public. Speculation turned to Alibaba. When would it IPO?

Before raising fresh capital, Alibaba reshaped its management[1] in preparation for a new phase, beefing up its team with new executives from Pepsi, Walmart, and KPMG[2] and a new head of strategy, Dr. Zeng Ming. Alibaba also appointed a Shanghai-born executive, David Wei (Wei Zhe), with experience in finance and retail, as CEO of the B2B business Alibaba.com. He would serve as CEO of Alibaba.com for more than four years,[3] including overseeing Alibaba's first IPO.

Taobao was wildly popular with consumers, but a commitment to free listings ensured that the business was still loss-making. So, instead, Alibaba decided to list only its original B2B business: Alibaba.com.[4] Founded in 1999, these companies were now eight years old. Alibaba.com had more than 25 million registered users in China and overseas. It was a stable and profitable, if unexciting, business.

IPO 1.0

Yet such was the buzz around Jack that the November 2007 IPO of Alibaba.com in Hong Kong generated a frenzy of interest in the stock not seen since the dot-com boom. One analyst slammed the psychology of Hong Kong investors who "trade stocks like they're playing at the baccarat table." That was an accurate description of many of the individuals who lined up to buy the shares, such as sixty-five-year-old Lai Ah-yung, who told the Associated Press: "People said buy, so I buy."

Although the B2B business of Alibaba.com was really a sideshow, excitement about China's booming Internet—now numbering more than 160 million users—and its vibrant economy meant that few people bothered to make the distinction.

Jack described Alibaba's business in language that resonated well in Hong Kong, a market obsessed with property speculation: "We're almost like a real estate developer," he explained. "We make sure the space is cleared, the pipes are laid, the utilities work. People can come in and put up their buildings on our site." But there was much more to come, he said, adding that if Alibaba did things right "we have the chance to build a platform that could become the Internet ecosystem for all of China."

The bulk of the shares were sold to institutional investors in an exhausting, ten-day global road show that finished up in San Francisco. The schedule was so packed that David Wei had no time to eat. Jack unexpectedly ducked out of their last investor meeting, calling David soon after to invite him to an airport restaurant where he'd ordered all the noodle dishes on the menu.

When they landed back in Hong Kong, they already knew from their road show that the offering would be a blowout success. The stock market there had already rallied 40 percent in the previous three months, but to ensure a strong start Yahoo had committed to buy[5] 10 percent of the offering, along with seven other "cornerstone" investors, including local real estate tycoons.[6]

The offering of Alibaba.com, listing under the lucky number stock ticker "1688," sold 19 percent of the company for $1.7 billion. It was the largest Internet IPO since Google in 2004, and valued[7] the company at almost $9 billion.

Demand from individual investors, who were allocated 25 percent of the total, outstripped supply by 257 to 1. Those lucky enough to secure an allocation of shares saw them triple on the first day from the HK$13.5 offer price, closing at HK$39.5. Alibaba's B2B business was valued at $26 billion, a multiple of 300 times its earnings.

But the luckiest investors were those who sold right away, since the share price fell 17 percent the next day.

The buzz around Alibaba was focused on Jack and the other high-growth businesses like Taobao and Alipay. But these assets weren't part of the IPO; in fact most of the shares released in the IPO were from Alibaba.com's parent, Alibaba Group, which needed to raise cash to support them.

David Wei later looked back on the IPO and said, "Taobao was still burning money." From Yahoo's 2005 investment, Alibaba still had "maybe $300 to $400 million, but that was not enough. We still didn't know how to monetize Taobao." Of the $1.7 billion raised in Hong Kong, only $300 million went to the B2B business. Alibaba had topped up its coffers with the remaining $1.4 billion, giving it reserves of almost $1.8 billion. "That's an enormous war chest," David recalled, "and would last us a very long time to support Taobao. At that time Alipay was still burning money as well."

The former Alibaba.com CEO added that the 2007 IPO gave him two insights into Jack's approach. The first was something that Jack had often told him: "Raise money when we don't need it. When you need it don't go out to raise money, it's too late." The second was that the IPO allowed Alibaba to take care of its employees: "Jack understands people more than any business. He knows business well, but if you ask me the three skills Jack has amongst people, business, or IT? IT is the worst. Business second. First is people." Alibaba's B2B business was eight years old. Jack knew that he needed to give his employees an opportunity to cash in their shares. David remembers Jack telling his employees, "You need to buy a house. You need to buy a car. You can't wait to sell the stock to get married, to have a baby. Selling the stock doesn't mean you don't like the business. I encourage you to sell some, to build your life, to give a reward to your family. Because you have been working too hard, you've been away from your family. They need some reward."

Jack himself didn't sell shares for the first two years. But when he did sell, some $35 million worth, he explained to his colleagues he

Jack's fame was cemented with the Alibaba.com IPO: Jack's Australian pen pal, David Morley, at the Hangzhou Airport, 2008. *David Morley and Grit Kaeding*

wanted to give his family "a little sense of accomplishment." But Jack didn't wait to buy himself a $36 million home[8] in Hong Kong.

The IPO prospectus listed Jack's home address as the small Lakeside Gardens apartment where it had all started. But now he would trade up to deluxe apartment in the sky, atop the Mid-Levels district on the hillside of Hong Kong's famous Victoria Peak.

Jack had become a billionaire (based on the value of his stock), but the IPO prospectus illustrated—thanks to the three big investment rounds led by Goldman Sachs, then SoftBank and Yahoo—how much smaller a stake he held in his company than many of his peers. At their IPOs, William Ding held a 59 percent stake in NetEase and Robin Li a 25 percent stake in Baidu.

Global Financial Crisis: Silver Lining

But storm clouds were gathering that would send the company's shares into a tailspin. Alibaba.com depended on foreign trade, but the U.S. economy was weakening, hitting the business of the China exporters who made up the backbone of the B2B business. Alibaba's shares started to slide, dipping below the IPO price in March. When the global financial crisis gathered pace in September 2008, triggering the collapse of Lehman Brothers, Alibaba's shares plummeted, hitting a low of only one-third of its IPO price the following month. Only weeks after Beijing had staged the Olympic Games, it was facing a crisis as global trade volumes plummeted by 40 percent.

Alibaba's B2B business was vulnerable. It had an impressive sounding 25 million registered users, but only a handful paid to use the website. Just 22,000 subscribers of its Gold Supplier service accounted for 70 percent of total revenues.[9]

As CEO of Alibaba.com, David Wei was expecting the falling share price would trigger a lot of pressure from Jack. But, he remembers, "Jack never picked up the phone or came to see me about the share price. Never once. He never talked about profit growth." But there was one occasion when he did experience Jack's wrath. "The only time he ever called me after midnight was when our team changed the website a little bit. He was shouting, the only time he ever shouted at me. I had never heard him so angry. 'Are you crazy?' " Jack wasn't yelling at him about the stock price. He was angry about downgrading in prominence a long-standing discussion forum set up for traders to chat with one another. Jack demanded David move it back the next day. David pushed back, saying that Alibaba needed to focus on transactions, not discussions, adding that the space on the home page was very valuable for advertisers. But Jack was emphatic: "We are a B2B marketplace. Nobody comes to trade every day. We are more important a community than our marketplace. The same for Taobao; nobody comes to shop every day. If you downgrade this forum you are focusing too much on profits. Switch it back to a non-revenue-generating entry point to the business community."

Although its share price took a beating, Alibaba would survive the global financial crisis. And, as with SARS five years earlier, the crisis created some unexpected dividends for the company.

First, Jack realized that the downturn gave him a way to increase the loyalty of his paying customers. He initiated a dramatic reduction in the cost of their subscriptions, telling David, "Let's be responsible to our customers. They are paying fifty thousand yuan; we can give them thirty thousand yuan back."

"The stock market went crazy," David recalled, as investors called him up to complain, "What? You're losing sixty percent of your revenue." But there was a method to Jack's madness. Jack was serious about putting the customer first, but David emphasized Jack was not espousing "an ideology of 'let's give everything for free.'" Instead, Jack was "always trying to understand how to get the money back later. He's just not greedy about getting the money first." Looking back on the price cut, David concluded that the move was well timed. "Revenues didn't drop at all. Customer volume growth offset the price drop completely. And after the financial crisis was over we didn't raise the prices. We created an opportunity to sell them more value-added services, more of an Internet-style model. Jack actually told me he wanted to change it anyway. The crisis gave him the opportunity."

The second dividend was that the collapse in their traditional export markets forced China's factory owners to prioritize consumers at home instead. Increasingly goods "Made in China" for export would be "Sold in China" too. Taobao was perfectly positioned to benefit from this switch. Jonathan Lu, then president of Taobao, commented, "More and more consumers are flocking to the Internet in search of cheaper goods amid the economic slowdown, while many others choose to open online shops as secondary jobs." By the end of 2009, Taobao's market share had climbed to nearly 80 percent.

Finally, Taobao started to generate meaningful revenues, selling merchants advertising space[10] to help them promote their goods to the surging number of online shoppers.[11]

By September 2009, Alibaba was on a roll. At Alibaba's tenth anniversary celebration Bill Clinton was back in Hangzhou as a keynote speaker, but this time with iconic figures for China's new consumer wave, such as Nike-wearing NBA player Kobe Bryant and the CEO of Starbucks, Howard Schultz. At the celebration, Alibaba also launched its new cloud computing subsidiary, Aliyun.

As Taobao gained momentum, it was becoming Alibaba's main focus. Consumer e-commerce was outshining the company's legacy B2B business—which Alibaba was to later delist[12] from the Hong Kong stock market—and the fading Yahoo China portal asset.

Since the 2005 deal, as Taobao grew in strength Alibaba and

Kobe Bryant presents Jack with a pair of his Nike sneakers in Hangzhou, September 2009. *Alibaba*

Yahoo enjoyed a long honeymoon. But a surprise event in early 2008 brought that to a dramatic end. On January 31, 2008, Microsoft made an unsolicited offer to buy Yahoo for $44.6 billion.[13] If the deal went through, Jack realized, Microsoft would become his biggest shareholder. Although he had a good relationship with Bill Gates, Jack realized that in Microsoft he would have a very different partner to contend with, one known to get much more involved in the companies it invested in than Yahoo did. There was another risk: The Chinese government had contacted Alibaba for comment about the possible change in ownership.

Control Concerns

Microsoft and the Chinese government have long enjoyed an unpredictable, love/hate relationship. High points include the red carpet treatment President Jiang Zemin gave to Bill Gates on his visit to China in 2003 and the return favor Bill Gates gave to newly minted president Hu Jintao at a dinner hosted by Bill Gates at his home on Mercer Island, Washington, in 2006. But there had been tensions, too, with Microsoft expressing its exasperation at the rampant piracy[14] of its products and the Chinese government accusing Microsoft of monopolistic behavior.

In public, Jack insisted that Alibaba would remain independent regardless of what happened with the bid. "Alibaba has been independent for nine years. . . . No matter what happens, we will go in our own way."

But in private, he was alarmed. Alibaba wanted to trigger the "right of first offer" clause in the 2005 deal, which allowed it to buy back Yahoo's stake in the event of a change of ownership, as now appeared likely. Alibaba hired Deutsche Bank and legal advisers to prepare. But in early 2008, as the global economy weakened, raising finance would be difficult, and Alibaba was a company with many moving parts. Taobao and Alipay were growing rapidly but still losing money. The listed company, Alibaba.com, was dropping in value. But if Alibaba couldn't raise the money or agree on a price with Yahoo to buy back its stake, the 2005 deal stipulated that the price would be determined by arbitration instead—a long and unpredictable process.

In the end, in May 2008, Jerry Yang—now Yahoo CEO since the departure of Terry Semel the previous year—rejected Microsoft's offer. Investors in Yahoo were furious, as management had turned down an offer that valued the company at a 70 percent premium. Yahoo's share price started to drop, losing 20 percent in one day. Shareholder activists[15] built up stakes in the company in an effort to force through the deal, but to no avail. When the global financial crisis hit a few months later, Jerry's decision to reject the Microsoft bid looked like the height of folly. Investors called for his head. In November 17, 2008, Jerry announced he was stepping down as CEO, handing the reins over to Carol Bartz, the former CEO of software firm Autodesk.

Yahoo's decision to reject Microsoft had cost Jerry Yang his job and dented his pride. Yet Alibaba had dodged a bullet, the uncertainty of an interloper intruding on its relationship with Yahoo, which, now on the back foot with investors, would continue to be its largest shareholder.

Any sense of relief, though, would evaporate a few months later when Jerry's replacement, Carol Bartz, took up her position as CEO of Yahoo.

Bartz was in many ways the opposite of Yang. Jerry Yang was known as well mannered, amicable, even deferential. But Bartz was infamous for her aggressive style, frequently dropping the F-bomb in meetings.

When Jack and a delegation of his senior Alibaba executives traveled to Yahoo's headquarters in Sunnyvale in March 2009 he was met at the entrance by Jerry.[16] He welcomed them, then walked them to their meeting with Bartz. But on arriving Jerry made his excuses and left the room: Bartz was in charge now.

Alibaba proceeded to give Yahoo an update on the progress of the company, including the runaway growth of Taobao. But rather than congratulating them, Bartz lambasted Alibaba for the dwindling market presence of Yahoo in China under their watch, reportedly telling them, "I'm going to be blunt because that's my reputation. . . . I want you to take our name off that site." Jack later told a journalist,[17] "If you cannot make the business cool, you have no right to be angry with me."

The relationship between Jack and Bartz had instantly become frosty. Soon there were long periods when the two had no contact with each other at all.

Alibaba's efforts to buy back Yahoo's stake would increasingly take place in public, as did their ongoing disputes.

In September 2009, at the same time as Alibaba was celebrating its tenth anniversary, in a public vote of no confidence Yahoo sold[18] the shares it had purchased in the Alibaba.com IPO. Then, in January 2010, as Google faced off with the Chinese government in a bitter spat over censorship and hacking, Yahoo came out in support of Google: "We condemn any attempts to infiltrate company networks to obtain user information. . . . We stand aligned with Google that these kind of attacks are deeply disturbing and strongly believe that the violation of user privacy is something that we as Internet pioneers must all oppose."

Alibaba was livid to see its biggest shareholder square off against the Chinese government. Through a spokesman, John Spelich, Alibaba fired back, "Alibaba Group has communicated to Yahoo that Yahoo's statement that it is 'aligned' with the position Google took last week was reckless given the lack of facts in evidence. . . . Alibaba doesn't share this view."

Worse was yet to come. In September 2010, Yahoo's Hong Kong managing director said he was seeking mainland Chinese advertisers for the site, putting Yahoo in competition with Alibaba, which responded that they would reevaluate their relationship with Yahoo.

Alibaba.com CEO David Wei publicly questioned the relationship with Yahoo: "Why do we need a financial investor with no business synergy or technology?" He added, "The biggest thing that has changed is Yahoo lost its own search engine technology. The biggest reason for a partnership doesn't exist."

The relationship with Alibaba would never improve under Carol Bartz, who was fired by Yahoo in September 2011. But before she stepped down, Alibaba was buffeted by two crises that threatened to erode the company's most precious commodity: trust.

The first crisis was an internal incident, the discovery of fraud within Alibaba's B2B business, which damaged Alibaba.com's reputation with its customers. The second was the controversy over the transfer of the Alipay asset outside Alibaba ownership, which damaged Alibaba Group's reputation with some of its investors.

The fraud, in which an estimated one hundred Alibaba sales personnel were implicated, involved 2,300 merchant storefronts[19] who were certified as trusted suppliers by the corrupt employees. The merchants then took in $2 million in payments for orders of computers and other goods on alibaba.com—bestselling items that were offered at very low prices—that they never shipped to the customers overseas.

Alibaba outed itself, sending its shares down by 8 percent, but Jack was most angry about the damage it had done to consumers trust. The salespeople were fired, and the accounts of more than 1,200 paying members were terminated. Although an investigation cleared the senior management of any wrongdoing, because the fraud happened on their watch Jack asked for the resignation of CEO David Wei and the company's COO.[20] Jack told the media that Alibaba is "probably the only company in China" where senior management takes responsibility, which prompted *Forbes* to describe Jack as "something of a rare species" in a nation "steeped in corruption." When some accused him that the dismissal of the senior executives was a publicity stunt, Jack responded angrily, "I'm not the guy who created the cancer, I'm the guy curing it!"

David Wei didn't oppose the move, crediting it as helping spur a similar crackdown within Taobao shortly after. "People said, 'Wow it's that serious?' " he told me. "And this triggered other cleanups within the group. It started within B2B, then to consumers. I feel very proud of my resignation. Without cleaning up the business, the IPO in 2014 would not have been so successful."

But the other crisis, impacting its investors, would have a more pernicious and long-lasting impact on Alibaba's reputation. Even though the company insists it did nothing wrong, a position that many investors support, the controversy continues to serve as a lightning rod to the company's critics. This crisis centered on who owned the Alipay business.

Firestorm

Alipay was a critical cog in the Taobao machine, handling more than $700 million a day in transactions, more than half of the total market in China. As it was so integral to Alibaba, it was hard to put a value on the business, but one analyst estimated that Alipay was worth $1 billion.

But on May 10, 2011, it emerged that the Alipay asset had actually been transferred out of Alibaba Group the previous year. The business was now owned by a company, personally controlled by Jack, called Zhejiang Alibaba E-Commerce Company Limited. Jack owned 80 percent of the company, and Alibaba cofounder Simon Xie (Xie

Shihuang) held the rest. Investors first got wind of the transfer in a paragraph buried on page eight of the notes to Yahoo's quarterly earnings report. It read:

> To expedite obtaining an essential regulatory license, the ownership of Alibaba Group's online payment business, Alipay, was restructured so that a hundred percent of its outstanding shares are held by a Chinese domestic company which is majority owned by Alibaba Group's chief executive officer. Alibaba Group's management and its principal shareholders, Yahoo and Softbank Corporation, are engaged in ongoing discussions regarding the terms of the restructuring and the appropriate commercial arrangements related to the online payment business.

A business potentially worth $1 billion just went missing? Investors were alarmed. Yahoo's shares dropped like a stone—losing 7 percent on May 11 and 6 percent the day after—wiping $3 billion off its equity market capitalization. That evening, in an effort to limit the damage, Yahoo disclosed that neither it nor SoftBank had been told about the transfer of control until after the fact.

But ignorance wasn't much of a defense. In Yahoo's 2005 investment agreement, any transfer of assets or subsidiaries out of Alibaba Group that were worth more than $10 million required the approval of the company's board of directors or shareholders.

At Alibaba.com's annual general meeting in Hong Kong, Jack defended the transfer, arguing it was "a hundred percent legal and a hundred percent transparent." He added that discussions were ongoing with Yahoo and SoftBank "regarding the appropriate commercial arrangements related to the Alipay business," adding, "if we had not been doing everything aboveboard, we would not be where we are today."

Alibaba also released a statement confirming the transfer and explaining that it was made to comply with regulations from the People's Bank of China (PBOC), China's banking regulator. Specifically the PBOC had issued its "administrative measures for the payment services provided by nonfinancial institutions," which required, Alibaba explained, that "absolute controlling stakes of non-financial institutions must be domestically held."

On May 15, in an attempt to calm the waters after days of turmoil, Alibaba and Yahoo issued a joint statement: "Alibaba Group, and its major stockholders Yahoo Inc. and Softbank Corporation, are engaged in and committed to productive negotiations to resolve the outstanding issues related to Alipay in a manner that serves the interests of all shareholders as soon as possible."

But there was a gap between the public statements from Yahoo and Alibaba, opening up a series of troubling questions that were essentially: Who knew what? When?

Alibaba said the Alipay transfer had already happened. But Yahoo hadn't informed its shareholders for months, perhaps even years. How long had Yahoo (and SoftBank) known about the transfer? Alibaba insisted that Yahoo and SoftBank had been told in a July 2009 board meeting that "majority shareholding in Alipay had been transferred[21] into Chinese ownership." The Chinese business publication *Caixin* confirmed, after an investigation, that Alipay was sold in two transactions, in June 2009 and August 2010, to Zhejiang Alibaba E-Commerce Company Limited, the firm controlled by Jack. The total price paid was 330 million yuan ($51 million). Critics argued that Yahoo was either dishonest or incompetent. If Yahoo knew about the transfer, why hadn't they told their investors? If they didn't know about it, why not?

Other troubling questions were also raised by the crisis. Did Alibaba really have no choice but to transfer such an important asset out of the company? Furthermore, did that transfer have to be made to a company under Jack's personal control? And what was going to happen next?

Shareholders in Yahoo were exasperated, with one hedge fund manager telling the media, "It seems like this thing has evolved into a he-said, she-said battle via press releases. It doesn't make Yahoo's board look like they were on top of things."

Critics of the VIE structure, and of investing in Chinese companies in general, were having a field day. But did Alibaba in fact, as it was arguing, have no choice but to make the transfer?

Behind the scenes, when the crisis first broke Jerry Yang was upset, but he remained calm. Masayoshi Son, however, was incensed. What was Jack thinking? To figure out what was going on, Jerry offered to fly to Beijing. Meeting there with a senior official at the PBOC, he was told that it was best he just "accept the situation." When he pressed for an explanation, he was simply informed that the matter was "out of their hands."

It was true that PBOC had introduced new rules, in June 2010, governing domestic third-party payment platforms on the Internet. The rules set out a longer application procedure for foreign-funded companies than for wholly domestically owned applicants. PBOC had been debating the issue of foreign ownership of payment companies since 2005. But the rules did not exclude foreign ownership entirely.

Jack's defenders argue that he was simply first to see which way the regulatory wind was blowing. Parking the Alipay asset into a domestic company that he controlled could insulate Alibaba from the risk that new licenses expected to be issued by PBOC would be denied to foreign-invested companies. In an effort to clear up the matter in 2014 ahead of its IPO, Alibaba justified the transfer by explaining that the "action enabled Alipay to obtain a payment business license in May 2011 without delay and without any detrimental impact to our China retail marketplaces or to Alipay."

Indeed, on May 26, 2011, Alipay, now entirely domestically owned, was the first of twenty-seven companies to be issued licenses[22] and was awarded license number 001. But Jack's critics charge that because PBOC also issued licenses to foreign-invested companies, such as Tencent's Tenpay, and was the number two player in the market, then the argument that Alibaba had to transfer ownership of Alipay out of foreign hands doesn't hold water. To this, Jack's defenders argue that the comparison with Tenpay and other foreign-invested companies isn't valid: Alipay already had such a dominant share of the market that it could not have expected such leniency. There were thousands of companies active in the third-party payment market, but with the first batch of licenses issued in May, PBOC also issued a deadline—September 1, 2011—for all companies to either obtain their own licenses or merge with an existing license holder. Inevitably this generated a lot of tension. Companies that had operated in a gray area now found themselves being divided into black and white, based on whether they had foreign investment and had obtained a license. Those that had not yet received licenses faced the risk of going out of business, and those that had received licenses but were foreign-invested were concerned that Alipay's move threatened their own ability to have IPOs in the future, damaging the valuation of their business and, many feared, undermining the VIE investment structure on which so many Internet companies relied.

A number of Alipay's rivals described to me a meeting hosted by PBOC soon after the licenses were issued, at which Jack was present. Many vented their unhappiness at Alibaba, but Jack remained silent. Yet even without the licensing issue, the reality was that too many companies were chasing after the oasis of fortunes to be made in payment riches. This turned out to be a mirage: With fees as low as 1 percent of transactions, if licensing hadn't thinned out the field, then competition would have done the job anyway. In this light, the Alipay incident—and the PBOC licensing regime it triggered—merely accelerated the inevitable: Many payment companies found themselves stranded in the desert, soon to run out of funding. One executive summed it up for me: "There were more 'payment solution' companies out there than consumer e-commerce companies. It was like being in a kitchen where there were more chefs than diners in the restaurant."

In light of all of this, was Jack justified in making the transfer of Alipay to his control? Or are those who, to this day, criticize the transfer justified? Both sides of the argument relied on their interpretation of what the Chinese government, in the form of PBOC, had in mind. But that was clear as mud. PBOC had never said that foreign-invested entities could own payment platforms. But equally it had never said that they could not. One influential investor I spoke with summed it up: "PBOC were pissed. But Jack was very skilled at playing off different factions. No one could do anything about it because PBOC's rules were so vague to start with."

Was something else going on that drove Jack to take the risky move of transferring Alipay out of Alibaba? The deteriorating relationship between Yahoo and Alibaba certainly didn't help. Under Carol Bartz, relations had become so bad that she and Jack were not even on speaking terms. Instead they started to communicate with each other by issuing statements or in interviews with the media.

Eight months before the Alipay crisis erupted, Bartz stated that she had no interest in selling Yahoo's stake in Alibaba and that Jack was merely trying to get "some of his stock back" ahead of an IPO that would value those shares much higher. Alibaba immediately fired back, via the media, denying any plans to get an IPO and laying out its efforts at good faith negotiations[23] with Yahoo to buy back its stake.

The reality for Alibaba, though, was that if Yahoo didn't like the price Alibaba was prepared to pay there was little Jack could do about it.

Did this frustration play a role? Or was another looming issue the reason? Five years had passed since Yahoo's investment. Part of the investment agreement, conceded to by Alibaba only after intensive negotiations, gave Yahoo the right to appoint a second director to Alibaba's board in 2010. Furthermore, the agreement also stipulated that a majority of the board could replace Alibaba's senior management. If a hostile Bartz gained the support of Jerry Yang, who although no longer CEO still sat on Alibaba's board, and enlisted the support of Masayoshi Son, she could outvote Jack and Joe, imperiling their positions. This was improbable—given Jack's relationship with Jerry and Masayoshi Son, not to mention the difficulty for a foreign company to try to gain control over such an iconic company as Alibaba—but not impossible, especially if Bartz could strengthen her hand in negotiations over a sale of Yahoo's stake. Yet even threatening such a move would have been highly destructive for Yahoo. "Then their investment would be worthless" is how another China Internet founder I spoke with put it.

In any case, the "nuclear option" never happened. As criticism of the transfer mounted Alibaba had little choice but to reach an agreement with Yahoo as quickly as possible. A number of domestic commentators were even harsher than foreign critics. In their eyes, the dispute threatened the interests of other entrepreneurs in China by undermining confidence in the VIE structure, and foreign investment in the country in general. After first criticizing the government for the vague and lengthy approval process for licensing payment providers, respected local magazine *Caixin* slammed Jack personally for "violating contract principles that support the market economy." Jack had tarnished his international business reputation and diminished Alibaba's long-term growth prospects, Caixin argued, by transferring an asset "to a concern under his name, for a price too low to be fair." One China Internet company founder I spoke with, four years after the controversy, told me that even if that was the motivation, Jack was justified in doing it: "I perfectly understand it. Is it right? If I were Jack, I would have done the same thing. If he hadn't resolved the incentive problem, Alibaba wouldn't be today's Alibaba." Although few Chinese business leaders publicly endorsed that view, a number posted links to the *Caixin* article on social media.

Soon after its publication, Jack communicated with Hu Shuli, *Caixin*'s influential editor-in-chief, through a flurry of mobile text messages to discuss the issues she had raised. Their first texting session lasted two hours. Jack texted her to say he was very disappointed that *Caixin* published the comments without knowing the whole picture. He said that he "had no interest in politics at all," he just wanted "to be himself" and "to be accountable to himself and to others."

Jack said that "today's situation is not designed [by us], but [we are] compelled to do it. The complexity of decision making of shareholders and the board is also a problem of corporate governance in the future." He added, "I have three principles of doing things: first, one hundred percent legal; second, one hundred percent transparent; third, I must let the company develop sustainably and healthily."

Interestingly, Jack revealed to Hu that Alibaba's relationship with Yahoo was stronger at that point than with SoftBank: "The problems between me and Yahoo are easy to solve. They are problems of interests. But the issues between me and Masayoshi Son are not only issues of interests." Beyond the Alipay dispute, at the height of the controversy, Jack disclosed[24] that he had fundamental disagreements with Son on a range of HR issues, including employee incentive schemes and staff training:

> He thinks that employees can be replaced at any time. I believe that we should give opportunities to young people in China, sharing the future with them. He thinks that's not the case in Japan: I pay you wages anyway, so if you want to do it that's fine, but if not there will be others. First of all, I don't think [what happens in] Japan is necessarily right; second, this is totally wrong in China. I believe customers first, employees second. We wouldn't have this company without our staff. We have completely different principles on this issue. . . . The issue has been there since day one.

Jack revealed that his disagreement with Son was long-standing, that they had been "fighting over it regularly in the past few years." Jack also contrasted his approach to equity ownership. "Seventeen thousand employees at Alibaba all have shares," he said. "You see that from the day that Alibaba was established until today, my share has been getting smaller and smaller." Jack argued that Son, by contrast, had a stake in Alibaba of "thirty percent from day one, and now it is over thirty percent." In a sign of the tension that had erupted between the two men, he invited journalists to look at Son's approach to his own employees at SoftBank: "You can check if he's given anything to his employees. . . . If he [Son] is asked to take out one percent [of his stake], it's like pulling out a tooth from a live tiger."

While Jack professed his admiration for Son's skills of negotiations, he also said Son is the world's number one "iron rooster" (*tie gongji),* a Chinese idiom describing people who are extremely stingy: Meaning, there is no chance whatsoever to pull out even one hair from an iron rooster.

Because many of the facts were disputed, and the stakes were so high, efforts to resolve the dispute dragged on for weeks, then months. Midway through the crisis,[25] Jack described the negotiations over the compensation to be paid for the Alipay transfer as "very complicated," comparing them to "peace talks at the United Nations."

But reaching a settlement was becoming urgent. By the end of July, Yahoo's shares had dropped 22 percent since the dispute began. A few weeks earlier, high-profile investor David Einhorn of Greenlight Capital sold his entire position in Yahoo, which he had built up because of its exposure to China, saying that the dispute "wasn't what we signed up for."

Finally, on July 29, an agreement was reached. The transfer of the assets would stand. But Yahoo, benefiting through its continued stake, would receive compensation of $2 to $6 billion from the proceeds of any future IPO of Alipay. Alibaba, Yahoo, and SoftBank were ready to put the dispute behind them. But investors in Yahoo were underwhelmed, particularly by the cap of $6 billion,[26] and its shares fell 2.6 percent on the news. But in a call explaining the agreement to investors Joe Tsai pushed back vigorously, saying that the transfer was made to stay in line with government regulations: "If you own a hundred percent of the business that cannot operate, you own a hundred percent of zero."

The Alipay episode left a bitter taste, but the compensation agreement had put an end to months of uncertainty. Now Alibaba could focus on its next priority: buying back as much as possible of Yahoo's stake.

On September 30, 2011, Jack accepted an invitation to Stanford University to give a keynote speech at the China 2.0 conference series, which I had cofounded with Marguerite Gong Hancock a few years earlier. After I had introduced him onstage, I settled into a seat in the front row to watch what turned out to be a vintage performance of "Jack Magic." Speaking in English, Jack started by acknowledging the elephant in the room—the company's relationship with Yahoo. He said he was very tired from the events of the past few months, then, raising his right hand and looking at the audience, he said, "I still don't know what the VIE is, right?" Of course it was obvious Jack knew all about the investment structure—it had been center stage of the Alipay controversy—but feigning ignorance was his way of winning over the crowd, even if the lawyers in the audience couldn't contain their incredulity. Jack then ventured onto safer ground using some of his stock stories, before I started to field questions for him from the media. Asked, "Are you going to buy Yahoo?" Jack replied, "Yes, we're very interested in that." When Kara Swisher of Dow Jones's AllThingsD asked him if he wanted to buy back just Yahoo's stake in Alibaba, or all of Yahoo, Jack replied, in a sound bite that quickly went around the world: "The whole piece. Yahoo China is already ours right?" Then putting his right hand in his pocket he added, "It's already in my pocket!" He concluded by adding that the situation was complex and would take time.

In the end, it would take nine months before a deal was completed. On May 21, 2012, the terms were made public: Alibaba would pay Yahoo $7.1 billion ($6.3 billion in cash and up to $800 million in preferred stock) to buy back half of Yahoo's stake, or 20 percent of Alibaba, netting Yahoo some badly needed cash: $4.2 billion after tax. Alibaba also made a commitment to buy back a quarter of Yahoo's remaining stake by 2015, or let Yahoo sell the stake in a future IPO[27] of Alibaba Group. Yahoo and SoftBank also agreed to cap their voting rights on Alibaba's board below 50 percent. Jack and Joe could feel secure in their seats. They set a course for their IPO (2.0).

Chapter Twelve

Icon or Icarus?

The communists just beat us at capitalism!

—Jon Stewart

IPO 2.0

On September 8, 2014, two days before Jack's fiftieth birthday, Alibaba Group Ltd. kicked off its global roadshow in New York City.

Fifteen years after climbing the rough, cement staircase inside the Lakeside Gardens apartment complex, I walked up the polished marble steps of the Waldorf Astoria hotel in Manhattan. I had come to witness the birth of "BABA."

Live-broadcast satellite trucks and black SUVs lined the block outside the hotel. Inside Jack, Joe, and the rest of the senior management team prepared to make their pitch. I walked alongside a line of investors that snaked all the way from Forty-Ninth Street up through the lobby to the hotel's gilded elevators. Today was all about the New

China. The venue was fitting, as the venerable Waldorf Astoria itself was acquired[1] shortly after, for $2 billion, by a Chinese company.

On reaching the upstairs ballroom, the investors were issued with wristbands that determined whether they would hear the Alibaba pitch in the main ballroom or in one of the overflow rooms outside. One investor said it reminded him of an iPhone launch.

All eyes were on Jack. Although Jonathan Lu, as CEO,[2] was the main front man for the presentation, Jack remained—as he does today—the personification of Alibaba. When it was his turn, Jack told the investors the story of his first, unsuccessful fund-raising trip with Joe to the United States fifteen years earlier. Seeking $2 million from venture capitalists, he returned, he said, empty-handed. But now he was back, and asking for a little more.

On that first trip Joe tried, without success, to convince Jack to present something to the investors they had flown to the United States to meet. But this time they came prepared. Each of the investors was handed a weighty, three-hundred-page prospectus. The bright orange cover's cartoonlike graphics at the front made it look more like a children's book than a serious document for grown-ups. But flipping past the artwork, the investors found the sobering text outlining the "Risk Factors"—standard for any public offering. The section ran thirty-seven pages long, detailing "intangible"[3] and "tangible" risks, such as the company's dependence on Alipay, a business it no longer owned. Jack addressed the issue of the Alipay transfer head-on, saying he had been given no choice. The decision, he said, was one of the hardest of his life, but one in retrospect he would make again.

The risk factors also included a discussion of the controversial but enduring VIE investment structure. But the offering had added, on top of the VIE, another layer of complexity for investors: the "Alibaba Partnership." The partnership[4] comprised thirty individuals, mostly[5] members of Alibaba's management team. Six,[6] plus Joe Tsai, were original cofounders of Alibaba. The explicit goal of the partnership is to help Alibaba's senior managers "collaborate and override bureaucracy and hierarchy," to ensure "excellence, innovation, and sustainability." In December 2015, Alibaba appointed four new partnering members, taking the total to thirty-four.[7]

Of course the implicit reason for the partnership is control. Even after becoming a public company, Alibaba wanted to ensure that the founders remained masters of their own destiny.

This had already caused controversy for Alibaba, prompting the Hong Kong Stock Exchange and its regulator[8] to turn down Alibaba's application for an IPO in the territory. Hong Kong was concerned that allowing the structure would signal a weakening of its commitment to the "one shareholder, one vote" system.

Alibaba countered that the partnership could not be compared to the narrow concentration of control of the "dual-class" or "high vote" share structures used by tech company peers in the United States like Google and Facebook. Instead it was proposing a new, more sophisticated form of corporate governance that gave each member of a larger group of managers a vote. But the distinction failed to convince the Hong Kong authorities, and Alibaba opted for an IPO on the New York Stock Exchange instead.

Saying "no" to Alibaba was costly for Hong Kong, depriving the city's bankers and lawyers of a huge windfall. Joe Tsai didn't pull his punches: "The question Hong Kong must address is whether it is ready to look forward as the rest of the world passes it by."

So, Alibaba found itself in New York. Selling 12 percent of the company, it raised $25 billion, the largest IPO in history. Credit Suisse and Morgan Stanley, two of the six banks hired to lead the deal, raked in $49 million each. The haul for an army of lawyers on the deal was more than $15 million.

In New York, the deal caught the attention of Jon Stewart at Comedy Central. First he joked about Alibaba's business, connecting buyers with sellers: "Craigslist with better graphics, is that what it is?" Then he poked fun at Alibaba's convoluted ownership structure: Investors in the IPO were buying shares in Alibaba Group Holdings Limited, a company incorporated in the Cayman Islands, controlled by a partnership, which did not actually own the business assets in China. "So I paid for a share for something on an island, and I don't own it?" Stewart continued, "You're selling us a time share, is that what it is? A time share in a company. Without giving us a free vacation to sit through your pitch?" Finally, Stewart noted that Alibaba was listing in New York because it couldn't list in China: "The communists just beat us at capitalism!" Stewart concluded by pretending to phone his broker to get his hands on, in vain, some BABA shares.

But this IPO[9] was not about individual investors; it was all about big institutions, for whom ninety percent of the shares were reserved. Seventeen hundred institutional investors subscribed to the shares, including forty who each put in orders for over $1 billion. In the end the bulk of the shares were allocated to just a few dozen institutions.

Jack Magic, and the appeal of Alibaba's huge business, worked. Demand[10] for BABA shares outstripped supply by over fourteen times. A healthy first-day pop was inevitable. Demand was so strong that it took the New York Stock Exchange half an hour even to determine the opening trade. The stock was listed at $68 but the initial quotes came in at just under $100. BABA closed the day 25 percent higher than the initial price, valuing the company at over $230 billion, more than Coca-Cola. Among Internet companies, Alibaba was second only to Google, higher even than Amazon and Facebook. In the following weeks, its shares continued to climb, its valuation far surpassing Walmart and Amazon, almost breaking the $300 billion mark in early November. Mirroring his record-breaking $36 million purchase of an apartment in Hong Kong after Alibaba

.com's IPO in 2007, less than a year after the 2014 IPO, Jack bought another trophy asset, for $190 million this time, in the shape of a ten-thousand-square-foot, three-story house perched even higher up Hong Kong's Victoria Peak.

However, just as Alibaba.com's IPO in 2007 had sizzled, then fizzled, BABA-boom soon become BABA-bust: Alibaba Group's shares sank by 50 percent before the summer of 2015 was out. In late August, they fell below the $68 IPO price for the first time. By September, Alibaba's valuation had sunk[11] by almost $150 billion from its November 2014 peak, in what Bloomberg described as "the world's biggest destruction of market value."

Newly appointed CEO Daniel Zhang reminded the company's employees, "Our values do not waver with the fluctuations in stock price," and that they were not just fighting a battle, but were "in it for 102 years to win the war." Thanks to the anticipated future IPO of the parent company of Alipay, renamed Ant Financial,[12] Alibaba would also continue its practice of creating regular opportunities for employees to cash out some of their shares. Although Ant Financial's IPO (on a domestic stock exchange) is likely still a year or two away, Alibaba has already started to distribute shares in the financial unit.

After a strong first few months, why did Alibaba's shares fall so fast and so far? The sharpest drop was triggered by a public dispute between Alibaba and a Chinese government agency, a development that came as a shock to the foreign investors who had assumed that Jack was somehow the ultimate insider, immune from such entanglements.

Fighting over Fakes

On January 28, 2015, the State Administration for Industry and Commerce (SAIC), China's business and licensing authority, posted a report[13] on its website that detailed complaints, leveled the previous July, that accused Alibaba of selling fake goods and its employees of taking bribes from vendors in order to boost the rankings of their products. The report also detailed a subsequent SAIC investigation into the sale of counterfeit items on six leading e-commerce sites, including Taobao and Tmall. The SAIC found that of its sample purchases on Taobao only 37 percent were considered authentic, adding, "For a long time, Alibaba hasn't paid enough attention to the illegal operations on its platforms, and hasn't effectively addressed the issues." Worse still, the report asserted that "Alibaba not only faces the biggest credibility crisis since its establishment, it also casts a bad influence for other Internet operators trying to operate legally."

When the media picked up the story, Alibaba's shares fell by more than 4 percent.

Alibaba was furious, questioning the SAIC's methodology and its motivations. Remarkably, both the SAIC's report and Alibaba's response to it were on full view to the public. In China, discussions between the government and companies are typically conducted in private, as the opacity of PBOC's intentions and interactions during the Alipay crisis had already illustrated. But here was one of China's largest companies directly criticizing the government. More spectacularly, a posting by a Taobao customer service representative on the company's official social media[14] account even named the individual SAIC official[15] involved: "Director Liu Hongliang! You're breaking the rules, stop being a crooked referee!" The post continued, "We are willing to accept your God-like existence, but cannot agree with the double standards used in various sampling procedures and your irrational logic."

Although the post was deleted by Alibaba a few hours later, it was replaced by an official communication that was still remarkable for its frankness: "We are open to fair supervision, and are opposed to no supervision, misconceived supervision, or supervision with malicious aims." Alibaba also indicated that it had filed a complaint against the SAIC official for misusing procedures and using erroneous methods to get a "non-objective conclusion," adding, "We believe Director Liu Hongliang's procedural misconduct during the supervision process, irrational enforcement of the law and obtaining a biased conclusion using the wrong methodology has inflicted irreparable and serious damage to Taobao and Chinese online businesses."

For Alibaba the timing of the dispute was particularly inopportune, coming one day before[16] the release of its quarterly earnings report. Alibaba reported sales of 40 percent,[17] but investors were unimpressed by its numbers, sending its shares down a further 8.8 percent. Tens of billions of dollars had been wiped off its valuation in just two days. In the earnings call, Joe Tsai, now executive vice chairman, fought back: "At Alibaba we believe in fairness. We support rigorous supervision of our company, but we also feel compelled to speak out when there are inaccurate and unfair attacks being leveled against us."

And the tit-for-tat wasn't over yet. SAIC then disclosed that it had kept private the details of the July 2014 meeting in order not "to impede Alibaba's preparations for its initial public offering." This was particularly unhelpful to the newly public Alibaba because it raised the ugly possibility that management had failed to disclose the dispute to investors ahead of its IPO, something that should have formed part of the (already voluminous) risk factors section of the prospectus. But Alibaba denied the accusation, saying it neither had prior knowledge of a white paper nor had requested SAIC to delay publication of any report, adding that meetings with regulators were a normal occurrence. Unsurprisingly all of this triggered a class-action lawsuit against Alibaba the following week.

Finally, the mudslinging had become too much. SAIC deleted the report from its website. Jack flew to Beijing to meet with the regulator's head, Zhang Mao.[18] There the two men, in public at least, buried the hatchet. Jack promised to "actively cooperate with the government and devote more technology and capital" to rooting out the sale of fake goods. Zhang Mao praised Alibaba for its efforts to safeguard consumer interests and said SAIC would look to develop new tools to oversee the e-commerce sector.

Looking back at the incident, one former senior Alibaba executive told me the company would have been better off not responding to the SAIC announcement in the first place: "Alibaba is still relatively young, but to some they've become such a big monster. Even the government doesn't know how to manage them. In the future, there will be a lot of conflicts. That's natural. Because this government has never had to deal with a company this influential."

For Alibaba, and any private company, the Chinese government itself is a multiheaded hydra of agencies, often competing with one another for influence, licensing fees, or other forms of rent to justify their existence, often lacking sufficient central government support to finance their operations. These agencies exist at both the national level and at multiple levels below. Some are replicated all the way down through the provinces to municipalities and finally to the level of rural counties.

Jack often repeats a line about his relationship with the Chinese government: "Fall in love with the government, don't marry them—respect them." With so many departments, if he were truly to marry the government, he'd end up a polygamist. Jack revealed[19] that Alibaba had hosted in 2014 alone over forty-four thousand visits from various government delegations in China.

Yet, short of marrying, even respecting the government can be a challenge. Jack once explained to a friend that he was never really sure of his schedule from one day to the next. If the party secretary of Zhejiang, for example, requested he travel with him as part of a business

Jack receives Xi Jinping, the Communist Party Secretary of Shanghai, at Alibaba in Hangzhou, July 23, 2007. *Alibaba*

delegation to Taiwan, then he would have little choice but to make the trip. Owning a Gulfstream G650 jet is quite a privilege, but unlike his tycoon peers in the West, for Jack there is always a lurking sense of not knowing where to tell the pilots to fly it.

Respecting the government also involves cultivating good relations with a wide range of officials, including future leaders of the country who might one day hold huge sway over the company. A typical feature in the lobby of any large company in China, whether state or privately owned, is a wall of photos memorializing meetings between the boss and various government dignitaries. Alibaba is no exception. At the entrance to its VIP visitor suite there is a photo[20] from July 2007 of Jack welcoming Xi Jinping to Alibaba. Xi today of course is president of China but back then he was Communist Party secretary of Shanghai.[21]

Entrepreneurs in China can never eliminate the risk for their business of arbitrary regulations or actions. Instead they can try to shield their companies by helping the government do its job.

Part of the SAIC's job is to stem the flood of pirated goods.[22] Online or offline, fighting piracy is like a game of Whack-A-Mole: Whack one molehill, and the moles will pop up somewhere else. To turn the page on its dispute with SAIC, Alibaba increased the number of staff dedicated to combating counterfeiting, from 150 to 450 people, including a team of "secret shoppers" to root out fakes. Alibaba operates a "three strikes you're out" system to sanction vendors. Selling the same fake good on three occasions[23] gets a merchant kicked off the platform. To weed out merchants who later resurface with another name—the "whack a mole" problem—Alibaba has adopted some creative countermeasures. Similar to the "proof of life" tactics used by hostage negotiators, the company asks merchants to prove their identities by taking a photo of themselves with their ID card and today's newspaper. They may even ask them to adopt a particular "pose of the day" in the photo as an extra security measure.

At a closed-door dinner in London in October 2015, Jack summed up the problem as follows: "Maybe one percent of the merchants on our platform are bad guys." Yet with nine million merchants on Taobao, that works out at ninety thousand "bad guys." An investor present at the dinner, David Giampaolo, summarized Jack's message that evening: "He is focused on solving the problem. However, few people, especially overseas, appreciate the enormity of the task."

In Beijing on Singles' Day 2015, Jack went further: "Every consumer that buys one counterfeit on our site, we lose five customers. We are also victims of [counterfeits]. We hate this thing. . . . We have been fighting for years, but we are fighting human nature, human instinct." Explaining that piracy had been rampant in China's offline retail sector for the past thirty years, Jack added, "We are fighting online and helping fighting offline. We have two thousand people working on it, we have fifty-seven hundred volunteers working on it. With special task forces, with the technology we have, we are making progress. I think the opportunity is whether we should work together to fight against these thieves. We are running a platform for more than ten million businesses. They [the pirates] are tiny; they are everywhere."

Some of Jack's rivals are sympathetic to his predicament. One told me: "When you're managing a platform with nine million merchants on it, you're running a country."

A key part of Alibaba's response is its Internet Security Team, headed by ex-cop Ni Liang. The team operates a "notification and take down" system that merchants can use to flag fake products[24] being sold on Alibaba's sites. Using techniques such as "price point analysis," brand owners can identify large quantities of high-margin items such as luxury bags being sold at impossibly low prices. But this method doesn't work well for high-volume, low-margin items such as soap or shampoo, where it can be hard to sort legitimate products from fakes. So Alibaba is looking to the power of Big Data: Company names, addresses, trading history, and bank accounts can all be useful to establish patterns of distribution and go after infringers. The power to deny them the use of Alipay as a payment tool on other platforms can also be an effective deterrent.

The reality is that, for piracy, e-commerce is both part of the problem and part of the solution. The Internet is more effective at distributing fake goods than offline methods, but also more effective at identifying and combating infringers.

Taobao, dominated by mostly mom-and-pop store owners, is less easy to police than Tmall. So with events like the November 11 Singles' Day, Alibaba is spending more marketing dollars on Tmall than Taobao. Tmall sets a higher bar[25] for merchants to trade. Also Alibaba generates commission fees on Tmall, meaning that shifting business away from Taobao makes more money for Alibaba as well.

But not all brands are convinced. A few months after the SAIC controversy the American Apparel & Footwear Association (AAFA), which represents more than a thousand brands, was again pushing for Taobao to be added back to the USTR's list of notorious markets; the association complained about the "rampant proliferation" of fake goods on Taobao and the "slow, sluggish, and confusing systems" that Alibaba has put in place to remove them. Yet despite AAFA's action, a number of its members, including Macy's and Nordstrom, continue to work closely with Alibaba on initiatives including Singles' Day, revealing a lack of consensus about the way forward. In November 2015, Juanita Duggan, the person who as CEO and president had spearheaded the complaint, resigned from her post.

Alibaba faces criticisms from some brand owners in Europe, too. In May 2015, Kering, the French luxury goods holding company of brands including Gucci and Yves Saint Laurent, filed a lawsuit against Alibaba alleging violations of its trademarks and racketeering laws. Part of the complaint included allegations that when customers enter the word *Gucci* in Alibaba's search engine, it returns links to fake products branded "*guchi*" or "*cucchi.*" Alibaba is fighting the suit, countering that Kering has "chosen the path of wasteful litigation instead of the path of constructive cooperation." In an interview on Singles' Day 2015 with Bloomberg, Jack was even blunter, revealing his frustration with lawyers: "Don't send lawyers. These lawyers don't understand business; they don't understand e-commerce." The following month, Alibaba stepped up its IP enforcement efforts by appointing Matthew J. Bassiur as head of Global Intellectual Property Enforcement. Bassiur had previously overseen anticounterfeiting operations at the pharmaceutical company Pfizer after several years with Apple Computer. Prior to his corporate career, Bassiur served as a federal prosecutor in the U.S. Department of Justice.

Fake goods weren't the only issue weighing on Alibaba's share price after its IPO. Some investors fretted about fake trades, too. Also known as "brushing," fake trades involve merchants shipping empty boxes to ghost customers to boost their rankings.[26] Local brands—particularly those in highly competitive sectors like apparel, cosmetics, and electronics goods—are the main culprits. Rather than carrying out the fake trades themselves, these merchants typically hire "click farming" companies to generate the fake purchases for them. They can also hire the same click farms to generate fake, positive product reviews to influence real purchasers. By one estimate, four click farms[27] interviewed each claim to control at least five million Taobao buyer accounts. These firms no doubt exaggerate their influence—to boost their appeal to potential customers—but collectively the click farm companies claim that in 2015 they accounted for double digit percentages of the total merchandise volume of Singles' Day purchases in 2015. Alibaba and other e-commerce players are on the lookout for these companies—monitoring traffic and transaction patterns to root out suspicious activity. (Although the click farms claim they can circumvent these attempts, they assent that these methods are not rigorously applied.) As with the battle against fake goods, Alibaba and other e-commerce players are engaged in a cat-and-mouse game. Like piracy, brushing cannot be eliminated entirely, unless the algorithms that rank merchants based on sales volume are abandoned. The e-commerce players can, and do, act to increase the costs of bad actors. Tmall's "anti-brushing" systems monitor behavior to establish if a purchaser is a real person, for example, by ensuring that the session involves clicks on a range of products—suggesting actual browsing of goods on sale—and sufficient time spent on each web page, concluding with a purchase deemed to be a reasonable amount for one person to make. In response, the click farms have increased the sophistication of their service, charging as much as thirty yuan ($4.70) per faked order, compared to the typical range of ten to twenty yuan ($1.56–3.12) per order, depending on the costs involved, such as commissions, payment fees, and generating fake logistics information. Tmall is more prone to brushing than Taobao, as the competition to secure high-ranking sales—and the publicity these can generate—in promotions like Singles' Day is so intense.

Alibaba's e-commerce platforms have become so large that policing the huge volume of goods and transactions is becoming ever more complex. Yet this size is also Alibaba's great strength. Merchants on Alibaba's sites are increasingly willing to spend money to upgrade their stores. Even merchants who prefer to sell goods on other sites still keep a presence on Taobao because it means consumers trust them more.

Competitors in the Wings

Nevertheless Alibaba is facing rising competition in a number of categories like clothing,[28] cosmetics,[29] books,[30] and food.[31] To buttress its position in electronics and electrical appliances, Alibaba has even started to make investments in traditional retailers as part of the new trend, mentioned earlier, called "omni-channel" or "online to offline," abbreviated as "O2O." In August 2015, Alibaba shelled out more than $4.5 billion to buy a stake[32] in Suning, an electronics and white goods retailer. But some analysts questioned the logic of buying into a company with more than 1,600 stores across the country that, like Best Buy in the United States, were at risk of becoming merely expensive showrooms used by customers to try out products that they would later buy online. Alibaba made the investment in Suning in part to counter its biggest competitor in e-commerce, a well-funded company called JD.com,[33] which went public in the United States four months before Alibaba. JD is a threat to Alibaba in part because it represents a competition of ideas. Unlike Alibaba, JD is more closely modeled on Amazon, purchasing and selling its own inventory. In addition, while Alibaba has kept one step removed, JD owns and operates its own logistics network. While Alibaba argues that JD will never rival it in scale due to the costs of owning inventory and shifting physical goods, JD counters that its model ensures a higher quality of product and speed of delivery to its customers.

JD clearly riles Jack. In early 2015 he turned his guns on the founder of JD, Richard Liu. Although he spoke the words to a friend in what he thought was confidence, Jack's criticism of the company was posted on social media: "JD.com will eventually be a tragedy and this is a tragedy I have warned everyone about from day one. . . . So I've told everyone in the company, don't go near JD.com." Soon after the incident, Jack apologized, joking, "The next time I have a conversation, it'll be in a public bath."

The Big Two

Another reason why Jack has trained his guns on JD is that it enjoys the backing[34] of Tencent, Alibaba's main Internet rival. As Alibaba extends into new territory beyond e-commerce, it is increasingly bumping into Tencent, whose valuation in 2015 at times surpassed that of Alibaba. Tencent makes most of its money in online games but is a threat to Alibaba because of the phenomenal success of WeChat,[35] the mobile application it launched in 2011 that has amassed more than 650 million regular users. WeChat is the primary mobile messaging platform in China, benefiting from—and even driving—China's smartphone boom. WeChat has been described[36] as "one app to rule them all." Without WeChat a cell phone in China loses much of its utility. The WeChat app effectively has made the contact book redundant. Most users check the application at least ten times a day. But WeChat is about far more than chat. Chinese consumers use it[37] for a much wider range of services than their peers in the West (who use Apple's iMessage, Facebook's Messenger, or WhatsApp). The power of Tencent's ability to innovate was demonstrated most dramatically in 2014 with WeChat's Lunar New Year "red packet" *(hong bao)* campaign.

In just two days, WeChat users sent out more than 20 million virtual envelopes[38] of cash. Jack even compared the psychological impact of WeChat's campaign on Alibaba to Pearl Harbor. Alibaba fought back in 2015 but despite doling out $100 million in cash-and-coupon promotions, it was able to rack up only a quarter of the red packets sent by WeChat users.

WeChat exposed a critical gap in Alibaba's armory that it tried to close with its own mobile social app, Laiwang. Throwing everything it could at promoting Laiwang, Alibaba even required every employee to sign up one hundred users in order to qualify for their annual bonus. But Laiwang launched two years after WeChat. By then it had already lost the battle. Today even Alibaba's senior executives use WeChat, resorting to Laiwang only for official communications with colleagues.

Alibaba is spending billions of dollars on investments, acquisitions, and marketing to shore up its mobile strategy, from investing in its YunOS,[39] to buying stakes in Sina Weibo,[40] the Twitter-like service, and Meizu, a smartphone manufacturer, to acquiring UCWeb, China's leading mobile browser company,[41] and AutoNavi, a leading online mapping company to boost Alibaba's position in location-based services. Alibaba has already shifted a lot of its core business to mobile. Half of all purchases made on Alibaba's websites are made on mobile devices. But Alipay, the leading online payment provider in China, is Alibaba's most important asset in its rivalry with Tencent to tackle the next frontier: the mobile wallet.

Control the wallet, the thinking goes, and you control the battlefield for a vast array of new opportunities beyond e-commerce, with financial services being the most lucrative. Alibaba's runaway success with the Yu'e Bao (meaning "leftover treasure") mutual fund is one example. But online banking is another. Alibaba is actively pushing MYbank. Tencent is responding with WeBank, which has already started to issue consumer loans[42] within fifteen minutes to individuals over their mobile phones, in amounts ranging from twenty thousand to three hundred thousand yuan (from $3,100 to $31,000).

Other fronts are also opening up in the Alibaba versus Tencent conflict, including proxy wars between firms backed by the two companies. In 2014, the contest over Uber-like ride-booking apps became what one analyst described as "the first battle in the world war of the Internet." Alibaba backed a company called Kuaidi Dache[43] while Tencent backed its rival, Didi Dache[44] in a conflict that raged out of control with $300 million poured in to fund tips and marketing subsidies. The battle became so intense that Kuaidi even offered taxi drivers a free case of beer for referring fellow drivers. As the red ink flowed on both sides, a truce was called in early 2015 when the two transportation companies merged in a $6 billion transaction to form Didi Kuaidi, although they retained the two separate operating units. With a $16 billion valuation and $3 billion in new capital, the new entity took on Uber, which had thrown its lot in with Baidu.[45] The "taxi wars" have even taken on international proportions, as Alibaba, Tencent, and Didi Kuadi have all invested in Lyft, Uber's principal U.S.-based competitor.

In 2015, Alibaba and Tencent also decided to combine two other proxies, Groupon-style companies Meituan and Dianping, in a $15 billion merger that some saw as also directed at Baidu and Nuomi, its proxy. Baidu also lacks a meaningful presence in payment, in contrast with the dominance of Alipay and Tenpay.

Alibaba and Tencent are so powerful today that the talk of the "Big Three" (with Baidu) is beginning to shift to talk of a "Big Two." But if the trend of Alibaba and Tencent combining forces to create dominant proxies continues, there is a risk that consumers would be alarmed if subsidies are withdrawn or fees increased for popular services like booking rides or ordering food, prompting intervention by the Chinese government to restrict their market power.

No doubt mindful of the risks, since the SAIC incident, Alibaba appears to be trimming its sails ever closer to the prevailing government winds. In September 2015, Alibaba elevated its Beijing office to become its "second headquarters" along with Hangzhou. The symbolism of a powerful company in southern China announcing a new "coheadquarters" in Beijing is obvious, although the city is much more than just a political center—it is an essential business hub as well.[46] There are also practical reasons for the move. Alibaba describes adding Beijing to Hangzhou as its "twin hub" a strategy to sharpen its edge in northern provinces in the face of increasing competition: By the end of 2015, JD.com had surpassed Tmall by some estimates to become the leading e-commerce player in Beijing.

Upgrading its office in Beijing is important for recruitment, too. Already home to over nine thousand employees, Beijing has a deeper pool of prospective talent for the company to draw on. The capital is home to some of the country's most prestigious universities and about one million students. In the competition for top talent, offering the ability to work in Beijing reduces the risk of losing candidates who prefer not to move to Hangzhou,[47] which by comparison is a much smaller, provincial city.

Yet on Singles' Day 2015, there were signs, too, that Alibaba is stepping up its efforts to cultivate government support. Hours before the launch of Singles' Day, Alibaba reported that Chinese Premier Li Keqiang's office had contacted Jack "congratulating and encouraging the creation and achievement of the 11/11 event." As the day began inside the Water Cube, the upper-right section of the screen that was recording transactions on Tmall was reserved for a map and a data feed displaying the purchases in countries like Belarus and Kazakhstan, two of sixty-four countries and regions along the "One Belt, One Road" (OBOR[48]), also known as the "Belt and Road" initiative, a centerpiece of President Xi Jinping's foreign and economic policy.

Whatever the risks, Jack professes confidence in Alibaba's future. While the government can play a role in stimulating exports and boosting investment in the economy, he stated, "Consumption is not done by government—it's done by entrepreneurship and the market economy. So, we have a great opportunity. Now it's our turn, not the government's turn."

Alibaba is going all out to grab the opportunity available to the private sector. In recent years, Alibaba's deal making has been so frenzied that one journalist friend in Beijing complained to me that he had little time to cover anyone else and had spent many an evening or weekend writing up the company's latest conquest. Covering Alibaba is complicated because the deals often involve a web of relationships, including those linked to Jack's own private equity fund, Yunfeng Capital.

Yunfeng: Billionaire's Boys Club

Yunfeng is a private equity company in which Jack holds an approximate 40 percent stake and serves as a partner.[49] Yunfeng[50] was launched in 2010 by Jack and cofounder David Yu[51] and others.[52] It is a sort of "billionaire's boys club," something that the fund promotes as a core strength, calling itself the "only private equity fund launched by successful entrepreneurs and industry luminaries." To those who criticize deal making between Alibaba and Yunfeng, Yunfeng is at pains to point out that Jack plays no role in the investment decisions of its various funds. Alibaba emphasizes that Jack will forgo any gains made from his involvement in Yunfeng.

The fact that most of the billionaires involved in Yunfeng have roots in Zhejiang or Shanghai is instructive. Just like the "cluster cities" in Alibaba's home turf, these entrepreneurs have a deep-seated tendency to club together. Now "investment clusters" are emerging in China's New Economy, too, with Alibaba the most prominent of all.

The company can make the case that when buying Yunfeng-invested companies[53] Alibaba is investing in companies that Jack already knows, making the fund a form of advance due diligence.

Yet each new deal struck between Alibaba and Yunfeng-related companies introduces further complexity,[54] potentially obscuring the true nature of Alibaba's relationships with the outside business world.

Is this the way Alibaba will maintain its competitive edge and innovative capacity? If transactions between Alibaba and Yunfeng-invested companies are not carefully explained, and the valuations clearly justified, public investors in Alibaba might not be fully aware of the hidden risks involved. This concern, amid some indications of tension between Yunfeng and Alibaba's in-house M&A team, appeared to have prompted Jack to relinquish his role as an executive[55] in Yunfeng, maintaining only a passive interest as an investor[56] in the fund.

During its IPO road show Alibaba emphasized three central growth drivers for the future: cloud computing/Big Data; expansion into rural markets; and globalization/cross-border trade.

Three Core Drivers

Cloud computing is an obvious direction for Alibaba. Investors in Amazon value highly the "virtual" revenue streams of its Amazon Web Services business. Although for Alibaba cloud services represent only 3 percent of revenues today, it is investing over $1 billion to expand them. Alibaba also talks often about the shift from the information technology era to a data technology era, "from IT to DT." Alibaba looks to "DT" to help toward another favorite buzzword for the company: "C2B," or "consumer-to-business." This is the idea that DT, including Big Data, can help Chinese manufacturers improve communication throughout the supply chain to predict demand, potentially eliminating inventory. By exploiting the information flowing across Alibaba's e-commerce, logistics, and finance businesses—for example predicting consumer trends and investment opportunities—the company hopes to leverage the "iron triangle" to even greater effect. Aliyun, Alibaba's cloud computing business, operates data centers in Beijing, Hangzhou, Qingdao, Shenzhen, Hong Kong, and Silicon Valley as well as a newly established international hub in Singapore. The company plans, according to its president, Simon Hu, "to overtake Amazon in four years, whether in terms of customers, technology, or worldwide scale."

In rural markets, Alibaba hopes to unlock new tiers of consumers and merchants. China is home to more than 700 million rural residents, but only one-quarter are online. As Internet and mobile penetration increases, Alibaba is opening up kiosk-like service centers in rural areas, committing over $1.6 billion to the effort.

The first pilot county project for Alibaba's "Rural Taobao" initiative is Tonglu, the same county where Jack's U.S. adventure began, and the birthplace of the country's major private courier companies. Alibaba's own research arm, AliResearch, predicts that rural online shopping will reach 460 billion yuan ($72 billion) by the end of 2016.

Cracking this market is not easy, since it's complicated by poor logistics and the lower levels of education of rural residents.

Former Alibaba.com CEO David Wei believes that for the group to "go rural" is more critical than for it to "go global." "If they don't get into India, Alibaba is still Alibaba. But if they miss the countryside in China, home to six hundred to seven hundred million people, then another Alibaba could emerge." Alibaba's rival JD.com has launched its own rural initiative—"Wildfire of a Thousand Counties"—and its core products such as washing machines and refrigerators are among the most craved items by countryside dwellers.

In any case, Alibaba has little choice but to "go rural." China's State Council has unveiled a major new initiative to promote e-commerce in the countryside—echoed by Premier Li Keqiang's "Internet +"

vision—and after the SAIC debacle, Alibaba can't afford to be seen as unsupportive. In July 2015, Jack led a delegation of Alibaba executives to Yan'an in Shaanxi Province. This rural location has tremendous significance in China as it lies near the end of the route of the Long March,[57] and served as a key base from 1936 to 1948 for the Communist Revolution. Jack's delegation included over thirty senior Alibaba executives including Polo Shao (Shao Xiaofeng), a former criminal investigator who is senior vice president and director for the Office of the Chairman at Alibaba Group and is also believed to serve as secretary of the Communist Party committee of the company.

In discussions with local Communist Party secretary and government officials, the delegation explored ways Alibaba could help promote economic development in the area, from establishing data centers to offering loans to local entrepreneurs to promoting the sale of locally grown apples. But Jack also used the visit to attend a lecture given by local Communist Party officials, after which he said that he just wanted to "come and take a look. The conditions were extremely hard in Yan'an at that time," and that he was keen to learn how "the Communist Party could stick to revolution romanticism and revolution heroism under such conditions."

Such speeches are of little help in promoting the third of Alibaba's core drivers, expanding in overseas markets. Yet in doing so Alibaba is also in step with the Chinese government's call to "go global," encouraging Chinese companies to go beyond simply exporting to extending their operations and influence overseas. This is nothing new for Alibaba, a company that started out with an international orientation in 1999. But with the success of Taobao starting a decade ago, Alibaba's focus turned inward. In 2010, the profile of international markets started to increase again with the launch of AliExpress, connecting sellers in China with consumers overseas. At first Alibaba expected the United States to be AliExpress's key market. But Alibaba discov-

Jack Magic comes to 10 Downing Street. Jack *(left)* regales a crowd, including British prime minister David Cameron *(second from left)* and the author at a reception at 10 Downing Street in London on October 19, 2015, shortly after Jack was named a member of the UK's Business Advisory Group. *10 Downing Street*

ered that America was a market with sophisticated players, both online and offline. After the early disappointments, then-Alibaba.com CEO David Wei instructed his team to look at countries with the lowest efficiency in their retail sector.

Without AliExpress even opening offices there, but with Russian and Portuguese language capabilities added to the AliExpress website, Russia and Brazil became early success stories. Demand from Alibaba's customers in Brazil at one point exceeded over three hundred thousand packages a day, before a slowing economy and the weakening real hit the company's business there. Demand in Russia, especially for clothing and consumer electronics, was so strong that AliExpress reportedly even broke the Russian postal service, leading to the dismissal of its boss. Today Russia accounts for a fifth of AliExpress's sales.

In 2015, Alibaba appointed former top Goldman Sachs executive J. Michael Evans as its new president, charged with leading international development efforts. These include its growing presence in Western Europe, where Alibaba aims to entice brands to target Chinese consumers through its websites.[58] At an event hosted in October 2015 by British prime minister David Cameron at 10 Downing Street in London, Jack was named as one of Cameron's business advisers.

Alibaba announced it was upgrading its office in the city to become its European headquarters, headed by Amee Chande, a former Walmart executive. Alibaba is also opening a network of "business embassies" in France, Germany, and Italy. Paris is headed by Sébastien Badault, formerly of Amazon and Google; Milan is headed by Rodrigo Cipriani Foresio, who previously worked at Buon Italia, an online food store; and Munich is headed by Terry von Bibra, a former executive with leading German retailer Karstadt. Alibaba's growing presence in Europe brings it closer to the headquarters of many of the brands most coveted by Chinese consumers. Any success stories it can generate—bringing European brands to the fast-growing consumer market in China—will no doubt also be an opportunity to strengthen its hand with its most vociferous critics, like Kering, the parent company of Yves Saint Laurent and Gucci.

The United States is also a key market for Alibaba's overseas efforts, mostly as the focus of its international investments. Alibaba has poured hundreds of millions of dollars into high-profile companies such as Lyft, Snapchat, Zulily, and a range of smaller players.[59] But these investments are more focused on absorbing new technologies or know-how to be deployed in China than they are a concerted effort to break into the U.S. market. The one Alibaba effort that did explicitly target the U.S. market, 11Main.com, was a conspicuous failure.[60] Speculation by some analysts that Alibaba would make a bold move in America, including an acquisition of eBay or Yahoo, has so far proved off the mark. Instead Alibaba's emphasis remains firmly on developing cross-border trade.

Alibaba has been actively ramping up its own presence in the

States, setting up a string of four offices along the length of the West Coast: an office just off Market Street in San Francisco, which houses Alibaba's international corporate communications team, headed by former PepsiCo executive Jim Wilkinson;[61] a new Alibaba Group office in San Mateo, California, where Michael Evans is based; an office in Pasadena, California, which serves as the U.S. home of Alibaba Pictures; and a small presence in downtown Seattle, just one block away from the U.S. Bank building, where Jack first logged on to the Internet back in 1995. In 2016 Alibaba is rolling out new offices in New York City, bringer it closer to U.S. brands, retailers, and advertisers, as well as in Washington, D.C., beefing up its lobbying and communications capacity, headed by Eric Pelletier, former GE executive and White House staff member.[62]

Despite its growing physical presence in the country, during a visit to New York and Chicago in the summer of 2015, Jack dismissed talk of any "Alibaba invasion" of America. He said he was often asked, " 'When are you coming to invade America? When are you going to compete with Amazon? When are you going to compete with eBay?' Well, I would say, we show great respect for eBay and Amazon, but I think the opportunity and the strategy for us is helping small business in America go to China, sell their products to China."

On that same trip to the United States, Jack also discussed the strain of running a public company. He complained that his life after the IPO was more difficult than before, and that "[i]f I had another life, I would keep my company private." Some in the audience in New York expressed surprise that Jack would voice regrets about listing so soon after Alibaba's blockbuster IPO. But this contrarian stance is vintage Jack.

From Philosopher to Philanthropist

Jack already has a reputation as China's philosopher CEO, and increasingly he is seen as a philanthropist and environmentalist, too. Six months ahead of the 2014 IPO, Jack and Joe together pledged 2 percent of Alibaba Group—from their personal holdings—to create a new Alibaba philanthropic trust.[63] The pledge was made in the form of stock options with an exercise price of $25 (some $43 below the initial offering price), creating overnight what became one of the largest philanthropic organizations in China. Jack also committed to endow the trust with more of his personal fortune in the future.[64]

The trust will focus primarily on China's environment and health care—two issues about which Jack has become increasingly vocal in recent years. China's rapid industrialization and urbanization have wrought havoc on the country's environment and people's health. At a conference for entrepreneurs in 2013,[65] Jack delivered a call to arms, his message distilled in an article later published by the *Harvard Business Review*: "Cancer—a rare word in conversation thirty years ago—is now an everyday topic." Jack often talks of the growing incidence of cancer among his employees, friends, and their families,[66] including in his Q&A session with President Obama. "Without a healthy environment on this earth, no matter how much money you make, no matter how wonderful you are, you will have a bad disaster."

With his activism, and the symbolism of the lake he built on the Wetlands headquarter campus, Jack is demonstrating that "[s]omebody has to do something. . . . Our job is to wake people up."

Jack isn't shy about criticizing the old industrial model: "Chinese people used to feel a sense of pride for being the world's factory. Now everyone realizes what it costs to be that factory. Our water has become undrinkable, our food inedible, our milk poisonous, and worst of all, the air in our cities is so polluted that we often cannot see the sun."

In his article, Jack also took aim at the government's inaction toward the environmental crisis: "Before, no matter how hard we appealed to the privileged and the powerful for attention on water, air, and food security issues, nobody wanted to listen. The privileged still got their privileged water and privileged food.[67] But everyone breathes the same air. It doesn't matter how wealthy or powerful you are, if you can't enjoy the sunshine, you can't be truly happy." Like many of the other superrich in China, Jack bought himself a pristine patch of paradise abroad. In 2015, with the help of the Nature Conservancy, an environmental foundation founded by a former Goldman Sachs banker, Jack purchased the $23 million Brandon Park estate in New York State's Adirondack Mountains; the estate is part of a holding that once belonged to the Rockefeller family. In his interview with Jack at APEC in Manila in November 2015, President Obama hailed Jack for taking an interest in the environment: "I know that in addition to the work that you have been doing with nonprofits recently, you have also been in conversations with Bill Gates about the potential of really turbo-charging investment in research and development around clean energy." Shortly afterward, on the eve of COP21, the UN conference on climate change in Paris, Jack announced his support for the "Breakthrough Energy Coalition." Led by Bill Gates, Jack was joined by his investor Masayoshi Son and former sparring partner Meg Whitman, along with Mark Zuckerberg and Jeff Bezos, among the twenty-eight investors pledging to help fund research into new technologies to reduce carbon emissions.

Health and Happiness

Jack's focus on the environment and people's health goes beyond a sense of corporate responsibility: Alibaba has business aspirations, too. In 2014 the company invested in CITIC 21CN, a Hong Kong–listed, pharmaceutical data business. As it has since been renamed, Alibaba Health seeks to profit from the inefficiencies of state-owned providers in the sector, including making appointment bookings easier for patients, as well as making it easier for doctors, clinics, and consumers to access information about and to order pharmaceuticals. The focus on health care is one of two long-term investment areas that Jack summarizes as the "2 H's": health and happiness.[68]

In addition to making people healthier, he aims to make "young people enjoy their lives, to be optimistic in the future. All the heroes in Chinese movies die. In American movies, all the heroes survive. I ask people, 'If all the heroes die, who wants to be a hero?'" Why the interest, for an e-commerce company, in entertainment?

True to his roots as a teacher, Jack often talks about taking care of the needs of the younger generation. In an interview with Charlie Rose he shared his view that, in China, "lots of young people lose hope, lose vision, and start to complain." Alibaba is increasingly active in areas that Jack hopes could provide the answer: sports and entertainment.

In November 2015, Alibaba sponsored the first regular-season U.S. college Pac-12 Conference basketball game in Shanghai, between the University of Washington Huskies and the University of Texas Longhorns, and announced it would host a game between Stanford and Harvard universities a year later. Alibaba has also started to buy sports teams. In June 2014, he made a $200 million investment in the Guangzhou Evergrande soccer team, a deal negotiated, the team's owner[69] later revealed, while Jack was drunk. Jack justified the investment: "I think not understanding soccer doesn't matter. . . . I also didn't understand retail, e-commerce, or the Internet, but that didn't stop me from doing it anyway." He said he was not investing in soccer, he was "investing in entertainment."

Alibaba is one of China's leading investors in film, television, and online video. The company's biggest outlay in traditional media so far is its $800 million investment in a Hong Kong–based film and TV studio[70] that it rebranded Alibaba Pictures. In 2014 Alibaba tapped Zhang Qiang, then vice president of the powerful, state-owned distributor China Film Group, to head up its entertainment business in China. Alibaba is also jointly invested[71] with Tencent in Huayi Brothers, a Beijing-based film and TV studio and acquired cinema ticketing company Yulekei. But Alibaba has made its biggest splash in Internet-based media, including investing in and then[72] acquiring Youku Tudou, a company founded by former Sohu executive Victor Koo.[73] More than 430 million people in China regularly watch videos online, mostly on their mobile devices, with some shows reaching larger audiences than the country's state-owned terrestrial broadcasters. The market used to be rife with pirated content, but today major online video platforms like Youku are pushing hard to become the local equivalent of Netflix, featuring programs such as popular Korean dramas or hit shows from the United States like *2 Broke Girls*. The $4 billion online video market—generated mostly by advertising, but also some subscription revenue—is still a challenging place to make money given the cost of licensing content. Youku Tudou never made a profit. Some investors questioned the impact of the acquisition on Alibaba's cost structure, but Alibaba justifies it to compete with rival platforms from Tencent, Baidu, and others. Also Alibaba had already announced plans to launch its own streaming service, "Tmall Box Office," or "TBO," in conjunction with cable TV player Wasu Media, in which Jack had already invested personally. The idea behind TBO is to be as disruptive a player on TV production in China as Netflix is in the United States. Already close to half a billion people[74] watch videos online on sites controlled by Alibaba, Baidu, Tencent, and others. Yet in another sign of the limits imposed on entrepreneurs when they encroach on its turf, in November 2015, the government imposed new restrictions on the amount of imported content—previously capped at 30 percent—they can offer on their platforms. In an effort to promote more homegrown content, Alibaba is also looking to explore new ways to finance shows, including harnessing crowdfunding through a company it acquired called Yulebao.

With its newly established U.S. base in Pasadena, California, Alibaba Pictures has big ambitions. Jack has said that he wants nothing less than to make Alibaba "the biggest entertainment company in the world." Leading the charge for Alibaba's overseas investments in entertainment is Zhang Wei, appointed in 2015 as president of Alibaba Pictures. An alumna of Harvard Business School, Zhang once hosted a business show on China Central Television (CCTV) and worked as a media executive with CNBC and Star Television before joining Alibaba in 2008. Alibaba Pictures has yet to release its own film but it has already financed movies like *Mission: Impossible—Rogue Nation*. In an interview with *The Hollywood Reporter*, Zhang revealed the initial resistance from studios to working with Alibaba: "The first thing everyone wonders is what an e-commerce company can actually do for them. One of the biggest disconnects the studios face is that they never really know, in a detailed, comprehensive way, who is coming to see their movies. Even the filmmakers would probably like to know this. How old are they? Where are they from? Do they have kids? What are their other interests? What's their living situation? What type of people are they? We talk about demand-driven entertainment. Bringing the Internet deeper into the entertainment business is the best way to solve that puzzle." Zhang added that Alibaba can utilize Alipay, used by many people to buy cinema tickets online, to gain a greater understanding of moviegoers: "The movie audience is much younger in China, as going to the movies is a lifestyle change. The generation before went to karaoke. Now they go to the movies as a primary source of entertainment."

More tangibly, merchandising is an area that ties together

e-commerce and entertainment. Zhang explains, "In the U.S., theatrical makes up maybe 30 to 40 percent of revenue. In China, theatrical is the majority by far. There's so much value that has not been developed yet in the merchandising space." Zhang points to the *Mission: Impossible* tie-ins as an example, selecting qualified merchants to manufacture licensed goods: "We came up with about thirty products with Paramount's merchandising team, sending them designs and samples throughout the whole process. We showed many directly to Tom Cruise as well, to make sure he was OK with how they represented the *Mission: Impossible* brand. This is our value: connecting both parties. In the past, how does a backpack maker in Zhejiang Province connect with Paramount and Tom Cruise in such an efficient and reliable way? It was just impossible."

Inevitably, given Jack's big plans in entertainment, Jack has been asked whether Alibaba intends to buy a Hollywood studio. Viacom's Paramount Pictures is one rumored target, which as the studio behind *Forrest Gump* might give Jack just the perch—or bench—that he craves in Hollywood. So far Alibaba has denied its intentions to buy a studio outright: "Well, I don't think they want to sell. It's better we partner. You can never buy everything in the world."

Yet barely a day goes by when Alibaba, or Jack himself, is not listed as a potential buyer of a company, somewhere in the world. In December 2015, Alibaba confirmed it was purchasing the *South China Morning Post* (*SCMP*), the main English daily newspaper in Hong Kong. Some saw the purchase of the 112-year-old publication as a means for Jack to burnish his credentials as a mogul. After all, Amazon founder Jeff Bezos had personally acquired the *Washington Post* two years earlier. Was Jack simply following suit?

Others saw signs of something deeper: that Jack was buying the paper to curry favor with Beijing. Almost two decades after the United Kingdom handed back the territory in 1997, the Chinese government is grappling with a yawning political and social divide[75] in Hong Kong. In 2014 the territory was brought to a standstill by the Occupy Central movement (also known as the Umbrella Revolution), a student-led movement protesting a lack of democracy and other freedoms. Although the crisis ended peacefully, the underlying tensions that fueled it remain ever present. The *SCMP* had reported extensively on the protests. Critics speculated that Jack had offered his services to bring the paper to heel—or even that he had no choice but to comply with a directive from Beijing to do so.

Jack dismissed the conspiracy theories: "I have always encountered speculation from other people. If I had to bother about what other people speculated about, how would I get anything done?" He vowed to respect the editorial independence of the newspaper: "They have an independent platform and they can have their own beliefs."

For the newspaper, the backing of a well-funded and influential business group on the mainland has obvious attractions. Like many print publications, the subscription-based business model of the *SCMP*, although still profitable, has suffered in the face of free online content. In line with Alibaba's longtime commitment to offer services for free, Alibaba will remove the newspaper's subscription paywall, allowing wider distribution and unlocking new business opportunities. In a Q&A with the newspaper, executive vice chairman Joe Tsai explained, "Our vision for *SCMP* is to build a global readership. . . . Even though some say the newspaper industry is a sunset industry, we don't see it that way. We see it as an opportunity to use our technological expertise, and use our digital assets and know-how to distribute news in a way that has never been done before." In business terms, the downside for the purchase is relatively limited, and a turnaround could win Jack plaudits.

For Alibaba, the deal is not large in terms of money: They paid just over $200 million for the business. Yet given the intense scrutiny that it invites, the transaction is not without risks. In his Q&A Joe explained that if the *SCMP* can help the world understand China better, this will also be good for Alibaba—a company based in China but listed in the United States: "China is important; China is a rising economy. It is the second-largest economy in the world. People should learn more about China." Yet in comments that both revealed his frustration and emboldened those critical of the deal, he added, "The coverage about China should be balanced and fair. Today when I see mainstream Western news organizations cover China, they cover it through a very particular lens. It is through the lens that China is a communist state and everything kind of follows from that. A lot of journalists working with these Western media organizations may not agree with the system of governance in China and that taints their view of coverage. We see things differently; we believe things should be presented as they are. Present facts, tell the truth, and that is the principle that we are going to operate on."

Whatever Jack's motivations for the acquisition are, by becoming a newspaper proprietor in Hong Kong he is wading into deeper waters. Yet he has never shied away from challenges before. Jack's fame stems from the story of how a Chinese company somehow got the better of Silicon Valley, an East beats West tale worthy of a Jin Yong novel. His continued success, though, is becoming a story of South versus North—of a company with roots in the entrepreneurial heartland of southern China testing the limits imposed by the country's political masters in Beijing.

Since Xi Jinping became president of China in 2012, high-profile entrepreneurs have found themselves increasingly subject to scrutiny and sanction from the Chinese government. One high-profile real estate entrepreneur, Vantone Holdings's Feng Lun, even blogged—then later deleted—the following message: "A private tycoon once said, 'In the eyes of a government official, we are nothing but cockroaches.

If he wants to kill you, he kills you. If he wants to let you live, he lets you live.'" The temporary and still unexplained disappearance in December 2015 of Fosun chairman Guo Guangchang—once feted as a "Warren Buffet of China"—further illustrates those risks.

Jack is already the standard-bearer for China's consumer and entrepreneurial revolution. Now he is advancing on new fronts, such as finance and the media, that have long been dominated by the state.

Forged in the entrepreneurial crucible of Zhejiang and fueled by his faith in the transformative power of the Internet, Jack is the ultimate pragmatist. By demonstrating the power of technology to assist a government confronted with the rising expectations of its people for a better life—from the environment, education, and health care to continued access to economic opportunity—Jack aims to create the space for him to fulfill even greater ambitions.

One leading Chinese Internet entrepreneur put it to me like this: "Most people think of Alibaba as a story. It's not just a story, it's a strategy."

Acknowledgments

For my father, David Clark, and my partner, Robin Wang.

I am deeply grateful for the inspiration, encouragement, and friendship of Amy Tan, Lou DeMattei, and the whole team at Tandema.

I would like especially to thank Mei Yan, for her friendship and for working so tirelessly on this project throughout, and my former collaborators at Stanford University: Marguerite Gong Hancock, for encouraging me to write this book, and Professor Bill Miller, for his insights into what makes Silicon Valley tick.

Many thanks to our research assistant Chang Yu at Peking University, now completing her Ph.D. in Hong Kong for which I wish her the best of luck.

At BDA, Meiqin Fang was very generous with her time and guidance, along with Dawson Zhang. Thanks also to Van Liu and Shi Lei. I'm very grateful to Wilbur Zou, for his leadership at BDA, enabling me to devote myself to this project. My assistant Joyce Zhao has always helped me keep on track, no matter where in the world I was writing.

The maps were designed by the Beijing-based artist Xiaowei Cui.

My sincere thanks to those who provided invaluable assistance but who preferred to remain anonymous. I'm very grateful to David

Morley, for giving his time so generously to share the Morley-Ma family story and photos; Heather Killen, for her recollections and the photos from Yahoo China's early days; Alan Tien for his insights into the eBay/PayPal story in China; and my friend and fellow monkey Roger Nyhus, for his warm introduction to the Seattle community.

I'm grateful for the support of all the Alibaba pioneers and veterans who helped me along the way, for the support of Jennifer Kuperman and team in San Francisco, and for the generous time afforded by Joe Tsai and colleagues in Hangzhou.

Thanks to my sisters, Terri, Alison, and Katie, for their support; to my editor, Gabriella Doob, at HarperCollins; and to the team at Sandy Dijkstra Literary Agency.

In memory of my mother, Pamela Mary Clark; my mentor, Professor Henry S. Rowen, from Stanford University, who was cycling on campus until the day he passed away in November 2015 at age ninety; and Miles Frost, a young and talented entrepreneur I had only recently befriended before his own story was cut so tragically short, at age thirty-one.

Notes

Introduction

1. The firm "BDA" originated as BD Associates, the name derives from the first initials of my Chinese partner in the venture, Dr. Bohai Zhang, and my first name, Duncan. The chairman of Morgan Stanley Asia, Jack Wadsworth, and Theodore S. Liu, former head of the China investment banking team, were instrumental in the launch of my venture, by giving me a one-year retainer to set up shop in Beijing.
2. A disclosure, although I'm no longer a shareholder, under the "friends and family" program, Alibaba did allow me to purchase some shares in the Alibaba.com IPO in Hong Kong in 2007 and in the Alibaba Group IPO in New York in 2014.

Chapter One: The Iron Triangle

1. Some caution should be exercised in assessing the final volume, given that some goods might be returned for full refunds the next day by customers—mostly for legitimate reasons, such as being damaged in shipping or customers changing their minds—and the practice by some merchants on the platform of inflating their own sales by hiring third parties to boost their rankings (a phenomenon known as "brushing," which is discussed in Chapter 12).
2. Originating as Bachelors' Day in the early 1990s when single students launched an "anti–Valentine's Day," the date 11/11 was chosen to symbolize single people.
3. For Alibaba's "business-to-consumer" website www.tmall.com.
4. A term copyrighted by Alibaba in 2012 to distinguish its own festival from

the earlier common name for the festival of "baresticks holiday" (*guanggun jie),* chosen for the resemblance of 11/11 to two pairs of chopsticks.

5. In a TV interview with Emily Chang of Bloomberg West on Bloomberg TV.
6. The phrase echoes the Chinese saying "*wanneng de shangdi,*" which describes an omnipotent God.
7. The original meaning of the character "*tao*"—to pan for gold—had fallen into obscurity.
8. Tmall carries some inventory in selected categories such as Tmall Supermarket.
9. True to Jack's passion for Chinese tradition, the name is an ancient term for servants.
10. The unfortunately named in English *ali wangwang.*
11. First launched in 2008 as Taobao Mall, it later became tmall.com.
12. Tmall also charges an annual fee.
13. In fiscal year 2015.
14. Offering a limited selection of items, mostly at entry-level prices.
15. Groupon itself entered China in 2011, but quickly ran into trouble and failed to gain traction.
16. Translates as "Super Good Deal."
17. Twenty-eight square feet per capita in the United States, 16 in Germany, and 14 in the United Kingdom.
18. In 2009.
19. The list details marketplaces that reportedly "engage in and facilitate substantial copyright piracy and trademark counterfeiting."
20. Including hiring its former general counsel.
21. Founded in Shenzhen in 1993 and sometimes described as the "FedEx of China."
22. The word *cainiao* originates in Taiwan and literally means "green bird," but it also has a military connotation, meaning "rookie soldier."
23. Via 1,800 distribution centers and 97,000 delivery stations.
24. The company itself is registered in Shenzhen.
25. Shen, a close friend of Jack Ma, built his fortune in the China Yintai Group, a mining, retail, and real estate concern that includes the sixty-six-story Yin Tai tower in Beijing, which houses the city's Park Hyatt hotel, where Shen has regularly hosted Jack for social events. Shen also controls a Hong Kong–listed retail subsidiary called InTime Department Stores, in which Alibaba has invested $700 million.

26. A local network of couriers in first- to third-tier cities, supplemented in less dense, and underdeveloped areas by more than 20,000 "self pickup" stations.
27. A nationwide logistics network.
28. *JD* is short for Jing Dong, with *Jing* the word for "capital," as in *Beijing*, and *Dong* the character for "East," but also derived from the given name of the company's founder, Liu Qiangdong, known in English as Richard Liu. Liu founded his company in 1998 as a disk drive company, then in 2004 launched a B2C website called 360buy.com, which he later rebranded JD.com.
29. 1.5 million square meters in total compared to Cainiao's one million.
30. For orders placed by 11 A.M. and next day for orders placed by 11 P.M.
31. $778 billion in the year to June 2014.
32. A story explored in Chapter 11.
33. In 2014 it generated 11 billion yuan ($1.8 billion) in revenues.
34. Managed by brokerage Tian Hong Asset Management, which Ant Financial had recently purchased.
35. Via Ant Financial.
36. In 2013, Jack Ma teamed up with two other Mas (although they are unrelated): Pony Ma, Jack's friend and CEO of Alibaba rival Tencent, and Ma Mingzhe, the chairman of Ping An Insurance. Together they launched China's first and largest online insurer, Zhong An, signing up more than 150 million customers within a year.
37. The system checks the faces of prospective customers against police databases, although this has led to delays in the service's rollout due to concerns by regulators.

Chapter Two: Jack Magic

1. The Club Med–owning chairman of Fosun Group.
2. In a conversation with the journalist Charlie Rose.
3. Jan "Jens" Van der Ven.
4. A stand-up comedian in Shanghai reportedly sources some of his material from Jack's speeches.
5. Rivals like Baidu rely more on telesales.
6. To the *China Daily,* May 11, 2015.
7. Selected examples include: Chen Qi is the founder of juandou.com and mogujie.com, was a product manager at Taobao, and worked on UED

(user experience design). Among Mogujie's four founding team members, three came from Taobao. Apart from Chen Qi, the other two are Mogujie's CTO Yue Xuqiang and CMO Li Yanzhu. Chen Xi is the founder of LavaRadio, an ambient music radio station, worked at Yahoo, and left about a year after Alibaba acquired Yahoo China. Cheng Wei is the cofounder of Didi Dache and worked at Taobao's B2C unit. Gu Dayu is the founder and CEO of www.bong.cn, a smart sports bracelet, and worked at Alibaba's International User Experience unit, Laiwang, and YunOS. Jiang Haibing was Alipay's second employee and is the founder of mabole.com, an online merchant recruitment service company. Lai Jie is the founder of Treebear, a commercial Wi-Fi provider. Alibaba led Treebear's Series A round in August 2014, taking a 10 percent stake. Lan Lan is the founder and CEO of 1kf.com, an O2O service platform to find physical therapists and masseurs, which was launched in March 2015. Li Liheng is the cofounder and CEO of chemayi.com, a localized auto/life-service platform. Li worked at Alibaba for eight years starting in 2002. The other two cofounders of chemayi.com are also Alibaba veterans, Lin Yan and Fan Qinglin. Li Zhiguo, the main developer of TrustPass, left Alibaba in 2004 to found koubei.com, a classified listing and community website. Alibaba invested in koubei.com in October 2006 and acquired the company in 2008, merging it into Yahoo China. Li, whose nickname was "Bug Li" at Alibaba, moved to AliCloud in February 2009 before quitting Alibaba again in September 2010. He then became an angel investor and is now CEO of wacai.com, an online financial management platform. Toto Sun (Sun Tongyu) is the former president of Taobao and cofounder of www.hezi.com, a virtual entertainment and education community for kids ages six to fourteen and their parents. Wang Hao is the cofounder and CEO of xiaom.com, a music streaming site. Xiaom was acquired by Alibaba in 2013, becoming part of AliMusic. David Wei (Wei Zhe) is the cofounder of Vision Knight Capital. Xu Ji is the founder and CEO of mangguoyisheng.com, an app for community doctors. Xu was Alibaba's seventy-second employee. Wu Zhixiang is the founder and CEO of ly.com, a travel-booking website. Wu worked in Alibaba's sales department for a year from 2001 to 2002. Ye Jinwu is the founder and CEO of yingyinglicai.com, a financial product purchasing app and worked at Alipay. Zhang Dou is the founder and CEO of yinyuetai.com. Zhang Hang is the cofounder of Didi Dache. Zhang Lianglun is the cofounder and CEO of mizhe.com and founder of BeiBei, a maternal and infant product e-commerce site. Zhou Kaicheng is the cofounder and CEO of Xingkong Qinang (www.xkqh.com), an O2O piano class service platform. David Wei's Vision Knight Capital participated in its Series C funding in October 2015. Zhu Ning is the founder of youzan.com, a platform to open WeChat stores, cofounder of guang.com, an e-commerce site (already closed), cofounder of cafebeta.com, and worked as chief product designer at Alipay.

8. itjuzi.com.

Chapter Three: From Student to Teacher

1. A "*baozhang*."
2. The work involves five elements: *taolu* (solo hand and weapons routines/forms), *neigong* and *qigong* (breathing, movement and awareness exercises, and meditation), *tuishou* (response drills), and *sanshou* (self-defense techniques).
3. "Benke."
4. "Zhuanke."
5. Although he probably coined the phrase much earlier.

Chapter Four: Hope and Coming to America

1. Classified as *getihu* (literally "single body units") or individual businesses, and *siying qiye*, or privately owned businesses.
2. Formerly named Lin'an, it was the capital of the Southern Song dynasty from 1138 to 1276. In the thirteenth century, when Europe was in the Dark Ages, Hangzhou is thought to have been the most populous city on earth, with more than one and a half million inhabitants. Marco Polo and famous Arab adventurer Ibn Battuta are both believed to have visited the city.
3. China Post only guaranteed delivery in three days, but exporters needed to get shipping forms to the port overnight. By taking the midnight train from Hangzhou, Nie delivered the forms in time, charging multiple exporters 100 yuan for each form but paying only once the 30 yuan needed for the train ticket.
4. Yunda, YTO, and ZTO.
5. As the Communist Party appointed both the senior bank officials and the senior executives of the SOEs, for better or worse there was no need for independent credit assessments and controls.

6. By the late 1990s Hong Kong and other overseas Chinese entrepreneurs had set up more than 50,000 factories in Guangdong Province, which has links to a diaspora of overseas Chinese numbering 20 million people. After Deng Xiaoping's southern tour, which established a number of special economic zones, including Shenzhen, the overseas Chinese, including many rich entrepreneurs, provided a ready supply of financing and export markets. Guangdong's location, adjacent to Hong Kong, and the world's busiest shipping routes gave it a further edge over Zhejiang.
7. Written by journalist Zhou Jishan.
8. According to a September 1995 article in *Hangzhou Daily.*

Chapter Five: China Is Coming On

1. One of Jack's early cards lists him as "marketing director."
2. Starting in the late 1980s, Dr. Walter Toki at the Stanford Linear Accelerator Center played an instrumental role, after he reached out to the Chinese-born American physicist and Nobel Prize laureate T. D. Lee about establishing an Internet connection with scientists in China.
3. Via a satellite uplink from an AT&T ground station at Point Reyes, California.
4. In its first edition.
5. Called the "Golden Dove Project."
6. John Nathan Hosteller, a Republican member of the House of Representatives from Indiana, and Democratic senator Bill Bradley of New Jersey.
7. The *Qianjiang Evening News.*
8. A sample listing from the site illustrates its simple nature: "Hydrofluoric acid with different concentrations packed in plastic drums of 25kgs" accompanied by the contact information for the Ningbo Material General Corporation.
9. Including a *Hangzhou Daily* article that appeared on October 18, 1996.

Chapter Six: Bubble and Birth

1. To *The Economist.*
2. CIECC had been established two years earlier to pursue "EDI" (Electronic Data Interchange) projects for MOFTEC.
3. She would later become chair, CEO, and Communist Party secretary of Chinese state-owned telecom manufacturer Putian. There she would actively promote China's own standard for 3G mobile telephony, called TD-SCDMA, which failed to gain market acceptance.

4. Jasmine Zhang from Yinghaiwei asserts that Jack chose the name because it sounded like Ariba.com, another high-profile e-commerce website at the time.
5. Both domain names were registered under Jack Ma's mother, Cui Wencai. On August 17, 1999, Cui transferred the ownership to Alibaba Ltd.
6. Alibaba.com was launched in April 1999, replacing the earlier alibaba-online.com and alibabaonline.com sites that had gone online in January. The company would later describe the site as a "trial" when unveiling an upgraded site at a formal launch ceremony the following October.
7. At China Pages, Jack had been joined by his wife, Cathy, Toto Sun (Sun Tongyu), Wu Yongming, James Sheng (Sheng Yifei), Ma Changwei, Lou Wensheng, and Simon Xie (Xie Shihuang), who had met Jack when working for Dife. Others from Hangzhou who had joined him in Beijing included Lucy Peng (Peng Lei, who quit her job as a teacher in Hangzhou when she married Toto Sun), Han Min, Jane Jiang (Jiang Fang), Trudy Dai (Dai Shan), and Zhou Yuehong.
8. For forty hours of access from ChinaNet.
9. Nearly all of the advertisers were technology firms, such as Intel, IBM, Compaq, Microsoft, Legend, and Founder.
10. Or "New Wave" (*xin lang* in Chinese).
11. Jack Hong, Benjamin Tsiang, and Hurst Lin. Sinanet had some users in Taiwan but struggled to make headway in China, and was blocked at times by the Chinese government.
12. From Dow Jones, Intel, and Morningside, an affiliate of the Hong Kong property developer Hang Lung run by Gerald Chen.
13. Only Raymond Lei had studied overseas, at Purdue University in Indiana, where he received a master's degree in computer science.
14. *Xiao Ao Jiang Hu* in Chinese.
15. According to Chen Xiaoping, a professor at the University of Washington in Seattle.
16. Cai Chongxin, or in Taiwanese romanization, Tsai Chung-Hsin.
17. His father, Dr. Paul Tsai, is the founder of the Tsar & Tsai Law Firm, whose origins in 1965 make it one of the oldest partnership law firms in Taiwan.
18. Alumni include the playwright Thornton Wilder (*Our Town*), the former CEO of Walt Disney Michael Eisner, the singer Huey Lewis, former White House press secretary Jay Carney, and most recently Song Andong, the first Chinese player drafted by the NHL. Joe is now a trustee of the school.

19. His ancestral home was Huzhou, near Hangzhou.
20. In 1996, Joe married Clara Wu, a Stanford- and Harvard-educated professional born to Taiwanese parents in Kansas.
21. Galeazzo Scarampi, chief executive of Investor Asia Ltd.
22. As one shareholder, Raymond Lei, had left the company the eighteenth slot was available for him. Eighteen is a lucky number in China, but Joe decided to leave it vacant, and he became employee No. 19. "Nineteen has always been my lucky number. My lacrosse jersey number was nineteen. I was born on January nineteenth."
23. A Cayman Islands company registered in June 1999 called Alibaba Group Holding Limited.
24. Joel Kellman at Fenwick & West helped set up some meetings.
25. The name "8848" was chosen because it represented the height of Mount Everest in meters.
26. Touting the first foreign-held license to operate Internet services in China.
27. He also wrote the seminal 2004 article, which later became a book, about the "long tail" as it applies to retailing online.
28. After receiving an MBA from Wharton, Yip had built up and sold a systems integration company in the United States before moving to Hong Kong and joining CIC.
29. These had been registered by a Hong Kong–born, UCLA computer science graduate named James Chu.
30. Despite Xinhua's backing, his site china.com was repeatedly blocked in China by rival agencies.

Chapter Seven: Backers: Goldman and SoftBank

1. Ted and I took turns writing the "Beijing Byte" column about tech developments in China, taking over from Kristie Lu Stout, who is now an anchor at CNN International in Hong Kong.
2. The initial wave of foreign employees included a number of young China adventurers. One of the earliest, employee number forty, was David Oliver, who grew up on a farm on the South Island of New Zealand and had been working in China for a few years. After he saw Jack give a speech in Singapore in March 1999, David was so impressed that he flew to Hangzhou, and by September he had started working for Alibaba. He joined the company at a very low salary by Hong Kong standards—$20,000 a year—so low that he

was later unable to afford to exercise his healthy allocation of options, priced at a mere five cents. Belgian Jan Van der Ven joined the company after building a number of trade websites in Shenzhen before moving to the factory town of Dongguan, Guangdong. Another early recruit, number fifty-two, was Brian Wong. Originally from Palo Alto, California, Brian is now a vice president in the chairman's office, constantly at Jack's side on his frequent trips overseas. Alibaba then added a tier of MBAs including Todd Daum and Sanjay Varma. Alibaba organizes occasional gatherings of the earliest employees, issuing hats displaying the order of precedence of joining. (Jack is #001.)

3. Jack's wife, Cathy, played an instrumental role in the international operations of the company for a number of years. Annie Xu, a UC Berkeley grad from Shanghai, has worked as general manager for Alibaba in the United States since May 2000. Abir Oreibi oversaw the company's European business for eight years from 2000.
4. "Pre-money."
5. Involving a "participated preferred feature."
6. She was a member of the bank's principal investment area (PIA) team launched in Asia by Henry Cornell. In addition to large investments in China such as in Ping An Insurance in 1994, after the bank had made some successful tech investments in Silicon Valley, Shirley was involved in placing small bets on tech companies in Asia, too. Shirley was named managing director at the bank the following year, at age thirty-two.
7. Investing in a company called ChinaRen.com, founded by three Stanford returnees. ChinaRen was later acquired by Sohu.
8. In 2015 he became the comanager of Joe Tsai's multibillion-dollar family investment office.
9. Adding to the company's existing Taiwan and Hong Kong sites.
10. Here at the company's tenth anniversary.
11. At Alibaba, Aliren (literally "Alibaba People") are employees who have stayed with the company for over three years.
12. Initially alibaba.com.cn, in 2010 becoming 1688.com.
13. Asia Business Conference.
14. In a 2003 interview with Zhejiang Satellite TV, he said, "Ten years ago I applied for Harvard twice and was rejected. I always wanted to go to Harvard and talk to the people there. . . . Until today I don't care too much about the academic qualifications from elite universities around the world. I think Hangzhou Teachers College is pretty good."

15. Originally from Shanghai, Wu had studied computer science in the United States and joined Yahoo early, in 1996.

Chapter Eight: Burst and Back to China

1. One of them was Edward Zeng (Zeng Qiang), the founder of a chain of Internet cafés. PR savvy, attracting a visit from First Lady Hillary Clinton, Zeng claimed to have built the "leading e-commerce enabling service in China."
2. Nobel Peace Prize recipient Liu Xiaobo has also described the Internet as "God's present to China. It is the best tool for the Chinese people in their project to cast off slavery and strive for freedom."
3. The "CCF" (China-China-Foreign) structure was set up to allow foreign investment into the new SOE telecom operator China Unicom. But Wu considered it a threat to his authority and declared the $1.4 billion of foreign investment illegal.
4. Joseph Tong (Tong Jiawei).
5. Appropriately enough its former CEO now runs a travel-related business in the region.
6. It had conducted a scaled-down "backdoor" listing on the Nasdaq in April 2000.
7. Kwan had worked for fifteen years at GE Medical Systems.

Chapter Nine: Born Again: Taobao and the Humiliation of eBay

1. The event would be the first in a series of annual conferences Alibaba still holds to this day, which they refer to as the "AliFest." Jin Yong was the first of a parade of VIPs that has since included President Bill Clinton, Kobe Bryant, Arnold Schwarzenegger, numerous CEOs, celebrities, and a parade of Nobel and Pulitzer prize winners.
2. A move that for a few days appeared to imperil the VIE structure: Wang lost his job in Sina's offshore-listed company but retained key licenses in China, then agreed to relinquish control of those, too.
3. Dangdang, run by Peggy Yu and her husband, Li Guoqing, was backed by VC investors including SoftBank. Joyo's CEO was Diane Wang, but the company was a spin-off from the software maker Kingsoft, which was engineered by Lei Jun, famous today as the founder and CEO of the high-profile Chinese smartphone manufacturer Xiaomi.
4. Neither Dangdang nor Joyo would become the Amazon of China, but Joyo

would at least become Amazon in China. In 2004, Joyo was acquired by Amazon for $75 million.

5. Known in Chinese as *yìqùwang*, whose meanings include "interesting exchanges network."
6. Since 1949.
7. Four hundred thousand dollars in angel backing from investment bankers George Boutros, Bill Brady, and Ethan Topper, who had all worked at Morgan Stanley with legendary deal maker Frank Quattrone.
8. All her possessions were in New York, but she didn't go back to pick them up—they would stay in storage for more than a year until EachNet could afford to ship them to China.
9. From Whitney, AsiaTech, and Orchid.
10. There were more than a dozen, including ClubCiti and Yabuy, founded by veterans from Federal Software who had backed 8848.
11. Whitman later attributed the delay to eBay's costly site outage in the United States the summer before.
12. With the purchase of a controlling stake in Internet Auction Company.
13. eBay paid $9.5 million for Taiwan auction site operator NeoCom Technology.
14. Behind the United States, Japan, Germany, and the United Kingdom.
15. eBay took two seats on EachNet's board. Bo held one of the other three.
16. The contrast between eBay's travails in China, where it had made an outright acquisition, and its triumph in Latin America, where it had made a minority investment in 2001 in local player Mercado Libre, would speak for itself. Today Mercado Libre is the most successful commerce player in Latin America, worth more than $6 billion, and eBay owns over 18 percent.
17. Initially through a joint venture with Alibaba in which SoftBank invested $50 million, with the additional investment in the form of $30 million in convertible notes that they could later convert into ordinary shares.
18. Shou Yuan.
19. "Taobao" was not the first choice of name for the new business. The original name was "Alimama," subsequently used for the company's online marketing technology platform.
20. Toto Sun was known as "the God of Wealth" (or "Cai Shen" in Chinese). His staff liked to call him "Uncle of Wealth." Sun hoped that the nickname would bring good luck to this new addition to the Alibaba family. Zhang Yu, a vice president in charge of operations, was known as Yu Yan, one of the leading female roles in Jin Yong's novel *Demi-Gods and Semi-Devils.*

21. For the impact of her regular publication *The Internet Report*, first released in 1995 in the run-up to the groundbreaking Morgan Stanley IPO of Netscape Communications.
22. In trying to imagine what an itinerant merchant of the Yiwu variety would look like in the United States, I thought of a movie from my childhood, the 1987 film *Planes, Trains and Automobiles,* starring John Candy and Steve Martin. Candy plays Del Griffith who is trying, and failing, to make a living traveling the country selling plastic shower-curtain rings.
23. Individual buyers—and sellers—who dominated the platform were less likely to pay taxes such as VAT, putting business-to-consumer websites at a disadvantage.
24. In 2004.
25. MIT, *Sloan Management Review*, 2012, Puneet Manchanda (University of Michigan) and Junhong Chu (National University of Singapore Business School).
26. "In the introduction phase, the platform's growth is primarily seller-driven: seller growth induces buyers to register, which in turn leads to more sellers to register, which further encourages more buyers to register, etc."
27. Meaning "Ali prosper."
28. Senior Vice President Bill Cobb, Chief Financial Officer Rajiv Dutta, and deal specialist Bill Barmier.
29. At the firm's annual analyst day on January 20, 2005.
30. Like eBay's acquisition of EachNet, this too ended in failure, resulting in its sale at a $600 million loss in 2009 to investors that included Silver Lake Partners, Index Ventures, and Andreessen Horowitz. Embarrassingly for eBay, just eighteen months later this team sold Skype to Microsoft for $8.5 billion.
31. Along with Tom Online itself, which was taken private shortly after.

Chapter Ten: Yahoo's Billion-Dollar Bet

1. With David Filo.
2. In the first nine months of the year.
3. Launching gbchinese.yahoo.com ("GB" standing for *guo biao*, or national standard) and another chinese.yahoo.com in the complex characters used by Chinese speakers outside the mainland.
4. For a period of fifty years under the Basic Law, part of Deng Xiaoping's "One Country, Two Systems" formula.
5. Qu Weizhi.

6. Later CEO of the Chinese online video company Youku.
7. Acquired in 1998 by AOL for $407 million.
8. A market that would dramatically reverse the fortunes of NetEase and propel the rise of another online games specialist based in Shanghai, called Shanda (Shengda in Chinese), which was listed on the Nasdaq in 2004.
9. Today they represent $18 billion in online revenues, bigger than China's $5 billion movie box office, and accounting for 13 percent of all Internet revenues in the country.
10. Including major portals like Sina, Sohu, and Tom.
11. By the end of 2009, Baidu had captured 63 percent of the Chinese search market, almost double Google's 33 percent share. In March 2010, when Google decided to quit the Chinese market amid bitter accusations of hacking and the pressures of censorship, Baidu would reign supreme with over 75 percent of the market by the end of the year.
12. Zhou had accused the CNNIC of lacking a legal foundation.
13. Called Yisou.
14. To improve its advertising business by matching it more closely with its users' search queries, Yahoo made a $1.3 billion purchase of Overture in 2003.
15. Qihoo 360, which went public on the Nasdaq in March 2011, would become best known for its free antivirus software, which would bring Zhou once again into conflict with Baidu and others, including Yahoo. In China, and among some former Yahoo colleagues in the United States, Zhou Hongyi developed a reputation as "the father of malware in China," a label he vigorously disputed. In December 2015, Zhou led a consortium of investors to take Qihoo back into private hands for $9.3 billion, with plans to delist the company from the New York Stock Exchange in the first half of 2016.
16. In May 2015, Yahoo injected its 384 million shares in Alibaba, worth more than $33 billion, just shy of Yahoo's total valuation, into a new entity, "SpinCo," in an effort to avoid paying over $10 billion in U.S. taxes.
17. The gathering was an off-site summit hosted by the Hua Yuan Science and Technology Association (HYSTA), a group of Silicon Valley–based entrepreneurs and engineers mostly hailing from China, ahead of their annual conference at the Santa Clara Convention Center.
18. The Yahoo-Alibaba transaction has proved so successful that many have claimed responsibility for teeing up the Jack-Jerry meeting at Pebble Beach. Jack has credited, among others, Wu Ying from UTStarcom, Liu Erfei of

Merrill Lynch, and Deng Zhonghan of Vimicro Corporation. Joe Tsai says, "Of course eighteen different people took credit for putting together that meeting. It was the Hua Yuan event [that] took credit. Everybody did." He added, "If you knew each other . . . you were at the same conference."

19. Traveling to Beijing with Jerry were Yahoo CEO Terry Semel and CFO Sue Decker and corporate development executive Toby Coppel.
20. A twenty-four-year veteran of Warner Bros., where he rose to become chairman and co-CEO.
21. Li, a protégé of Jiang Zemin, was in charge of propaganda for the Communist Party, a post he was appointed to in 2002. He served in that capacity for a decade, overseeing the extensive system of censorship for the Internet.
22. The company had listed the year before and had a market cap of more than $2.2 billion, with revenues of $165 million.
23. Instead, he dreamed of turning his company into the Disney of China, having earlier that year taken a 19.5 percent stake in Sina as the first step in a hostile takeover (which never materialized).
24. After selling part of its 40 percent stake in Taobao to Alibaba for $360 million.
25. In a talk at the Computer History Museum in Mountain View, California, hosted by HYSTA, whose conference had helped tee-up the original deal.
26. Yahoo also bought out a SoftBank investment in Taobao for $360 million, half of which SoftBank then used to acquire more shares in Alibaba, in addition to another $30 million to exercise convertible notes it had purchased in 2003.
27. The amount was so large that, on hearing the news of the investment, one CEO of a smaller e-commerce player recounted to me, "I thought the news must be fake, many people did. One hundred million dollars would have been a big number, but one billion dollars? I had never imagined such a large number."
28. Now CEO of Shazam.
29. Once he had established Qihoo 360, using the proceeds of Yahoo's investment, Zhou set about building a product designed to help users uninstall the very product he himself had built at 3721, which had since been rebranded Yahoo Messenger, but which he now described as malware that should be removed.
30. huoyan-1989@yahoo.com.cn.
31. The Beijing State Security Bureau issued a Notice of Evidence Collection

and requested "email account registration information for huoyan-1989 @yahoo.com.cn, all login times, corresponding IP addresses, and relevant email content from February 22, 2004," from Yahoo China's offices in Beijing.

32. Including Human Rights Watch, the Committee to Protect Journalists, and Reporters Without Borders.
33. Who had already taken flak from Alibaba's rival eBay for committing to the event.
34. The House Foreign Affairs Committee.
35. After fielding an enquiry from the U.S. embassy about the background of Google's decision, I found myself being quoted later on in a cable leaked by Wikileaks. Rather disappointingly, no one took much notice.

Chapter Eleven: Growing Pains

1. A number of Alibaba veterans left the firm, including cofounder Toto Sun, CTO John Wu, and COO Li Qi, whom Jack had first worked with at China Pages.
2. Maggie Wu (Wu Wei), who still serves today as the company's CFO.
3. Before starting his own private equity fund, Vision Knight Capital.
4. And its domestic site alibaba.com.cn.
5. And hold for two years.
6. Peter Woo's Wharf, Robert Kuok's Kerry Properties, and the Kwok family's Sun Hung Kai Properties.
7. The offering priced Alibaba's shares at more than 106 times its 2007 forecast earnings versus forty-one times for Google, or forty-five times for its old rival Global Sources.
8. A five-bedroom, 7,000-square-foot property for which he paid more than $5,400 per square foot. He purchased the penthouse apartment complete with private roof garden from developer Kerry Properties, one of the cornerstone investors in the IPO.
9. The previous year Alibaba.com generated $170 million in revenues and $28 million in net profit.
10. On its Alimama platform.
11. In September 2008, Alibaba launched the first phase of its "Big Taobao Strategy," integrating Taobao.com and the online advertising platform Alimama to build "the world's largest e-commerce ecosystem."
12. After a four-and-a-half-year life span as a publicly listed company, in June

2012 Alibaba.com was absorbed back into parent Alibaba Group, with shareholders paid the same price as in the original 2007 IPO.

13. Valuing Yahoo's shares at a 61 percent premium over the market price.
14. Estimated at over 99 percent.
15. Including Carl Icahn. But Yahoo's efforts to strike a search deal with Microsoft's rival Google killed any prospect for the deal.
16. Who was still the representative for Yahoo on Alibaba's board.
17. Gady Epstein at *Forbes*.
18. The sale for about $100 million netted them a pretax paper gain of $98 million. The sale released cash Bartz badly needed to shore up investor support.
19. In 2009 and 2010.
20. Elvis Lee.
21. Alibaba said that majority ownership was transferred in 2009 to comply with regulations, then full ownership transfer completed in 2010.
22. Governing Internet payment, mobile phone payment, bank card–related services, issuance and acceptance of prepaid card payments, and currency exchange.
23. The talks had been initiated with Jerry Yang and were continued by the two companies' CFOs before breaking down that summer.
24. In an interview on July 7, 2011, with *China Entrepreneur* magazine (*Zhongguo Qi Ye Jia).*
25. In a June 2011 interview at the *Wall Street Journal*'s All Things Digital conference in California.
26. By June 2015, when Alipay was valued by private investors as high as $50 billion, the $6 billion cap on a stake then worth more than $18 billion would look like a very raw deal for Alibaba investors like Yahoo.
27. Three months earlier Alibaba had announced it would take its Hong Kong–listed subsidiary Alibaba.com back into private hands, paying the same price for the shares as the company had listed in 2007 (a 60.4 percent premium on the shares). This cleaned the way for the IPO of the whole Alibaba Group in 2014.

Chapter Twelve: Icon or Icarus?

1. Losing in the process the long-standing arrangement to hosting U.S. presidents visiting New York City.
2. A year earlier Jack had become chairman of Alibaba, with Joe Tsai becoming executive vice chairman. Jonathan Lu would last barely two years in the

job. Both he and his successor, Daniel Zhang, would face the unenviable task of trying to fill Jack's shoes.

3. Including any impairment of the "trusted status of the ecosystem" or Alibaba's "culture, mission, and values."
4. The ranks of the Alibaba Partnership can be refreshed through the admission of new partners each year. Those appointed typically have more than five years' service, and their election is subject to the approval of 75 percent of all partners. A Partnership Committee of five, including Jack and Joe, administers the structure.
5. Drawn from Alibaba's finance and logistics affiliates.
6. Jack, Lucy Peng (Peng Lei), Trudy Dai (Dai Shan), Jane Jiang (Jiang Fang), Jin Jianhang, and Eddie Wu (Wu Yongming).
7. The new members are: Yongfu Yu, president of Alibaba's mobile business unit and its advertising platform Alimama; Junfang Zheng, Alibaba Group's deputy CFO; Ying Zhao, vice president of Ant Financial; and Lijun Sun, general manager of rural Taobao marketplace. This is the first time that Alibaba has added new members to its partnership since the IPO in September 2014. In its prospectus, Alibaba said that to be eligible for election, a partner candidate must have "continued service with Alibaba Group and/or our related companies or affiliates for, in most cases, not less than five years," in which case Yongfu Yu is an exception. Yu was the chairman and CEO of UCWeb, a mobile Internet technology and service provider that was acquired by Alibaba in 2014.
8. The Securities and Futures Commission.
9. In 2007 in Hong Kong, one-quarter of the Alibaba.com IPO shares went to individual investors.
10. After New York, Alibaba's global road show took in Boston, San Francisco, Hong Kong, Singapore, and London. Management divided up into two teams, each fronted by Jack or Joe.
11. As the company approached the one-year anniversary of the IPO, concerns grew about the expiration of the "lockup"—shares that key investors were not permitted to sell for the first year—of 1.6 billion of its 2.5 billion shares.
12. In November 2013, Zhejiang Alibaba E-Commerce Company Limited was restructured to become Alibaba Small and Micro Financial Services Group. Jack saw his shareholding reduced from 80 percent to about 8 percent in the new company, or no greater than his shareholding in Alibaba Group.
13. Variously described as a "white paper" or as merely minutes of a meeting.

14. Sina Weibo.
15. The head of the SAIC's department of online commerce.
16. And one day after Yahoo announced it was creating a new structure—which it hoped would minimize its tax liabilities—to spin off a 15 percent stake in Alibaba.
17. Revenue rose 40 percent to $4.22 billion, but came in below the average estimate of $4.45 billion, according to Thomson Reuters.
18. Zhang is the son-in-law of Gu Mu, a former key aide to Deng Xiaoping who had accompanied him on his tour of southern China, opening the door to entrepreneurs.
19. At a dinner in London in October 2015.
20. Which given anticorruption campaigns requires careful curation.
21. Xi had recently finished up a stint as party secretary of Zhejiang Province.
22. China has a reputation as a wild west for a lack of respect for intellectual property rights, justified by the rampant piracy in the market. But it isn't due to a lack of laws. Since its accession to the World Trade Organization in 2001, China has set up an elaborate framework of trademark, patents, and copyright laws. A survey conducted in 2015 by the American Chamber of Commerce in China found that 85 percent of respondents believed China's IPR enforcement had improved in the last five years, but 80 percent were concerned about ineffective enforcement.
23. Or selling a range of fake items on four occasions.
24. Where merchants are suspected of committing a criminal offense, Alibaba will escalate the case to the local Administration of Industry and Commerce or to the police, which has an officer stationed at Alibaba headquarters who is dedicated to tracking the sale of illicit goods, or the sale of illegal products such as guns.
25. Tmall merchants are required to furnish more evidence of their authorization to trade from brand owners.
26. Taobao's and Tmall's search algorithms are heavily driven by historical trading volumes.
27. Known as the "Big Four Unions," based in Hangzhou and other locations.
28. VIP Shop, Melishuo, and Mogujie.
29. Jumei.
30. Dangdang and Amazon.cn.
31. Womai and Yihaodian, invested by Walmart.

32. 19.9 percent. Suning, shelling out 14 billion yuan—$2.3 billion—became a 1.1 percent stakeholder in Alibaba.
33. Also known as Jingdong, formerly 360Buy.
34. In the run-up to JD's IPO, Alibaba rival Tencent took a 15 percent stake and folded its own struggling e-commerce offerings into the company.
35. *Wei xin* (micro message) in Chinese.
36. By Andreessen Horowitz.
37. WeChat's popularity owes much to its personalized feel, tailored to the needs and mind-sets of China's mobile masses. But users can control the information they share with strangers, and unlike the Twitter-like Weibo the total number of followers on WeChat is capped at 5,000. Building on Weibo's success as a home for celebrities and brands, WeChat also offers more than 8.5 million public accounts.
38. A modern twist on the traditional seasonal offerings of money to family and friends.
39. The initiative ran into headwinds in 2012 when its launch partner, the Taiwanese hardware company Acer, pulled out. This was reportedly following pressure exerted from Google, which leveled accusations that Alibaba was deploying a "noncompatible" version of Android.
40. Alibaba acquired an 18 percent stake in Sina Weibo in 2014. But by this point Weibo had lost much of its luster to WeChat.
41. UCWeb.
42. *Weilidai* ("a tiny bit of loan").
43. Meaning "quickly hail a cab."
44. Meaning "beep beep, hail a cab."
45. Uber was next to step up to the subsidy plate, shelling out an estimated $1 billion in China in 2015 to win over drivers and customers, aided by a $1.2 billion fund-raising exercise.
46. Some foreign observers make the mistake of believing that "Shanghai is New York City and Beijing is Washington, D.C.," but this vastly understates Beijing's importance as a business hub—and understates the fact that local government in Shanghai is much more of a force in local business than in Beijing.
47. Even recruiting talent from Shanghai for Alibaba's Hangzhou headquarters can be a challenge, as the office lies some distance from the city's train station. To attract and retain Shanghai-based talent, Alibaba offers special

buses to and from Shanghai each weekend to ferry employees, who stay in Hangzhou only four nights a week.

48. Describes the twin-pronged strategy comprising the "Silk Road Economic Belt," a series of land routes from China across central Asia to the Middle East, Africa, and Europe, complemented by "The Twenty-First-Century Maritime Silk Road" to reinforce existing sea trade routes.
49. General partner.
50. Yunfeng's name in English translates as "cloud and the cutting edge of a sword." The combination of Jack's first name "Yun" and David Yu's given name "Feng."
51. Yu first rose to prominence with the sale of his display advertising company Target Media to rival Focus Media in 2006.
52. Other partners include Shen Guojun from Intime Investment, Shi Yuzhu from gaming company Giant Interactive, Liu Yonghao of New Hope Group, Wang Yusuo from ENN Group, Jason Jiang from Focus Media, Xu Hang from Shenzhen Mindray Medical, Chen Yihong from China Dongxiang Group, Zhou Xin from e-House, Wang Jianguo from Five Star, Zhou Shaoxiong from Septwolves, Wang Xuning from Joyong Holdings, and Zhang Youcai from Unifront Holdings.
53. One example is the September 2015 announcement that Alibaba had established Alibaba Sports Group along with Yunfeng Capital and Sina (the parent of Sina Weibo, in which Alibaba is an investor) in an effort to "reshape China's sports industry through the Internet."
54. Cofounder David Yu, for example, also serves on the board of Alibaba-invested Huayi Brothers Media Group. His mother, Wang Yulian, is also a partner at Yunfeng and the largest shareholder in Ant Financial, after Jack and Simon Xie, holding a reported 4.6 percent stake.
55. As a General Partner.
56. As a Limited Partner.
57. The military retreat of the Red Army from 1934 to 1935.
58. As a sign of its commitment to boosting the sale of imported products in China, Alibaba branded Singles' Day in 2015 as the "11/11 Global Shopping Festival." Yet the company has a long way to go to secure a sufficient range of imported items to compete with the overseas sites that many Chinese shoppers have already discovered.
59. Including the mobile search player Quixey, Amazon Prime competitor Shoprunner, game developer Kabam, and mobile messaging app Tango.

60. Building on its earliest U.S. investments in e-commerce companies Auctiva and Vendio, Alibaba launched its own U.S. website, 11Main.com, in an effort to reach directly to American consumers. But the effort failed, and in June 2015 Alibaba disposed of its interest.
61. He also previously served in the George W. Bush administration, including as senior adviser on foreign affairs to Secretary of State Condoleezza Rice.
62. Deputy assistant to the president for legislative affairs, serving George W. Bush.
63. Since Alibaba donated 0.3 percent of its annual revenue to a company foundation, but the new trust is much larger.
64. Presumably to include the returns on his Yunfeng Capital investments.
65. In the northeastern city of Yabuli.
66. On social media in China, there has been intense speculation about the state of health of Jack's own family members, but Jack has not spoken publicly about this.
67. The Communist Party runs special farms, off-limits to the public and media, to ensure high-quality food supplies for its senior leaders, who also receive privileged access to the best medical care, provided by military hospitals.
68. To Bloomberg TV's Emily Chang in November 2015.
69. Real estate billionaire Xu Jiaxin.
70. ChinaVision.
71. 3.6 billion yuan ($565 million).
72. In a deal announced in October 2015 valuing Youku at more than $5 billion.
73. Victor founded Youku after working as COO of Sohu. Youku acquired its largest competitor to become Youku-Tudou.
74. 461 million people in mid-2015 according to CNNIC.
75. In 2014, the territory had been brought to a standstill by the Occupy Central movement, or Umbrella Revolution, a student-led protest against the lack of genuine democracy and other freedoms. Although the crisis ended peacefully, the underlying tensions that fueled it remain ever present.